Welcome to the

WEBELOS

Handbook

Hi! My name is Ethan. I'm a Boy Scout this year, but I had an awesome time working on the Webelos and Arrow of Light adventures. Now it's your turn to earn those ranks, and I've got plenty of hints and fun stories to help you out. So turn the page—you've got great adventures ahead!

33452
ISBN 978-0-8395-0046-9
© 2015 Boy Scouts of America
2015 Printing

Table of Contents

WEBELOS REQUIRED ADVENTURES

ARROW OF LIGHT REQUIRED ADVENTURES

WEBELOS AND ARROW OF LIGHT ELECTIVE ADVENTURES

Webelos Parent Introduction

The Cub Scouting Webelos program will open a new world of adventure for your son—a way to learn new skills, enjoy lots of outdoor activities, and most of all, have fun! This parent information section will give you a head start in understanding how the program works, and you'll learn about the many ways you can help your son and his Webelos den.

As a parent or guardian, you want the best for your son. You want a close relationship with him, and you want to help him grow physically, mentally, and morally. The Webelos program is geared to your son's developing abilities and changing interests. The program will provide your boy with a variety of new experiences that will help him assume responsibilities and gain maturity, knowledge, and skills. You'll find yourself growing closer to him as you encourage him in his advancement and take a turn assisting with Webelos den activities. Join him in these adventures!

In the front of this book, there should be an insert section for you on youth protection. If the insert is no longer in your son's copy of his handbook, talk with your den leader about finding one.

This insert, and the exercises included at the back, are required for each parent and son to read and discuss at each rank.

Your Son, Scouting, and You

As a parent or other caring adult, you want your Webelos Scout to grow up to be self-reliant and dependable, worthy and caring. Scouting has these same goals in mind for him.

The mission of the Boy Scouts of America is to prepare young people to make ethical and moral choices over their lifetimes by instilling in them the values of the Scout Oath and Scout Law.

Scout Oath (or Promise)	Scout Law
On my honor I will do my best To do my duty to God and my country and to obey the Scout Law; To help other people at all times; To keep myself physically strong, mentally awake, and morally straight.	A Scout is trustworthy, loyal, helpful, friendly, courteous, kind, obedient, cheerful, thrifty, brave, clean, and reverent.

The Scout Oath and the Scout Law are defined on pages 24 through 27 in the Bobcat requirements.

Since 1910, the Boy Scouts of America has been weaving lifetime values into fun, developmental activities. These activities are designed to help families teach their sons how to make good decisions throughout their lives and give them confidence as they become the adult leaders of tomorrow.

In a society where your son is often taught that winning is everything, Cub Scouting teaches him to DO HIS BEST, to help others, and to try to live his life according to the Scout Oath and the Scout Law. If a Cub Scout has done his best to satisfy a requirement, then he has met the standard for advancement in Cub Scouts. It is up to his parent and den leader to gauge whether he has offered his best effort.

The Character Compass, shown on page 18, will serve as a guide for your Scout as he discovers the meaning of the Scout Law. Take note of the Character Compass symbol as it appears throughout your son's handbook, and use each note as an opportunity for discussion about the specific point and how it relates to the adventure he is working on.

The Purposes of Cub Scouting

Cub Scouting is a year-round family-oriented part of the BSA program designed for boys who are in first through fifth grades (or are 7, 8, 9, and 10 years old). Parents, leaders, and organizations work together to achieve the Purposes of Cub Scouting.

1. Character Development
2. Spiritual Growth
3. Good Citizenship
4. Sportsmanship and Fitness
5. Family Understanding
6. Respectful Relationships
7. Personal Achievement
8. Friendly Service
9. Fun and Adventure
10. Preparation for Boy Scouts

What Is a Webelos Scout?

Your son has joined the part of the Cub Scouting program of the Boy Scouts of America that is for fourth- and fifth-grade boys. Webelos Scouts are older than boys in the Tiger, Wolf, and Bear levels of Cub Scouting. If a boy has completed third grade, or if he has not completed third grade but is 10 years old, he's the right age for this den. Boys who have completed the third grade work on the Webelos rank. Boys who have completed the fourth grade work on the Arrow of Light rank.

Most Webelos Scouts are in this program for about 18 months. This is preparation for his later participation in the great adventure of Boy Scouting. After your son's Webelos Scout experience, and after he has completed the fifth grade or is age 11, or has earned the Arrow of Light rank and is at least 10 years old, he'll be ready for more independence and adventure in a Boy Scout troop.

History of Webelos

In 1902, Ernest Thompson Seton started an outdoor program for boys called the Woodcraft Indians. In 1910, he became one of the founders of the new Boy Scout movement and one of its best-known promoters.

He later helped develop the Cub program. The new program adapted activities, games, and ceremonies from several youth groups, such as Seton's Woodcraft Indians, Wolf Cubbing (developed in England by the founder of the Scouting movement, Lord Baden-Powell), and the Boy Rangers of America. American Indian lore was emphasized.

The Boy's Cubbook was also published in 1930. In the book, Akela was an American Indian boy, son of the chief of the Webelos tribe. "Webelos" was explained as "a word with an inner meaning, signifying progress from Wolf through Bear and Lion Ranks to Scout: W-B-L-S...We'll Be Loyal Scouts." (The original Cub Scout ranks were Wolf, Bear, and Lion, with Webelos added in the 1950s.) The chief of the Webelos tribe was named Arrow of Light, which was adapted from the Arrow Park World Jamboree in London in 1929, when the Golden Arrow was made the symbol of world friendship.

The Cubbing story told of the boy Akela being taken on trips into the forest where he learned knowledge and skills from the wolf and the bear. Before he could become a Scout he had to look the lion in the eye and learn courage and determination. Then, he was admitted to the lower ranks of the young Scouts of the trail, advancing (at the age of 12) from the world brotherhood of Cubs into the world brotherhood of Scouts.

In later years, the name Akela was used for the chief of the tribe or pack. By 1980, a parent or another caring adult could be Akela and help the Cub Scout along the advancement trail.

In 1953, a Cub Scout advisory group began studying a proposed Webelos den plan to help create more variety in the program for older boys. In 1954, the Webelos den was created for 10 ½-year-old boys, with a new Webelos den badge. The first *Lion-Webelos Book* with meeting outlines for Webelos leaders was introduced in 1958.

In 1988, a two-year Webelos Scout program was recommended, and it was implemented the next year. The changes included an expanded outdoor program with more opportunities for boy leadership, which would provide a better vehicle for Webelos Scouts to progress into Boy Scouting.

Today's Webelos program remains an exciting adventure for boys, their families, and their leaders. The continued outdoor program, the opportunities for boy leadership, and the preparation for boys to leave Cub Scouting and embark on the adventure of Boy Scouting are all wonderful steps for boys to take on the road to becoming a First Class Boy Scout and then soaring on to Eagle.

Webelos Den and the Cub Scout Pack

If your son has been in Cub Scouting before, he already knows a little bit about the Webelos Scout den from his earlier experiences. If your son is new to Cub Scouting, he belongs to a small group called a Webelos den. The den is part of a larger Cub Scout pack that includes the boys in the Tiger, Wolf, and Bear dens along with the Webelos dens.

The Webelos den has three leadership positions. They'll need your help if the den is to be successful.

- ◆ The **Webelos den leader** is an adult who plans and directs the den activities. Appointed by the pack committee, the Webelos den leader must be at least 21 years old. There also should be an assistant Webelos den leader. Only the den leader or assistant den leader may sign off on your son's advancement.

- ◆ The **Webelos den chief** is a Boy Scout, Varsity Scout, or a Venturer. The den chief is trained to help the Webelos den leader, especially in leading games and teaching skills.

- ◆ The **Webelos denner** is a Webelos Scout elected by the other boys to help the den leader and den chief.

You can help as well by indicating to your son's leaders your skills and interests that may relate to an adventure area. For example, if you are an engineer, you could help lead the Engineer adventure. If you are skilled with hand tools and know about home repairs, you could help with the Build It and Fix It adventures. Read through the adventures in this handbook to get a better idea of how you could help.

The pack is operated by a community organization, such as a school, a church or other religious institution, a service club, or another group interested in helping youth. It's called the chartered organization because it holds a charter from the Boy Scouts of America National Council that allows it to operate the Scouting program.

In addition to their den meetings, Webelos Scouts take part in the monthly pack meetings led by an adult volunteer called the Cubmaster. Parents and other adult family members can serve on the pack committee, which plans pack activities. During a pack meeting recognition ceremony, your son will receive the adventure pin awards he has earned. Be sure to attend so you can help pin those awards on him!

Your Son's Advancement

Much of your son's progress will take place through activities centered on his advancement. He'll advance by earning adventure pins as he completes each adventure. The adventures focus on citizenship, leadership, outdoor skills, physical fitness skills, as well as understanding his duty to God and building his character. The entire den works together on an adventure each month, mostly in their meetings. There may be some of the adventure work that your son will need to complete at home with your help. Each adventure presents an array of hands-on activities and fascinating information that will enrich his life. By working on specific adventures and requirements, he will earn the Webelos rank. Later, he'll be eligible to work on the adventures and requirements for Cub Scouting's highest rank, the Arrow of Light. As the requirements for adventures and rank are completed, your son's den leader will sign off in the appropriate spaces.

If your Webelos Scout has a cognitive or physical disability that prevents him from attempting an adventure, talk to your Cubmaster and den leader.

There are a few differences in the younger age Cub Scout program and the Webelos program:

♦ When a Tiger, Wolf, or Bear Scout completes requirements, a parent or guardian signs his book along with his den leader. When a Webelos Scout completes requirements, he takes his book to the Webelos den leader. For projects that are done at home or with the family and are not easily transportable, the parent or guardian still may be asked to approve the Webelos Scout's completion of an adventure requirement.

♦ Webelos Scouts are encouraged to have several parent/son overnight camping trips during the year, as well as other activities that prepare them for becoming Boy Scouts. In the younger ranks of Cub Scouting, overnight camping is family camping.

♦ Webelos Scouts have some distinctive choices in their uniform. You can find more about this in your son's section about his Webelos uniform.

If Your Son Is New in Scouting

If your son joined Cub Scouting as a Webelos Scout, he must earn the Bobcat rank badge before receiving any other rank. The Bobcat badge requirements are on page 23. He will need your help to fully understand the Scout Oath and the Scout Law. When your son has completed the Bobcat requirements to your satisfaction, he'll receive his Bobcat badge at a pack meeting.

Your Responsibility to Your Webelos Scout

As your son travels along the Webelos and Arrow of Light adventures, take an interest in his activities. He needs to know that you approve of what he's doing, you're interested in what he's learning, you want to help him, and you're proud of his accomplishments. Your son sees Webelos Scouting as a chance to have fun, go camping, and make new friends. He also sees it as a step on the way to outdoor adventures in Boy Scouting.

But, Webelos Scouting is more than that. For you, it is a new way to grow closer to your son, to share his excitement about his expanding physical and mental skills and create a warm and open relationship with him. Join him on the Webelos adventures. Help him move toward the Boy Scouting adventures. You'll be glad you did.

Scouting and Duty to God

The Boy Scouts of America has always held steadfastly to the principle, embodied in the Scout Oath, that a Scout has a duty to God. The BSA does not promote any specific religion, and has always embraced all faiths. We do encourage youth members and their families to be active in their own faith, in keeping with the BSA's Declaration of Religious Principle.

It naturally follows that the leadership for your son's spiritual development, both within and outside Cub Scouting, must come primarily from your home and your family's religious leaders. Your son will look to you as his example of how to learn and perform his duty to God.

BOY SCOUTS OF AMERICA

The adventures related to duty to God in each rank of the Cub Scouting program provide support, and each boy has the opportunity to earn the religious emblem of his faith. The emblem is created and presented by your son's religious group. Most of the world's religions have an emblem of their faith. However, alternative requirements are available for boys whose faith institutions do not have an emblem or whose families are not affiliated with an organized religious group.

In addition, the staff at your BSA local council service center should be able to help. Many local councils and districts offer organized opportunities for Scouts to earn their religious emblems while meeting and sharing fellowship with other Scouts of their faith.

 Your den leader or local council service center can help you and your family learn more about the religious emblem for your faith. With an adult's permission, you can also visit **www.praypub.org** or **www.scouting.org/filestore/pdf/512-879_WB.pdf**.

Webelos Den Overnight Campouts

The policy of the Boy Scouts of America is to encourage several overnight camping trips and other challenging outdoor activities for Webelos Scouts. You'll always have a major part in Webelos den overnight campouts. Don't worry if you're not an experienced camper. The Webelos den leader and other adults will help you, and you and your son will have fun learning about camping together.

The cooperation of adults is essential. The Webelos den leader cannot be expected to take full responsibility for the health and safety of six or eight boys at an overnight campout. In most cases, the Webelos Scout will be under the supervision of a parent or guardian. In all cases, each Webelos Scout is to be responsible to a specific adult. Boy Scouts of America health and safety and Youth Protection policies apply.

> If your chartered organization does not permit Cub Scout camping, you may substitute a family campout or a daylong outdoor activity with your den or pack.

Planning Overnight Campouts

You'll have a hand in planning the details of each Webelos den overnight campout at a meeting of all participating adults. If you have special outdoor skills, the Webelos den leader may plan an activity in which you can instruct the Webelos Scouts.

Here are some of the topics for the meeting:

Where you're going. The site may be decided before the meeting. It won't be a rugged, pioneering type of camp. Your son won't experience that kind of camping until he's a Boy Scout.

Webelos den overnight campouts should take place in warm weather, at sites reasonably close to home. The events may be held at suitable public campgrounds, local council camps, or privately owned facilities. A location with a tested water supply, toilets, cooking facilities, and an area for indoor activity would be appropriate. Usually tents are used. Tent camping provides an element of adventure.

Each adult and boy team brings the tent and other equipment they'll use. Equipment can be borrowed from a Boy Scout troop or rented. Any nearby cabins or shelters should serve only as emergency protection and a base for toilet facilities, water, etc.

How you'll get there. At the meeting, you and the other adults will make plans to share transportation to the campsite.

Who will cook. You and your son will cook for yourselves, so bring food and cooking equipment from home. Plan simple menus together. (This *Webelos Handbook* has some suggestions.)

Cooking can be done on wood or charcoal fires in established grills or fire pits provided by the camp or in charcoal grills provided at the camp or brought from home. Adults who own propane and liquid fuel stoves or lanterns may use them, if allowed by local camping property authorities, but under no circumstances should boys be permitted to handle liquid fuels or stoves or lanterns fired by such fuel. Such equipment should be considered personal gear, and adult owners must assume full personal responsibility for these items and for fuel.

Welcome, Webelos Scout!

You're a Webelos Scout—one of the older boys in the pack! You'll go camping with your den, along with your parent, guardian, or an adult relative or friend. Everything in the Webelos Scout program is more challenging than the activities younger boys in the pack do. You'll earn adventure pins that only Webelos Scouts can wear. At the same time, you'll be getting ready to become a Boy Scout!

The Meaning of Webelos

The word Webelos (say WEE-buh-lows) has a special meaning. Webelos is made up of the first letters of these words: "**WE**'ll **BE LO**yal **S**couts." Loyal means you'll keep the Scout Oath and try to live by the Scout Law. Check out page 5 for the full story of how the WEBELOS name came to be.

Your Webelos Den

The Webelos den is part of Cub Scouting. It's for the older boys in the pack. The boys in your den are your same age or your same grade. You will be in this den for 12–18 months as you work on your Webelos and Arrow of Light rank badges. Your Webelos den will meet two to three times a month and then together with the entire pack once a month. The den meetings are where you'll learn new skills. Go to all the meetings so you won't miss any of the fun, excitement, new information, and adventures. Den meetings often include games, sports, and making things. Sometimes the den will go on special outings, like a nature hike or an overnight campout.

Your Leaders

Your Webelos den leader and Webelos assistant den leader understand boys your age, and they also know about Boy Scouting and can help you get ready for it. Your Webelos den leader can teach

you the right way to build a fire, cook a meal, pitch a tent, and many other skills that are fun. Webelos den leaders know the importance of the Cub Scout motto, "Do Your Best," and will teach you about the Boy Scout motto, "Be Prepared." They'll help you do your best in improving your skills and learning new ones. They know the

importance of Scouting. They believe in God and the greatness of the United States of America. They believe in you and your future. That's why they take the time to lead your Webelos den. Family members often help at the den meetings too, sharing their knowledge of certain adventure areas.

You may also have a Webelos den chief as a leader in your den. Webelos den chiefs are Boy Scouts, Varsity Scouts, Venturers, or Sea Scouts who help the Webelos den leader by leading games and teaching you many of the skills you'll need to know when you move into a Boy Scout troop.

You could help be a leader of your den by being a denner. The denner is a Webelos Scout who has been selected by the Webelos den for a short term. The denner helps the den leader and den chief at meetings and outdoor events. If you're elected to be the denner, do your best!

Pack Meetings

Your Webelos den plays an important part in the monthly pack meeting. You and your den might demonstrate the new skills you've learned in the past month or exhibit projects you've completed for an adventure. Each pack meeting includes a special ceremony for Webelos Scouts who have earned adventure pins during the month.

Your Uniform

As a Webelos Scout, you may choose between two uniforms. One is the blue uniform worn as a Tiger, Wolf, or Bear Scout. The other is the uniform you can take with you into Boy Scouting—the tan Boy Scout shirt and olive green trousers. You and your family choose which uniform you'll wear.

You'll have three special uniform parts to show you're a Webelos Scout: an olive green cap with a plaid front panel and the Webelos emblem, a plaid Webelos neckerchief, and a Webelos neckerchief slide. The navy blue Cub Scout belt may be worn with both uniforms; a Webelos belt buckle is available. The official Boy Scout olive web belt may be worn with the tan/olive uniform.

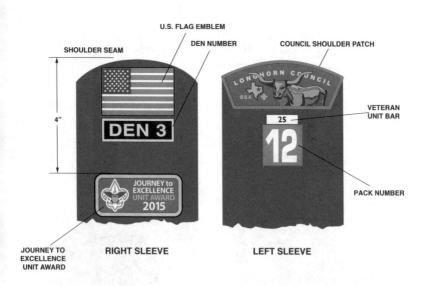

U.S. FLAG EMBLEM

SHOULDER SEAM

DEN NUMBER

COUNCIL SHOULDER PATCH

4"

DEN 3

LONGHORN COUNCIL
BSA

25

12

VETERAN UNIT BAR

PACK NUMBER

JOURNEY to EXCELLENCE UNIT AWARD 2015

JOURNEY TO EXCELLENCE UNIT AWARD

RIGHT SLEEVE

LEFT SLEEVE

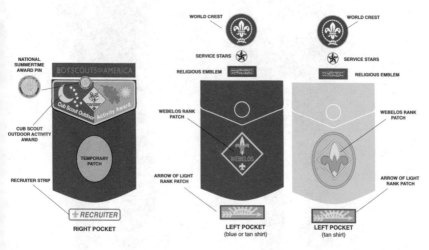

WORLD CREST

WORLD CREST

SERVICE STARS

SERVICE STARS

NATIONAL SUMMERTIME AWARD PIN

BOY SCOUTS OF AMERICA

RELIGIOUS EMBLEM

RELIGIOUS EMBLEM

Cub Scout Outdoor Activity Award

WEBELOS RANK PATCH

WEBELOS RANK PATCH

CUB SCOUT OUTDOOR ACTIVITY AWARD

TEMPORARY PATCH

WEBELOS

RECRUITER STRIP

ARROW OF LIGHT RANK PATCH

ARROW OF LIGHT RANK PATCH

RECRUITER

RIGHT POCKET

LEFT POCKET
(blue or tan shirt)

LEFT POCKET
(tan shirt)

You should be proud to wear your uniform at all Webelos den meetings and pack meetings. Wear your uniform on campouts, other den outings, service projects, and other den and pack special events. It shows you're one of the older boys in the pack, on the trail to Boy Scouting.

The diagrams here will show you where to place the Webelos Scout insignia for your uniform on the sleeves and pockets of the uniform.

Temporary insignia, such as an emblem from day camp, is worn centered on your right pocket.

The Webelos denner wears his shoulder cord suspended from the left shoulder of the blue uniform, or he wears it without the tab, under the left epaulet on the tan/olive uniform. The cord is removed when the term of office ends.

Adventures and Adventure Pins

Each month, the projects and many of the activities at den meetings are centered on one of the adventures that you can complete. The requirements for each adventure and adventure pin award are in this book, along with detailed information you'll need for each subject. You'll do much of your badge work with your den and some of it at home.

Adventure pins are colorful metal emblems you pin on the front of your Webelos cap or wear pinned to the Webelos colors, the gold, green, and red ribbons worn on your right sleeve.

Webelos Badge

As soon as you start earning adventure pins, you can look forward to earning the Webelos badge! The Webelos rank is the fifth rank in Cub Scouting, coming after Bobcat, Tiger, Wolf, and Bear.

There are two Webelos badge options: diamond-shaped and oval. Whichever you choose, you wear the Webelos badge on your left shirt pocket.

Arrow of Light Badge

Arrow of Light is the highest rank in Cub Scouting. Set your sights on it now. You'll wear your Arrow of Light rank badge below the left pocket. It is the only badge from Cub Scouting that may continue to be worn on the Boy Scout uniform. By the time you've earned the Arrow of Light rank, you'll have gained knowledge and skills in a lot of subjects, and you'll know a lot about being in a Boy Scout troop!

Character Compass

As you work on your Webelos adventures in your *Webelos Handbook*, you will notice this symbol:

A compass is a device that can guide a person from place to place. Character is how we act, and it guides our entire lives. This compass will be your guide to one or more of the 12 points of the Scout Law. Every time you check the compass, it will remind you of how the activities in each adventure are related to the Scout Law. This will also help you think about how the points of the Scout Law guide our way in

Cub Scouting and in daily life. Those points are all different, and each one is a treasure for you to find! You may also be asked to discuss your thoughts on the Character Compass during your den meetings.

A SCOUT'S RESPONSIBILITY TO THE OUTDOORS

Much of Scouting, including Cub Scouting, happens outside. In order to do their part in preserving the natural world, Scouts of all ages dedicate themselves to practicing the ideas held by two important sets of guidelines.

The Outdoor Code

For more than 60 years, the Outdoor Code has been a guide for Scouts in the outdoors. Remember to do your best by showing respect for the outdoors and by learning and upholding the Outdoor Code.

THE OUTDOOR CODE

As an American, I will do my best to—

♦ **Be clean in my outdoor manners,**

♦ **Be careful with fire,**

♦ **Be considerate in the outdoors, and**

♦ **Be conservation-minded.**

Being clean in your outdoor manners, careful with fire, and considerate means you can enjoy the outdoors in ways that do no harm to the environment. Being conservation-minded encourages the protection and thoughtful use of natural resources and doing your part to improve the condition of the land and the environment.

As a Cub Scout, you will learn to use the Leave No Trace Principles for Kids to help you take care of an area where you hike or camp.

LEAVE NO TRACE
PRINCIPLES FOR KIDS*

Center for Outdoor Ethics | LNT.org

1. **Know Before You Go.** Find out about the place you're going to camp ahead of time. Are there rules you need to know about? Are any activities against the rules? Is water available? Do you need to bring anything special?

2. **Choose the Right Path.** Always walk on trails, even if that means getting your boots muddy. Don't take shortcuts. Set up tents in marked camping areas.

3. **Trash Your Trash.** Use bathroom facilities when available. Follow campground rules for handling dishwater. Pack out all your trash unless the campground has trash pickup.

4. **Leave What You Find.** Leave any natural treasures where you find them so other campers can enjoy them, too. If you want a souvenir of your campout, take a picture. A good saying to remember is "Leave nothing but footprints, take nothing but pictures, kill nothing but time."

5. **Be Careful With Fire.** Cook on a camp stove or grill whenever possible.

It's easier and less messy than cooking over an open fire. Only build fires in designated fire rings. Always have someone keep an eye on your fire until it is dead out.

6. **Respect Wildlife.** Travel quietly and give animals enough space that you don't disturb them. Getting too close to an animal can potentially hurt the animal and you. Take pictures from a safe distance. You're visiting the animal's home, so be considerate.

7. **Be Kind to Other Visitors.** Be respectful of other visitors by keeping noise down and not entering other groups' campsites without permission. Be polite to other people you meet. Give them the respect you expect from them.

To help you remember the Outdoor Code and the Leave No Trace Principles for Kids, you can find them in the back of your handbook.

The member-driven Leave No Trace Center for Outdoor Ethics teaches people how to enjoy the outdoors responsibly. This copyrighted information has been reprinted with permission from the Leave No Trace Center for Outdoor Ethics: www.LNT.org.

Your First Rank—Bobcat!

If you haven't earned your Bobcat badge yet, this is where you start. When you've earned your Bobcat, you'll know the signs, symbols, and big ideas of Scouting. And when you know those, you're a Scout!

If you haven't already earned your Bobcat badge, you will need to start your Cub Scouting adventures by learning what it takes to become a Bobcat!

Read through the Bobcat requirements and practice several times what you have learned. When you think that you are ready, share what you've learned with your family, your den leader, and with your den at a pack meeting. Then give yourself a pat on the back and congratulate yourself on earning your Bobcat badge!

BOBCAT REQUIREMENTS

1. Learn and say the Scout Oath, with help if needed.

2. Learn and say the Scout Law, with help if needed.

3. Show the Cub Scout sign. Tell what it means.

4. Show the Cub Scout handshake. Tell what it means.

5. Say the Cub Scout motto. Tell what it means.

6. Show the Cub Scout salute. Tell what it means.

7. With your parent or guardian, complete the exercises in the pamphlet *How to Protect Your Children From Child Abuse: A Parent's Guide.*

*If the tear-out section is no longer in your handbook, talk to your den leader about finding one.

1 | Learn and say the Scout Oath, with help if needed.

One of the most important parts of earning Bobcat is understanding that all members of the Boy Scouts of America believe in, live by, and often repeat the Scout Oath and the Scout Law. We learn those words and believe in them as a way to live our lives and be good members of our families, our communities, and the Boy Scouts of America!

Scout Oath

On my honor I will do my best
To do my duty to God and my country

and to obey the Scout Law;
To help other people at all times;

To keep myself physically strong,
mentally awake, and morally straight.

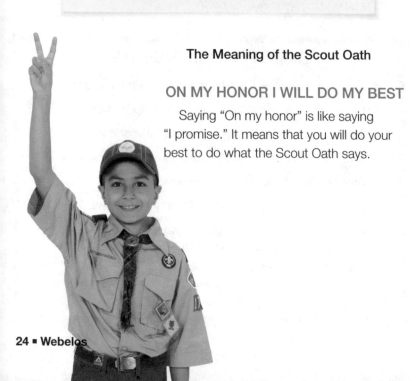

The Meaning of the Scout Oath

ON MY HONOR I WILL DO MY BEST

Saying "On my honor" is like saying "I promise." It means that you will do your best to do what the Scout Oath says.

**The Scout Oath has three promises.
Let's look at what they mean.**

TO DO MY DUTY TO GOD
AND MY COUNTRY AND TO
OBEY THE SCOUT LAW

A duty is something you are expected to do. At home, you might be expected to make up your bed or take out the trash. You also have duties to God and to your country. You do your duty to God by following the teachings of your family and religious leaders. You do your duty to your country by being a good citizen and obeying the law. You also promise to live by the 12 points of the Scout Law, which are described below.

TO HELP OTHER PEOPLE AT ALL TIMES

Many people need help. A friendly smile and a helping hand make life easier for others. By helping other people, you are doing a Good Turn and making our world a better place.

TO KEEP MYSELF PHYSICALLY STRONG,
MENTALLY AWAKE, AND MORALLY STRAIGHT

The last part of the Scout Oath is about taking care of yourself. You stay physically strong when you eat the right foods and get plenty of exercise. You stay mentally awake when you work hard in school, learn all you can, and ask questions. You stay morally straight when you do the right thing and live your life with honesty.

_____

Approved by

Scout Law

A Scout is trustworthy, loyal, helpful, friendly, courteous, kind, obedient, cheerful, thrifty, brave, clean, and reverent.

The Meaning of the Scout Law

The Scout Law has 12 points. Each is a goal for every Scout. He does his best to live up to the Law every day. It is not always easy to do, but a Scout always tries.

A Scout is TRUSTWORTHY. A Scout tells the truth and keeps his promises. People can depend on him.

A Scout is LOYAL. A Scout is true to his family, friends, Scout leaders, school, and country.

A Scout is HELPFUL. A Scout volunteers to help others without expecting a reward.

A Scout is FRIENDLY. A Scout is a friend to everyone, even people who are very different from him.

A Scout is COURTEOUS. A Scout is polite to everyone and always uses good manners.

A Scout is KIND. A Scout treats others as he wants to be treated. He never harms or kills any living thing without good reason.

A Scout is OBEDIENT. A Scout follows the rules of his family, school, and pack. He obeys the laws of his community and country.

A Scout is CHEERFUL. A Scout looks for the bright side of life. He cheerfully does tasks that come his way. He tries to make others happy.

A Scout is THRIFTY. A Scout works to pay his way. He uses time, property, and natural resources wisely.

A Scout is BRAVE. A Scout can face danger even if he is afraid. He stands for what is right even if others laugh at him.

A Scout is CLEAN. A Scout keeps his body and mind fit. He helps keep his home and community clean.

A Scout is REVERENT. A Scout is reverent toward God. He is faithful in his religious duties. He respects the beliefs of others.

Approved by _____

3 | Show the Cub Scout sign. Tell what it means.

Make the sign with your right hand. Hold your arm straight up. The two raised fingers stand for the Scout Oath and the Scout Law. The fingers look like the sharp ears of the wolf ready to listen to Akela! Remember that Akela (say Ah-KAY-la) means "good leader" to a Cub Scout. Your mother or father or guardian is Akela. So is your Cubmaster or your den leader. At school, your teacher is Akela.

Approved by

In a meeting with a mix of Cub Scouts, Boy Scouts and/or Venturers it is appropriate for a Cub Scout to use either the Cub Scout sign or the Scout sign.

4 | Show the Cub Scout handshake. Tell what it means.

When you shake hands with another Cub Scout, do this: Hold out your right hand just as you always do to shake hands. But then put your first two fingers along the inside of the other boy's wrist. This means that you help each other to remember and obey the Scout Oath.

Approved by

The Cub Scout motto is "Do Your Best."

A motto is a guiding principle and a rule for living. Do Your Best means trying your hardest, not just a little bit. Do your best all the time. Do your best in school and at home. Do your best when you play a game and help your team. Do your best as you work on your rank adventures!

Approved by _____

6 | Show the Cub Scout salute. Tell what it means.

Salute with your right hand. Hold your first two fingers close together. Touch your fingertips to your cap. If you aren't wearing a cap, touch your right eyebrow. You salute the flag to show respect to our country. Always use the Cub Scout salute when you are in your Cub Scout uniform, both indoors and outdoors. If you are not in uniform, you salute the flag by placing your right hand over your heart.

Approved by _____

7 | **With your parent or guardian, complete the exercises in the pamphlet *How to Protect Your Children from Child Abuse: A Parent's Guide.***

If your handbook does not include the pamphlet, talk with your den leader.

_____

Approved by

Congratulations on earning your Bobcat badge! You may now continue on the trail of your Webelos and Arrow of Light adventures! Let's take a look at what those adventures are called, what you need to do to earn your Webelos and Arrow of Light badges, and all the fun things you will explore as a Webelos and Arrow of Light Scout!

The Webelos and Arrow of Light Adventures and Requirements

The requirements to earn your Webelos rank and the Arrow of Light rank may be completed in any order. Akela (your den leader, parent, or guardian) will decide on the order for your den. You can do the electives any time you want. And you'll earn an adventure pin for each adventure you complete. Jump right in, Webelos Scout!

WEBELOS BADGE REQUIREMENTS

1. Be an active member of your Webelos den for three months. (Being active means having good attendance, paying your den dues, and working on den projects.)

_____/_____ (date)

2. Complete each of the following Webelos required adventures with your den or family:

Cast Iron Chef

_____/_____ (date)

Stronger, Faster, Higher

_____/_____ (date)

Duty to God and You

_____/_____ (date)

Webelos Walkabout

_____/_____ (date)

First Responder

_____/_____ (date)

3. Complete two Webelos elective adventures of your den or family's choosing. (See page 531.)

_____/_____ (date)   _____/_____ (date)

4. With your parent or guardian, complete the exercises in the pamphlet How to Protect Your Children from Child Abuse: A Parent's Guide and earn the Cyber Chip award for your age.*

_____/_____ (date)

* If your family does not have Internet access at home AND you do not have ready Internet access at school or another public place or via a mobile device, the Cyber Chip portion of this requirement may be waived by your parent or guardian.

ARROW OF LIGHT BADGE REQUIREMENTS

1. Be active in your Webelos den for at least six months since completing the fourth grade or for at least six months since becoming 10 years old. (Being active means having good attendance, paying your den dues, and working on den projects.)

_____/_____ (date)

2. Complete each of the following Arrow of Light required adventures with your den or family:

Building a Better World

_____/_____ (date)

Duty to God in Action

_____/_____ (date)

Camper

_____/_____ (date)

Scouting Adventure

_____/_____ (date)

3. Complete three Webelos elective adventures of your den or family's choosing.

_____/_____ (date)   _____/_____ (date)   _____/_____ (date)

4. With your parent or guardian, complete the exercises in the pamphlet How to Protect Your Children from Child Abuse: A Parent's Guide and earn the Cyber Chip award for your age.*

_____/_____ (date)

Once you have achieved all of the Webelos or Arrow of Light rank badge requirements and your handbook has been signed, you are ready to earn your Webelos or Arrow of Light badge! Let out a big GRAND HOWL, Webelos Scout!

CAST IRON CHEF

Do you like to eat? Of course you do. The Cast Iron Chef adventure is all about eating. Not food that your mom or dad cooks or that you get at a restaurant but food that you and your friends cook in camp.

Now, you can cook all sorts of stuff in camp, like ramen noodles or hot dogs, but you can cook some pretty awesome stuff over a campfire too. On my first troop campout, our senior patrol leader, Bill (he's the older Boy Scout who actually runs our troop), cooked a pineapple upside-down cake in a big cast iron pot called a Dutch oven. It smelled amazing when it was baking and tasted even better when it was done.

I went back for seconds— but there was nothing left! Luckily, Bill taught us how to make our own cake, which we did on the very next campout.

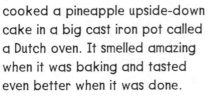

SNAPSHOT OF ADVENTURE

Eating right helps you grow, gives you energy, and keeps your mind sharp. In this adventure, you will learn to build a fire and explore different ways to cook in camp. You will also set nutritional goals for yourself and plan a menu for your den or family. Best of all, you'll get to eat the food you cook!

REQUIREMENTS

Do all of these: **Approved by**

1. At an approved time in an outdoor location and using tinder, kindling, and fuel wood, demonstrate how to build a fire; light the fire, unless prohibited by local fire restrictions. After allowing the fire to burn safely, safely extinguish the flames with minimal impact to the fire site. _____

2. Set personal nutritional goals. Keep a food journal for one week; review your journal to determine if the goals were met. _____

3. Plan a menu for a balanced meal for your den or family. Determine the budget for the meal. Shop for the items on your menu while staying within your budget. _____

4. Prepare a balanced meal for your den or family; utilize one of the methods below for preparation of part of your meal: _____
   - **A.** Camp stove _____
   - **B.** Dutch oven _____
   - **C.** Box oven _____
   - **D.** Solar oven _____
   - **E.** Open campfire or charcoal _____

5. Demonstrate an understanding of food safety practices while preparing the meal. _____

To start a fire, you need three things: heat, oxygen, and fuel. Heat comes from matches, oxygen comes from the air, and fuel comes from wood. Not just any wood will do, however. It needs to be dry and well seasoned—never freshly cut. Also, you can't just hold a match to a big log to start a fire. Instead, you must build your fire slowly using tinder, kindling, and logs.

- **To help protect the earth, never cut live trees for firewood. (Green wood doesn't burn well anyway.)**
- **Also, don't bring firewood from home. Doing that can spread pests that hurt trees.**
- **Webelos Scouts should only light fires under supervision of a den leader or another adult.**

Tinder is anything that burns as soon as you light it. It can include small twigs, dry leaves, pine needles, tree bark, wood shavings, paper, or even dryer lint you bring from home. (Really!) *Kindling* is small sticks, no bigger than a pencil, that will burn easily but not as fast as tinder. *Fuel wood* is bigger pieces of wood that will burn a long time. You don't need huge logs, by the way; look for pieces no thicker than your wrist.

Be Careful With Fire

- ✦ Clear anything that could burn from an area at least 5 feet in all directions from your fire.

- ✦ Never play in or around the fire.

- ✦ Never leave the fire unattended.

- ✦ Make sure the fire is completely out before you leave.

A Scout is trustworthy. You can show that you are trustworthy by following the rules of fire safety.

After you're done cooking, be sure to put your fire completely out. You can cover a small fire with a metal can. For larger fires, you can use water or sand and stir the coals. Carefully feel for heat. It should be cold to the touch.

To make a quick fire starter, put dryer lint inside an empty toilet paper roll and close each end with a piece of masking tape.

To lay a fire, first gather all the tinder, kindling, and fuel wood you think you will need:

1. Build a tepee out of kindling and put some tinder inside it. Add some fuel wood.

2. Light the tinder and blow gently or fan, if necessary, to supply oxygen.

3. As the kindling burns, have an adult help adding larger sticks and then small logs.

4. When the fire burns down to coals, you're ready to cook. Take plenty of time to let a good bed of coals form; it's hard to cook over open flames because you can't control the heat.

REQUIREMENT 2 | Set personal nutritional goals. Keep a food journal for one week; review your journal to determine if the goals were met.

Do you know what a balanced diet is? No, it doesn't mean resting your plate on your head! It means eating the right assortment of foods so you get all the nutrients you need for good health. For example, the calcium in milk and yogurt makes your bones strong. The vitamin A in carrots and dark leafy greens helps you see well. The protein in meat, nuts, and beans helps your body repair cells and make new ones.

GRAINS 5 ounces	VEGETABLES 2 cups	FRUITS 1½ cups	DAIRY 3 cups	PROTEIN FOODS 5 ounces
Make half your grains whole Aim for at least **3 ounces** of whole grains a day	**Vary your veggies** Aim for these amounts **each week:** **Dark green veggies** =1½ cups **Red and orange veggies** = 4 cups **Beans and peas** = 1 cup **Starchy veggies** = 4 cups **Other veggies** = 3½ cups	**Focus on fruits** Eat a variety of fruit Choose whole or cut-up fruits more often than fruit juice	**Get your calcium-rich foods** Drink fat-free or low-fat (1%) milk, for the same amount of calcium and other nutrients as whole milk, but less fat and calories Select fat-free or low-fat yogurt and cheese, or try calcium-fortified soy products	**Go lean with protein** Twice a week, make seafood the protein on your plate Vary your protein routine—choose beans, peas, nuts, and seeds more often Keep meat and poultry portions small and lean

Find your balance between food and physical activity

Be physically active for at least **60 minutes** each day.

Know your limits on fats, sugars, and sodium

Your allowance for oils is 5 teaspoons a day.

Limit calories from solid fats and added sugars to **120 calories** a day.

Reduce sodium intake to less than **2300 mg** a day.

Source: *www.choosemyplate.gov*

> **NOTE:** These amounts are for a Webelos Scout who weighs 60 pounds and needs to take in 1,600 calories per day. You can adjust the totals if you weigh more or less.

The chart on page 42 is from **www.choosemyplate.gov**. It shows how much of the five food groups you should eat every day. It helps if each meal contains at least three of the five food groups and each snack contains two groups.

What about sweets and other treats? Save those for special occasions and for after you've eaten the foods you need.

> When I did this adventure myself, I decided to try eating fish for the first time. It was delicious! Who knew?

After you've looked at the chart, talk with your parent or den leader and set some personal nutritional goals. For example, you might decide to eat more vegetables, cut back on red meat, or try something you've never eaten such as kumquats or kiwis or clementines. (Those are all fruits, by the way, and they taste great!)

Keep track of everything you eat for a whole week to see whether you've met your goals.

@ With permission from your parent or guardian, visit **www.choosemyplate.gov** for more information on nutrition and staying healthy. There are also many websites with nutritional information, such as calories, for popular foods.

Great meals don't just happen. Somebody has to plan them. Work with your family or other members of your den to plan a delicious breakfast, lunch, or supper. Remember to include three different food groups if possible.

Make a shopping list, and decide how much money you can spend. Then head to the grocery store and start shopping. Work to stay within your budget by checking prices as you go. If you need to make adjustments, that's OK: a Scout is flexible. (OK, that's not in the Scout Law, but it's still true.)

A Scout is thrifty. You can show that you are thrifty by finding ways to save money when shopping.

Here are some things to consider when you go shopping:

- ◆ Store brands are often less expensive than brands you see advertised on TV or online.

- ◆ Foods you make from scratch usually cost less (and are tastier) than processed foods.

- ◆ You should compare the price of fresh, canned, and frozen fruits and vegetables to find the best price.

- ◆ To really be sure you're getting the best deal, compare the price per ounce of different products.

SAMPLE CAMP MENU

BREAKFAST

Eggs in a bag: For each Scout, crack one or two eggs into a sealable, quart-sized plastic bag. Add 1 tablespoon milk and other ingredients—bacon bits, cheese, chopped green pepper, chopped onion, salt, pepper—to taste. Seal the bag, removing excess air, and then shake it. (Don't shake it before you seal it!) Place the bag into boiling water and cook for 3–4 minutes or until fully cooked. Use tongs to remove the bag from the hot water.

Fruit salad: Cut up apples, bananas, oranges, grapes, or other favorite fruits. Mix together and toss with a little lemon juice to prevent browning.

Biscuits: Arrange canned biscuits on a metal plate or pie pan. Carefully place the plate on several rocks in the floor of a preheated Dutch oven. Cook until golden brown.

Juice and milk

LUNCH

Peanut butter and jelly sandwiches
Carrots, apples
Juice boxes

DINNER

Dutch-oven pizza: Spread pizza dough on a metal plate. Cover with pizza sauce, sautéed vegetables, cooked meat, cheese, and other favorite toppings. (Anchovies, anyone?) Carefully place the plate on several rocks in the floor of a preheated Dutch oven. Cook until cheese is melted and crust is golden brown.

Salad
Drinks
S'mores: Roast a large marshmallow on a skewer over hot coals. Add a square of chocolate, and sandwich between two graham crackers. Delish!

A. Camp stove   **B. Dutch oven**   **C. Box oven**

D. Solar oven   **E. Open campfire or charcoal**

OUTDOOR COOKING METHODS

Camp Stove: A camp stove is a tabletop stove that uses liquid fuel or propane. Camp stoves work just like your cooktop back home. Be careful, however, because some can tip over easily. Always have an experienced adult help you light a camp stove.

Dutch Oven: A Dutch oven is a cast iron (or aluminum) pot that is heated by charcoal or hot coals. A camping Dutch oven has legs on the bottom and a rim around the lid. For baking, put 10–12 coals underneath and enough coals on top to cover the lid. For boiling, put more coals underneath. Either way, you can add or remove coals to adjust the temperature.

Box Oven: A box oven is sort of like a homemade Dutch oven. It's a foil-lined cardboard box that sits on top of a cookie sheet that is propped on four empty vegetable cans. Between the cans is a bed of coals, which provides the heat.

Solar Oven: A solar oven is a pizza box that's lined with aluminum foil and covered with black construction paper. It uses the sun's rays to cook what's inside. (Now you know why tents aren't made of black paper and aluminum foil!)

Open Campfire or Charcoal: Open fires are good for roasting marshmallows and grilling things like burgers. For best results, wait until the flames die down and cook over the coals. If using charcoal, let it burn down until it is covered with white ash. Charcoal is a good tool for learning outdoor cooking, because it is easy to light and keeps a steady, even heat.

Camp food is yummy, and camp cooking is fun. As part of this adventure, you'll get to try some really cool ways to cook food. Just don't try them all at home. Campfires in the kitchen are not a good idea!

However you cook, you need to do some things to keep from getting sick and making other people sick:

- **Clean hands and surfaces frequently.** Wash your hands with warm water and soap for at least 20 seconds before and after you handle food and after you use the bathroom. Wash your cutting boards, dishes, utensils, and countertops with hot soapy water after you prepare each food item and before you go on to the next food.

- **Don't cross-contaminate.** That's a fancy way to say you should keep raw meat, poultry, seafood, and eggs separate from other foods in your shopping cart, grocery bags, refrigerator, and ice chest. Also, never place cooked food on a plate that has held raw meat, poultry, seafood, or eggs.

- **Cook to proper temperatures.** Use a food thermometer, which measures the temperature inside cooked meat, poultry, and egg dishes, to make sure the food is fully cooked. Stick the thermometer into the middle of the food and don't let it touch the pan. Most cookbooks include the correct temperatures for different kinds of food.

- **Chill/refrigerate promptly.** Never let food sit out for more than two hours before putting it in the refrigerator, freezer, or ice chest. Never thaw frozen food at room temperature. Instead, thaw it out in the refrigerator, in cold water, and in a microwave oven using the defrost setting. Food thawed in cold water or in the microwave should be cooked immediately.

♦ **Maintain proper temperatures.** Keep cold foods in an ice chest or refrigerator until you're ready to use them. If you are going to use an insulated container to keep food warm, fill it with hot water, wait a few minutes, then empty it and fill it with hot food.

When I was a Webelos Scout, our den sometimes forgot to pack a few things. Like sauce for our spaghetti. And jelly for our PB&J sandwiches. Crazy, huh?

Over time we got better at planning and cooking and even washing dishes. Now, as Boy Scouts, we cook some great food. And that food gives us the fuel we need for some really awesome adventures.

See you at camp!

DUTY TO GOD AND YOU

I went to Boy Scout camp for the first time last summer. We did a lot of cool stuff like shooting and swimming, and we really had fun at the opening and closing campfires. But one of my favorite times was the chapel service we went to on Wednesday night.

During the service the chaplain pointed out that the camp chapel didn't have a roof or walls, which meant there was nothing to separate us from God above us or from the world around us. He said that even when we go back to our places of worship with their roofs and walls, we should keep working to stay connected to God and to God's people. That's what you'll learn about in the Duty to God and You adventure.

SNAPSHOT OF ADVENTURE

Understanding more about your religious beliefs and the beliefs of others can help you make sense of the world around you. The Duty to God and You adventure lets you learn about your own faith, plan and participate in a worship service, and explore ways to continue your faith practices in the future.

REQUIREMENT

Do either requirement 1 OR requirement 2.   Approved by

1. Earn the religious emblem of your faith for Webelos Scouts, if you have not already done so. _____

2. Complete at least three of requirements 2a–2d:

   A. Help plan, support, or actively participate in a service of worship or reflection. Show reverence during the service. _____

   B. Review with your family or den members what you have learned about your duty to God. _____

   C. Discuss with your family, family's faith leader, or other trusted adult how planning and participating in a service of worship or reflection helps you live your duty to God. _____

   D. List one thing that will bring you closer to doing your duty to God, and practice it for one month. Write down what you will do each day to remind you. _____

REQUIREMENT 1 | Earn the religious emblem of your faith for Webelos Scouts, if you have not already done so.

Most major faith groups that support Scouting have created religious emblems that Scouts can earn. Working on the emblem for your faith group will help you learn the meaning of duty to God, which is part of the Scout Oath.

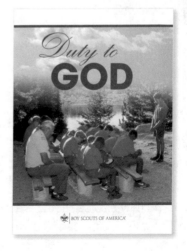

Once you earn your religious emblem, you can wear a special square knot patch on your uniform as a Webelos Scout, a Boy Scout, and even as an adult leader. That and the Arrow of Light are the only Cub Scout awards you can wear as a Boy Scout.

Your den leader or local council service center can help you and your family learn more about the religious emblem for your faith. With an adult's permission, you can also visit **www.praypub.org** or **www.scouting.org/filestore/ pdf/512-879_WB.pdf.**

Duty to **GOD**

BOY SCOUTS OF AMERICA

REQUIREMENT 2A | Help plan, support, or actively participate in a service of worship or reflection. Show reverence during the service.

You might plan to do a service at your faith organization, a family reflection, or an interfaith service. An interfaith service may be appropriate if members of more than one faith are gathered together. It lets you practice your faith and learn how others practice theirs. You can hold an interfaith service in your den, pack, or at a big event like a camporee.

Your den leader or another adult will help you plan your service. It might have a theme, such as peace, and include songs or readings about that theme. Or you might take turns praying the way you have been taught by your faith.

SAMPLE INTERFAITH SERVICE

Your interfaith gathering might include these parts:

- ◆ Welcome
- ◆ Thought to share/lesson
- ◆ Song
- ◆ Sharing time
- ◆ Prayer/meditation
- ◆ Helping others (like a collection for the World Friendship Fund)
- ◆ Benediction/sending forth

You will see that many faiths share similar practices, like praying, but you may also see some practices that are unfamiliar, like the use of incense. Even a practice that many faiths share can be done in different ways. Take praying. People may stand, sit, kneel, or lie facedown on the ground. They may close their eyes or leave them open. They may fold their hands or raise them in the air. They may take off their hats or wear special head coverings.

When you plan your service, be careful not to say or do things that will make other people uncomfortable. For example, instead of saying, "Please bow your head for prayer," you could say, "Please prepare to pray in the way you have been taught."

A Scout is reverent. During the service, be sure to show reverence. That includes doing your duty to God and showing respect for other people's beliefs.

Write down a plan for your interfaith service, worship service, or reflection.

Welcome: _____

_____

Thought/lesson: _____

_____

Song: _____

Sharing: _____

_____

Prayer/meditation: _____

_____

Helping: _____

_____

Closing: _____

_____

REQUIREMENT 2B | Review with your family or den members what you have learned about your duty to God.

REQUIREMENT 2C | Discuss with your family, family's faith leader, or other trusted adult how planning and participating in a service of worship or reflection helps you live your duty to God.

REQUIREMENT 2D | List one thing that will bring you closer to doing your duty to God, and practice it for one month. Write down what you will do each day to remind you.

Talk with your family or den members about what you learned as you completed requirement 2a. If you talk with other den members, listen to what they learned. Then you will have learned those things, too.

Here are some things to talk about:

♦ What does duty to God mean to me?

♦ What does reverence mean to me?

♦ How are the other faiths I learned about different from my own?

♦ How are they similar?

♦ What faith practice did I learn about that makes me feel closer to God?

FAITH PRACTICES

Here are some practices that many faiths share:

- Worship: going to a service at a church, temple, mosque, synagogue, or other place
- Prayer: talking to God (and listening)
- Meditation: clearing your mind to focus on your faith
- Service: helping other people
- Charity: donating money to worthy causes
- Fasting: giving up food or other things at certain times
- Confession: admitting things you've done wrong and asking for forgiveness
- Study: reading books of faith
- Observing holy days: setting aside days for your faith tradition that require special actions
- Obeying the rules set down by your faith tradition

What other practices does your faith encourage?

Working on this adventure, I learned that people of several different faiths fast during part of the year. Muslims don't eat or drink during the daytime for the whole month of Ramadan, and many Christians fast or give up certain foods during the season of Lent. I think it's cool how people of different faiths end up doing similar things to get closer to God. What did you learn in this adventure that was cool?

FIRST RESPONDER

PARAMEDIC 7 ENGINE

IRVING FIRE DEPARTMENT

My mom is an emergency medical technician, and she says First Responder is the most important Webelos Scout adventure. In fact, she told me the other day that her ambulance crew was able to save a man's life because his son—a Webelos Scout—saw that he was having a heart attack and called 911.

How cool is it that he was able to help? Wouldn't it be awesome to have the skills and confidence to be prepared to save somebody's life? Well, you never know. It just might happen. That's what the First Responder adventure is all about.

SNAPSHOT OF ADVENTURE

In this adventure, you will put the Scout motto, "Be Prepared," into action by learning about first aid. You'll also build your own first-aid kit and make emergency plans for your home or den meeting location. And you'll learn how professional first responders help keep you safe. By the time you finish this adventure, you should be ready to act if you are first on the scene when an emergency happens.

REQUIREMENT

Do all of these: **Approved by**

1. Explain what first aid is. Tell what you should do after an accident.   _____

2. Show what to do for the hurry cases of first aid:

    A. Serious bleeding   _____

    B. Heart attack or sudden cardiac arrest   _____

    C. Stopped breathing   _____

    D. Stroke   _____

    E. Poisoning   _____

3. Show how to help a choking victim.   _____

4. Show how to treat for shock.   _____

5. Demonstrate that you know how to treat the following:

    A. Cuts and scratches   _____

    B. Burns and scalds   _____

    C. Sunburn   _____

    D. Blisters on the hand and foot   _____

E. Tick bites   _____

F. Bites and stings of other insects   _____

G. Venomous snakebite   _____

H. Nosebleed   _____

I. Frostbite   _____

6. Put together a simple home first-aid kit.
Explain what you included and how to use
each item correctly.   _____

7. Create and practice an emergency readiness
plan for your home or den meeting place.   _____

8. Visit with a first responder.   _____

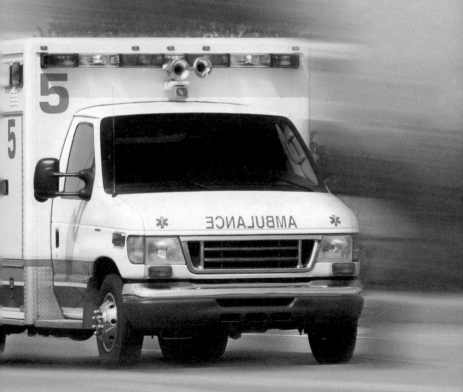

When people get hurt, they need help right away. That help is called first aid. It's the quick help someone receives before professional help can arrive. You might be the only person at the scene of an accident who can provide first aid, so it's important to know the right way to help.

> The Scout motto is "Be Prepared." One way to be prepared is to learn how to do first aid before an emergency occurs.

First aid is what happens when you remove a tick that's burrowed into your skin. First aid is what happens when, after you scrape your knee, your mom cleans and bandages the wound. First aid is what happens when a server in a restaurant saves a choking victim by giving abdominal thrusts. First aid is what happens when a Boy Scout performs CPR while he's waiting for an ambulance to arrive. First aid is what you will learn during this adventure.

What to Do After an Accident

If you come across an accident or medical emergency, do these things:

- **Check.** Make sure the scene is safe before approaching. You can't help anyone if you become a victim yourself.

- **Calm down and think.** Assess the situation and decide what needs to be done. Staying calm may be hard to do, but it's important. The victim will feel better knowing you are in control, and you will be able to make better decisions than if you were panicked.

- **Call.** If the victim seems badly hurt, send someone to call for medical help. If no one is there to do that, call for help, and offer to assist the victim.

- **Care.** Explain that you know first aid, and get permission to treat the victim before doing anything else.

When sending someone to get help, point at a specific person and say something like, "Juan, go call 911 and ask for an ambulance." Don't assume everybody knows what to do.

* Do not move a badly hurt person unless he or she is in further danger. It may be necessary to move a person if there is a nearby fire or if the person is lying in the road. But never move an injured person unless it is absolutely necessary.
* Check the victim for "hurry cases" (see page 66).
* Treat the victim for shock (see page 74).

A Scout is brave. But that doesn't mean bravery is something you're born with. You can train yourself to face emergencies with courage. In an emergency, remember to:
Be strong.
Be calm.
Be clear.
Be careful.

How to Get Help in an Emergency

In most parts of the United States, you can dial 911 to get help for all kinds of emergencies, including medical problems. Some communities may have different phone numbers for the police, fire department, emergency medical services (EMS), or rescue squad, so ask your parent or den leader for the right phone numbers for your community.

When you call for help in an emergency, remember the three W's: *who*, *what*, and *where*.

- **Who:** Give your name and the phone number you're calling from. (Some 911 systems can trace your phone number and location, but others can't.)

- **What:** Explain the situation. Is it a fire? A car accident? How many people are hurt? What are their injuries?

- **Where:** Give your exact location, using either the street address or the names of both streets at the nearest corner.

Never hang up until the operator tells you to. He or she may need more information. Don't worry; the operator can still send help.

Never call 911 except in actual emergencies. Calling in non-emergency situations is dangerous because it could prevent real emergency calls from getting through. To practice making 911 calls, use a toy phone or a cellphone that has been turned off.

My mom invited a real 911 operator she knows to one of our den meetings. He had us make pretend calls to him, which really helped us understand what to do in an actual emergency.

How to Get Help in Other Situations

At times, you may need to get help in non-emergency situations. Maybe you want to report a suspicious car nearby or a broken traffic light. Maybe you need help with a family problem.

Find out how to get help where you live, and make a list of the phone numbers. Post the list on your refrigerator so everyone can find the numbers quickly. It's also a good idea to put your list on a card and carry it with you.

Our home address _____

IMPORTANT PHONE NUMBERS

Keep a list of numbers for:

♦ Police or sheriff's department _____

♦ Fire department _____

♦ Ambulance or emergency medical services _____

_____

♦ Utility companies (electricity, gas, water)_____

_____

_____

_____

♦ Your family doctor _____

♦ Poison control center 800-222-1222

♦ Your religious institution (church, synagogue, mosque, etc.)

_____

♦ Your parent's or guardian's cellphone _____

_____

♦ Your parent's or guardian's workplace _____

_____

♦ A friendly neighbor who can help you _____

_____

REQUIREMENT 2 | Show what to do for the hurry cases of first aid:

A. Serious bleeding

B. Heart attack or sudden cardiac arrest

C. Stopped breathing

D. Stroke

E. Poisoning

A sprained ankle needs first aid, but it's not a life-threatening injury. Other medical problems—called "hurry cases"—require immediate help. Unless someone acts fast, gets help, and gives the right first aid, the victim can die within a few minutes.

3C THE THREE C'S

When dealing with hurry cases, remember the three C's.

- **Check:** Make sure the area is safe for you. Then check the victim to identify the problem. Is the victim breathing or moving? Tap the victim's shoulder and ask, "Are you OK?" Does the victim respond?
- **Call:** Call 911. Call out for for help, or send someone for help.
- **Care:** Care for the victim to the best of your ability while you wait for help to arrive. Some of the steps in treating hurry cases require special training to perform, but it's important to know what they are.

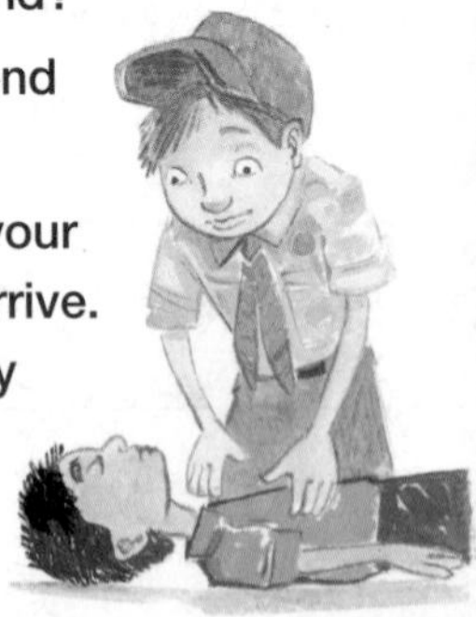

The five hurry cases are:

- **Serious bleeding.** When blood is spurting from a wound, it must be stopped quickly.

- **Heart attack or sudden cardiac arrest.** If someone's heart has stopped, it must be restarted quickly.

- **Stopped breathing.** If breathing has stopped, it must be restarted quickly.

- **Stroke.** If someone has a stroke (a blockage of blood flow to the brain), he or she must get medical attention quickly.

- **Poisoning.** If someone has swallowed poison, it must be made harmless quickly.

PROTECTIVE MEASURES TO TAKE WHEN GIVING FIRST AID

Treat all blood as if it contains germs that can make you sick. Do not use bare hands to stop bleeding; always use a protective barrier. If you have any cuts or scrapes, cover them with a bandage. Always wash your hands and other exposed skin with hot water and soap immediately after treating the victim. When possible, don't use a kitchen sink.

The following equipment should be included in all first-aid kits and used when giving first aid to someone in need:

- Disposable, latex-free gloves—to be used when stopping bleeding, dressing wounds, performing CPR, or treating a victim who is choking

- Plastic goggles or other eye protection—to prevent a victim's blood from getting into the rescuer's eyes in the event of serious bleeding

- Antiseptic—for use in cleaning exposed skin areas, particularly if soap and water are not available

HURRY CASE: Serious Bleeding

In a bad accident, you might see blood spurting out of a wound. It doesn't ooze or flow slowly; it gushes out like a fountain. It must be stopped immediately.

3C Activate the 3 C's

Put on disposable, latex-free gloves and eye protection (not just eyeglasses), then grab the wound with your gloved hand. Press hard. With your free hand, grab your neckerchief, handkerchief, or another cloth. Fold it into a pad, and press it on the wound. If you can, wrap the wound with gauze to hold the pad in place. If not, keep applying pressure with your hand. Don't remove the pad if it gets soaked with blood. Instead, put another pad and bandage over the first.

If the wound is on the arm or leg, raise that limb above the level of the victim's heart. That can help slow the bleeding. (Don't do this if there are other injuries such as a broken bone.)

HURRY CASE: Heart Attack and Sudden Cardiac Arrest

Heart attack is the No. 1 cause of death in the United States. Most heart attacks happen to adults, but sometimes even young people can experience them.

The most common symptom of a heart attack is pain in the center of the chest, but people can have other symptoms as well, including:

- Pain that radiates to the arms, back, neck, or jaw
- Sweating when the room is not hot
- Feeling like throwing up
- Feeling weak
- Sudden, sharp chest pain outside the breastbone
- Dizziness or lightheadedness

 Activate the 3 C's

If you think a person is having a heart attack, call for medical help at once. If the person becomes unresponsive, begin chest compressions immediately, as described below.

Another very serious heart problem is sudden cardiac arrest, which occurs when the heart stops pumping. In seconds, the victim will become unresponsive and will stop breathing or will gasp for breath. If you suspect sudden cardiac arrest, call for medical help, begin chest compressions, and locate an automated external defibrillator (AED) if available. (See page 70.)

Circulation

Cardiopulmonary resuscitation (CPR) is a way to keep the heart beating until medical help arrives. It requires instruction from a certified teacher. Your den leader can help you find more information.

The steps of CPR for adults include a cycle of 30 chest compressions followed by two rescue breaths.

1. Place the heels of your hands on the center of the victim's chest, one on top of the other. Lace your fingers together.

2. Position yourself over the victim with your shoulders over your hands and your arms straight.

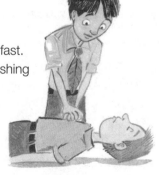

3. Give 30 compressions. Push hard and fast. Let the chest rise completely before pushing down again.

4. Perform two rescue breaths as described in the Breathing section on page 71.

5. Continue the cycle until one of the following happens:

    a. The victim shows signs of life (breathing).

    b. A trained adult or medical help arrives to take over.

    c. You are too exhausted to continue.

    d. An AED is ready to use.

    e. The scene becomes unsafe.

Defibrillation

Find out if there is an automated external defibrillator (AED) near the victim. If there is, you can help by retrieving it and turning it on. An AED is a special device that can shock the heart into beating normally again. AEDs are found in schools, shopping malls, airports, houses of worship, and other places where people gather. You have to complete training to use an AED; this training is usually part of CPR training.

HURRY CASE: Stopped Breathing

In drowning cases, electric shock, and some other accidents, the victim's breathing may stop. It must be started again quickly, or the person's heart will stop beating, and the person will die. You can help with these problems by providing care until professional medical help arrives.

③Ⓒ Activate the 3 C's

Here are the steps you can take:

Airway

With the victim lying on his or her back, open the airway by pressing down on the forehead and lifting up on the chin. This will keep the tongue from blocking the flow of air. Don't do this if you suspect a neck injury.

If the victim starts to vomit, roll him or her onto the side away from you so the vomit doesn't get inhaled into the lungs. Be sure to roll the body as a unit—not just the upper body. You'll need help to do this.

Breathing

When the victim's airway is open, check for breathing. Place your cheek 1 to 2 inches above the victim's mouth. Look, listen, and feel for movement and breathing. If the person is breathing, you will feel and hear the airflow on your cheek and see and feel the chest rising and falling. If there are no signals that a person is breathing, give two rescue breaths using the following procedure.

Rescue Breathing

Step 1 Place a CPR breathing barrier over the victim's mouth to protect both of you from any diseases that could be spread.

Step 2 While continuing to tilt the head, pinch the victim's nostrils, seal your mouth over his or her mouth, and blow into it to fill the lungs. The breath should last about one second. Watch to see if the person's chest rises. Remove your mouth, and then give another rescue breath.

Step 3 For an adult: If the victim does not start breathing again after two rescue breaths, his or her heart may stop beating, too. Immediately begin CPR. (Ask your den leader about procedures for children.)

HURRY CASE: Stroke

Stroke occurs when the blood supply is cut off to part of the brain. Brain damage and death can result if the victim doesn't get medical help.

Stroke can cause:

♦ Numbness or weakness in the face, arm, or leg—especially on one side

♦ Trouble walking, speaking, understanding, or seeing

♦ Dizziness

♦ Headache

3C Activate the 3 C's

A good way to remember the signs of stroke is with the acronym FAST:

- **Face drooping:** Does one side of the person's face droop? Is the person's smile uneven?

- **Arm weakness:** Is one arm weak or numb?

- **Speech difficulty:** Is the person's speech slurred? Does the person have a hard time speaking or repeating a simple sentence?

- **Time to call for help:** If you see these signs, call 911 immediately.

HURRY CASE: Poisoning

3C Activate the 3 C's

Poisoning can be caused by many things, including:

- Eating certain wild mushrooms or berries

- Swallowing household cleaning supplies, weed killers, insect poisons, or even things like nail polish remover

- Taking too much medicine

- Breathing in toxic fumes

If someone has swallowed or breathed in poison, call 911 or 800-222-1222 (the national Poison Help Line) immediately. Tell the operator what the poison is, if you know it, and follow the directions. Save the poison container so professionals can identify the poison.

If a person has breathed in smoke, gas, or other fumes, try to move him or her to fresh air. Be careful that you don't become a victim yourself, however. Make sure the area is safe first.

> It's important always to keep all household cleaners, medicines, weed killers, and insect poisons out of the reach of small children. Locked cabinets are best because children are curious and quickly learn to climb.

REQUIREMENT 3 | Show how to help a choking victim.

Choking on food or a foreign object can lead to unconsciousness and death. If you see someone choking, take action immediately.

When you see a person holding his hands to his throat and turning blue, ask if he is choking. If he can speak, cough, or breathe, encourage him to try to cough up what he has swallowed. If not, call 911, or ask a bystander to call 911. Tell the person you know first aid, and ask if you can help.

If the answer is yes, give back blows:

  ♦ Give five back blows between the shoulder blades with the heel of your hand.

If the object is not removed, give abdominal thrusts:

  ♦ Position yourself behind the person, and reach your arms around his or her waist.

  ♦ Make a fist with one hand just above the person's belly button. Cover the fist with your other hand.

  ♦ Make a series of five quick thrusts inward and upward to force air from the lungs. (Pretend like you're trying to pick the person up.)

  ♦ Alternate between abdominal thrusts and back blows until the object is dislodged, the person becomes unconscious, or medical help arrives.

Because of the possibility of injury, do not practice actual back blows or abdominal thrusts unless you are using a special simulator.

REQUIREMENT 4 | Show how to treat for shock.

When a person is injured or under great stress, the circulatory system might not provide enough blood to all parts of the body. That's called shock. The person will feel weak. The face may get pale. The skin will feel cold and clammy. He or she may shiver or vomit.

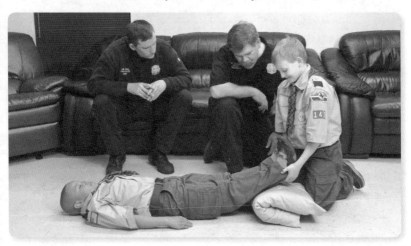

Don't wait for these signals to appear. Give any badly injured person first aid for shock:

- Call 911 for emergency help immediately.
- Have the person lie down on his or her back.
- Raise the feet slightly, unless you think there are injuries to the head, neck, back, hips, or legs. If you don't know, have the person lie flat.
- If the person is not awake, turn him or her on the side. But first, be sure the person has no head, neck, or back injuries.
- If the weather is cool, cover the person with a sheet. If it's hot, don't.
- Do not give the person anything to eat or drink.
- Stay with the person until help arrives.

A. Cuts and scratches
B. Burns and scalds
C. Sunburn
D. Blisters on the hand and foot
E. Tick bites
F. Bites and stings of other insects
G. Venomous snakebite
H. Nosebleed
I. Frostbite

Cuts and Scratches

Cuts and scratches are openings in skin. They can let in germs that cause infections.

When treating cuts and scratches, be sure to wear disposable, latex-free gloves and eye protection. Wash your hands thoroughly with soap and water after treating any wounds.

For small wounds, wash the wound with soap and water. Then apply antibiotic ointment to help prevent infection if you have the victim's permission and know that he or she doesn't have any allergy to the medicine. Keep the wound clean with an adhesive bandage. Change the bandage as often as needed, but at least once daily.

For larger cuts, first stop the bleeding by applying direct pressure. Keep the wound as clean as possible to limit infection. Cover an open wound with a sterile gauze pad or a clean cloth folded into a pad. Hold the pad in place with tape or a bandage made out of a neckerchief. Any bandage should be loose enough that you can slide two fingers between it and the person's body. An adult leader should evaluate any large wound. Once the bleeding has stopped, clean the wound as described above.

Anyone suffering a serious wound should be treated for shock and seen by a physician.

Burns and Scalds

Burns and scalds range from simple sunburn to very dangerous third-degree burns. What kind of first aid to give depends on the severity of the burn.

First-Degree Burns

First-degree burns only affect the outer surface of the skin, which gets red and sore. Put the burned area in cold water until the pain stops. If you don't have any water, cover the burn with a clean, dry, loose dressing.

Second-Degree Burns

With second-degree burns, which are also called partial-thickness burns, blisters form on the skin. Put the burned area in cold water until the pain stops. Gently dry the burned area. Cover it with a sterile gauze pad, and hold the pad loosely in place with a bandage. Be careful not to break open blisters, which could cause infection. Don't apply creams, ointments, or sprays. If needed, treat for shock. Second-degree burns should be evaluated by an adult to determine the need for additional medical help.

Third-Degree Burns

With third-degree burns, which are also called full-thickness burns, the skin may be burned away, and the flesh may be charred. The victim may feel no pain because nerve endings have been burned. You will definitely need to call 911 or local emergency responders and have an adult evaluate the situation. Don't remove clothing from around the burn. Wrap the victim in a clean sheet. Cover him or her with blankets if the weather is cool. Treat for shock if needed, and stay with the victim until professional medical help arrives.

SUNBURN

Sunburn is a common injury among people who enjoy being outdoors. Most sunburns are first-degree burns, although severe sunburn is a second-degree burn and should receive prompt medical attention. All sunburns are dangerous because they can lead to long-term skin damage and even skin cancer when you get older.

People with lighter skin are most at risk of getting sunburned, but no one is immune. You can prevent sunburn by using plenty of broad-spectrum sunscreen with a sun protection factor (SPF) of at least 30. Put it on 20 minutes before you go outside and every two hours while you're outside. Reapply it after swimming or if you are sweating a lot. A broad-brimmed hat, long-sleeved shirt, and long pants will give you even more protection.

You should wear sunscreen even on cloudy days. The ultraviolet radiation from the sun that causes a sunburn can pass through clouds.

Blisters on the Hand and Foot

Blisters are pockets of fluid that form as the skin's way of protecting itself from friction. Blisters on the feet are common injuries among hikers. You can avoid getting blisters by wearing shoes or boots that fit well, by changing your socks if they become sweaty or wet, and by paying attention to how your feet feel. A hot spot is a warning that a blister might be forming. As soon as you notice it, cover the hot spot with moleskin.

If a blister forms, you can protect it with a doughnut bandage. To make one, cut moleskin in the shape of a doughnut, and fit it around the blister. Shape several more doughnuts, and stack them on top of the first. Cover with an adhesive bandage.

Tick Bites

Ticks are small, hard-shelled arachnids that bury their heads in your skin. Protect yourself whenever you're in tick-infested woodlands and fields by wearing long pants and a long-sleeved shirt. Button your collar, and tuck your pant legs into your socks.

Inspect yourself daily, especially the warm and hairy parts of your body, and immediately remove any ticks you find. If a tick has attached itself, ask an adult to help you. The adult will grasp the tick with tweezers close to the skin and gently pull until it comes loose. It's important not to squeeze, twist, or jerk the tick, which could leave its mouth parts in the skin. Wash the wound with soap and water, and apply antibiotic ointment. After dealing with a tick, thoroughly wash your hands. If you develop a rash or flulike symptoms or otherwise feel ill in the next days or weeks after being bitten, talk to your doctor.

Bee and Wasp Stings

Scrape away a bee or wasp stinger with the edge of card, such as your Whittling Chip card, or ask an adult to help. Another method is to put a piece of tape on top of the sting to pull out the stinger. Don't try to squeeze it out. That will force more venom into the skin from the sac attached to the stinger. An ice pack might reduce pain and swelling.

Some people have severe allergies to bee and wasp stings. If someone has trouble breathing after being stung or feels his or her throat swelling or closing up, seek medical help immediately, and alert an adult. Find out if the person is carrying a kit for treating anaphylactic shock, and help him or her administer the medication.

Chigger Bites

Chiggers are almost invisible. Their bites cause itching and small welts. Try not to scratch chigger bites. You might find some relief by covering chigger bites with calamine lotion or hydrocortisone cream.

Spider Bites

Only a few types of spiders' bites cause serious reactions. Victims of these spider bites should be treated for shock and seen by a doctor as soon as possible. When possible, try to identify the spider, or take the dead spider to the physician's office. Be sure that you don't put yourself in danger to do so.

Black widow

The bite of a female black widow spider can cause redness and sharp pain at the wound site. The victim might suffer sweating, nausea and vomiting, stomach pain and cramps, severe muscle pain and spasms, and shock. Breathing might become difficult. The bite of a brown recluse spider doesn't always hurt right away, but within two to eight hours there can be pain, redness, and swelling at the wound. An open sore is likely to develop. The victim might suffer fever, chills, nausea, vomiting, joint pain, and a faint rash.

Brown recluse

Snakebite

Snakes are common in many parts of the country, but bites from them are rare. Snakes try to avoid humans and normally strike only when they sense danger. Snakebites seldom result in death.

Use a hiking stick to poke among stones and brush ahead of you when you walk through areas where snakes are common. Remember to stay on the trails. Watch where you put your hands as you collect firewood or climb over rocks and logs.

The bite of a nonvenomous snake causes only minor puncture wounds. You can treat these like other puncture wounds; just wash with soap and water, then apply antibiotic ointment and an adhesive bandage. Before applying medicine, put on disposable, non-latex gloves; ask about any drug allergies; and get permission. Get medical attention if you see signs of an infection.

The bite of a venomous snake can cause sharp, burning pain. The area around the bite might swell and become discolored.

If you think a person has been bitten by a venomous snake, call for help, and follow these steps:

- Keep the person calm and still.

- Do not let the victim walk unless it is unavoidable—for example, if you have to evacuate the area. If possible, have an adult carry the victim to a safer area or to medical help.

- Immobilize the part of the body that was bitten, and position it below the level of the heart.

- Remove any rings or jewelry from the bitten extremity.

Copperhead snake

- Clean the wound with antiseptic, and cover it with a clean bandage.

- Don't apply ice or a tourniquet.

- Don't cut the wound or try to suck out the venom.

- Don't give the victim caffeine or alcohol.

- Try to remember the snake's shape and color pattern so you can describe it later, but don't try to capture it.

Nosebleed

A nosebleed can look bad, but it will usually stop in just a few minutes. Have the victim sit up and lean forward to prevent blood from draining into the throat. Pinch the nostrils together for 10 minutes to maintain pressure on the flow and stop the bleeding. Apply a cool, wet cloth to the victim's nose and face above where you are pinching. (As always, wear latex-free, disposable gloves.) Watch for symptoms of shock and treat if needed. Call for help if the bleeding doesn't stop after 15 minutes.

Frostbite

Frostbite happens when the skin gets cold enough to freeze. A sure sign of frostbite is grayish-white patches on the skin. Some victims will complain that their ears, nose, fingers, or feet feel painful and then numb. Others won't notice anything.

If you suspect frostbite, get the person into a tent or building, then gently warm the affected area and keep it warm. If an ear or cheek is frozen, remove your glove, and warm the injury with the palm of your hand. Slip a frostbitten hand under your clothing, and tuck it beneath an armpit. Treat frozen toes by putting the victim's bare feet against the warm skin of another person.

Avoid rubbing frostbitten flesh. That can damage tissue and skin.

You can also warm a frozen part by holding it in warm—not hot—running water. Have the patient exercise injured fingers or toes, and don't let the injured area freeze again. Get the victim to a doctor.

What's the best way to avoid frostbite? Stay warm and dry. Wear warm gloves, socks, and a hat. Wool and synthetic materials will keep you warm when they get wet; cotton won't. Dress in layers so you can regulate your body temperature by adding or removing articles of clothing.

Every home and car should have a first-aid kit so that supplies will be there when you need them.

Home First-Aid Kit

Here are the things you should include:

- ◆ Tweezers
- ◆ Box of latex-free adhesive bandages (different sizes)
- ◆ Twelve each of 3-by-3-inch and 4-by-4-inch sterile pads
- ◆ Roll of 1-inch and roll of 2-inch latex-free adhesive tape
- ◆ Scissors
- ◆ Safety pins
- ◆ Two 1-inch roller bandages
- ◆ Two 2-inch roller bandages
- ◆ Three cravat, or triangular, bandages
- ◆ Two 17-inch splints of thin board
- ◆ Antibiotic ointment
- ◆ Calamine lotion
- ◆ Latex-free, disposable gloves
- ◆ Mouth-barrier device
- ◆ Goggles
- ◆ Hand sanitizer

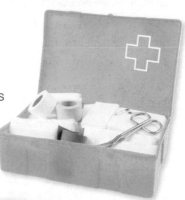

Car First-Aid Kit

All the items listed above plus:

- ◆ Small flashlight and spare batteries
- ◆ White handkerchief (to attach to the car so you can attract attention if the car is disabled)

- Blanket
- Large red and white sign that reads "Send help!" (Place in the front or rear window in an emergency.)

Personal First-Aid Kit

You should also make a first-aid kit to carry on outings. Include these items:

- adhesive bandages
- moleskin
- antibiotic ointment
- latex-free gloves

In addition to the basic items above, consider including:

- gauze pads
- adhesive tape
- soap
- scissors
- mouth barrier
- pencil and paper
- antiseptic wipes

Emergencies can happen at any time—even in the middle of the night. What would you do if you woke up and smelled smoke or heard your smoke alarm going off? It's important to have a plan.

Sketch a floor plan of your house or apartment. Figure out two possible escape routes from each room, and draw them on your floor plan. Now, decide on a place away from the building where everyone can meet once they are outside. Discuss your plan with your family, and practice what you would do in an emergency.

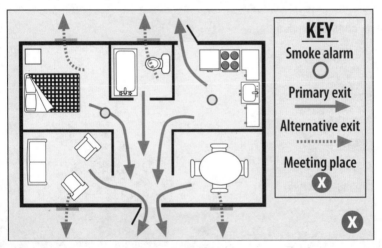

KEY

Smoke alarm
O

Primary exit
→

Alternative exit
▪▪▪▪▪▪▪▪▪▪▶

Meeting place
Ⓧ

Discuss these questions with your parent:

♦ Are our smoke alarms working?

♦ Are our windows easy to open? How could we get out through windows, such as picture windows, that don't open?

♦ Are there rooms on a second floor or higher? Should we buy escape ladders? Does our building have a fire escape?

♦ Would anyone in the family need special assistance in an emergency?

REQUIREMENT 8 | Visit with a first responder.

First responders are people who keep us safe. They include police officers, firefighters, EMS workers, and search and rescue professionals. Whenever an emergency happens or someone calls for help, they are the first people to respond.

Many first responders were once Webelos Scouts just like you. Some enjoyed learning about first aid and wanted to provide emergency medical care for a living. Others became police officers or firefighters because they wanted to help other people, just like the Scout Oath says.

In fact, first responders are helpful all the time, even when they aren't working. If an emergency happens in the woods, on an airplane, or in a restaurant, they quickly take action.

Meet with a first responder, and learn more about his or her work. If possible, meet at a place like a fire station or police station so you can see the equipment and vehicles the first responder uses. Ask the first responder what training or education he or she has had. Find out how you can be helpful in your role as a Scout first responder.

A Scout is courteous. When you visit a first responder, show good manners, follow instructions, and say "thank you" as you leave.

Maybe someday I'll be an EMT like my mom. But I can help my community, even if I don't become a first responder, because I know what to do in an emergency. In fact, Mom said people usually look to Scouts in emergencies because we have special training. I think I'm up to the task. What about you?

STRONGER, FASTER, HIGHER

Whew! Sorry I'm out of breath, but I just finished jumping rope. It's part of my plan to get ready for my Boy Scout patrol's 10-mile hike. Yep, we're planning to hike 10 miles in a single day. But that's nothing. Some of the older guys in my troop have hiked for 10 straight days at Philmont Scout Ranch, where they also got to do cool stuff like rock climbing, burro racing, and mountain biking.

You can start working toward hikes like that with the Stronger, Faster, Higher adventure. And you'll learn the building blocks of fitness so you can take other awesome adventures throughout your life.

SNAPSHOT OF ADVENTURE

The Stronger, Faster, Higher adventure will help you understand how to exercise in a healthy and safe way and show you some creative ways to be active every day.

REQUIREMENT

Do all of these: **Approved by**

1. Understand and explain why you should warm up before exercising and cool down afterward. Demonstrate the proper way to warm up and cool down. _____

2. Do these activities and record your results:

   A. 20-yard dash _____

   B. Vertical jump _____

   C. Lifting a 5-pound weight _____

   D. Push-ups _____

   E. Curls _____

   F. Jumping rope _____

3. Make an exercise plan that includes at least three physical activities. Carry out your plan for 30 days, and write down your progress each week. _____

4. With your den, prepare a fitness course or series of games that includes jumping, avoiding obstacles, weight lifting, and running. Time yourself going through the course, and improve your time over a two-week period. _____

5. With adult guidance, help younger Scouts by leading them in a fitness game or games as a gathering activity for a pack or den meeting. _____

6. Try a new sport that you have never tried before. _____

Have you ever felt really sore after you played hard? By warming up before doing physical activities and cooling down afterward, you reduce the chance that you'll get sore or hurt yourself.

The best way to warm up is to do a light aerobic activity like walking or jogging at an easy pace for 5 to 10 minutes. "Aerobic" is a fancy word that means "with oxygen." If you're breathing harder than usual — and using more oxygen — then you're doing an aerobic activity. Once your muscles are warmed up, stretch them, but don't strain them. Now, you're ready to exercise.

Simple Stretching Exercises

Here are some simple stretches that can keep you from getting hurt.

Forward Lunge: Stand and put your left leg about 2 feet in front of you. Lean toward your left knee, keeping your back straight, until you feel your muscles stretch. Hold for five seconds. Repeat three to six times, then switch legs.

Side Lunge: Stand with your legs about 2 feet apart. Bend your left knee and lean toward the left, keeping your back and right leg straight. Hold for five seconds. Repeat three to six times, then switch legs.

Cross-Over: Stand with your legs crossed and your feet close together. Keep your legs straight, and try to touch your toes. Hold for five seconds. Repeat three to six times, then switch legs (so the other one is in front).

Quad Stretch: Stand near a wall with your right hand on the wall and your knees together. With your left hand, lift your left foot up to your behind. Hold for five seconds. Repeat three to six times, then switch legs.

Butterfly Stretch: Sit with the soles of your feet touching. Lower your head toward your feet and hold for five seconds. Repeat three to six times.

When stretching, use smooth, steady motions. Don't bounce or jerk.

After your activity, cool down by stretching or walking at an easy pace for a few minutes until your heart rate gets back to normal. You can check your pulse by lightly pressing two fingers in the soft area beside your Adam's apple. You should count 30 to 50 beats in 30 seconds.

REQUIREMENT 2 | Do these activities and record your results:

Record your results for each activity in the "Start" column. If you choose to practice some of these activities for requirement 3, use the other columns to record your results.

Skill	Start	Week One	Week Two	Week Three	Week Four
a. 20-yard dash					
b. Vertical jump					
c. Lifting a 5-pound weight					
d. Push-ups					
e. Curls					
f. Jumping rope					

We all have things we naturally do really well. If you're small, you may be able to run very fast. If you're tall, you may be able to jump high or far. If you have strong arms, you may be able to lift weights. If you can hold your breath for a long time, you may be good at swimming underwater.

But you don't have to stick with what you're naturally good at. By learning other physical skills—and doing some practice—you can get stronger and faster and go higher, which is what this adventure is all about.

Use the chart under requirement 2 to track your progress, or create a new chart if you choose different activities. Write down how you do each week, and see how you improve.

My friend Davi and I were exercise buddies. Davi's really fast, so he helped me improve my time on the 20-yard dash. And I gave him tips for doing push-ups. It really helps when you have someone cheering you on!

20-yard dash

See how fast you can run 20 yards (60 feet). Measure off the distance first and have someone time you with a stopwatch. Running fast for short distances is called sprinting. Run as fast as you can because you don't need to save any energy for later, like you would in a longer race.

Vertical jump

Stand near a wall with a piece of chalk in your hand. Jump as high as possible and make a mark on the wall at the highest point. Measure from there to the floor to see how high you jumped.

Lifting a 5-lb. weight

Pick up a 5-lb. dumbbell or something around the house that weighs that much. You could use a milk jug about two-thirds full of water to do this. Hold your hand in front of you with your elbow at your side. Lift the weight toward your shoulder and then lower it back to the starting position. Count how many times you can lift it before your arm gets tired.

Push-ups

Lie face down on the ground or floor and put your hands flat next to your shoulders. Push up with your arms, keeping your back and legs as straight as possible. Then, lower your body and touch your chest to the ground.

Repeat as many times as you can, counting one push-up each time your chest touches the floor. (If you're having trouble, try keeping your knees on the ground instead of lifting your whole body.)

Curls

Lie on your back with your legs bent and your feet on the floor. Cross your arms over your chest. Have a partner hold your ankles to keep your feet on the floor. Sit up and touch your elbows to your thighs. Then return to the starting position, counting one curl each time you do.

Jumping rope

Get a weighted rope whose handles reach your armpits. Make sure you have plenty of room around (and above) you and jump as many times as you can without stopping. Count each time you jump over the rope. Only jump an inch or so into the air, bounce on your toes, and don't try anything fancy until you've mastered the basics!

In the Scout Oath, you promise to keep yourself physically strong. Regular exercise is a great start.

Exercise is a lot more fun when you make a game out of it. Some city parks have fitness trails with exercise stations along them. You run from one station to the next, doing activities like pull-ups or rock climbing.

You and your den can create your own fitness trail at your meeting place or a nearby park. First, think of some fitness activities you like to do. Here's a list to get you started:

- Climbing through a refrigerator box
- Doing curls
- Climbing a fence
- Jumping over an obstacle
- Jumping rope
- Doing the long jump
- Monkey bars

- Plank walking
- Doing push-ups
- Shooting a basketball
- Swinging on a rope
- Tumbling
- Weight lifting

Lay out a path for your fitness trail and set up your stations along it. Put a sign at each station saying what you're supposed to do there, like "Do Five Push-ups."

Now the fun begins! Take turns going through the course. Record your times. See who the fastest Scout is and who improves the most over two weeks.

A Scout is friendly. If someone in your den is having a hard time with a station, offer some encouragement or help.

REQUIREMENT 5 | With adult guidance, lead younger Scouts in a fitness game or games as a gathering activity for a pack or den meeting.

Don't keep all the fun to yourself! Pick a game that your den enjoys playing and teach it to younger Scouts, at either a pack or den meeting. You can invite them to come try your fitness trail!

Here are some tips for teaching your game:

- Make sure you have everybody's attention. (Use the Cub Scout sign.)
- Explain the rules.
- Demonstrate how to play.
- Ask if anybody has questions—and answer them!

It's OK to pick a game that has winners and losers, but don't focus on that too much. Remember that everybody is a winner when everybody has fun.

A Scout is clean. To be good at sports, steer clear of alcohol, tobacco, and drugs. They aren't cool.

REQUIREMENT 6 | Try a new sport you have never tried before.

Sports are a good way to become stronger and faster and reach higher toward better fitness. You may already play a sport, which is great, but try a new sport for this requirement. New sports open up new possibilities for fun and learning.

Not sure which sport to try? Ask your parent or den leader for help, or take a look at this list:

- Archery
- Badminton
- Baseball
- Basketball
- Cycling
- Cross country
- Golf

- Gymnastics
- Hockey
- Kickball
- Rowing
- Snow skiing
- Soccer

- Softball
- Swimming
- Tennis
- Track
- Ultimate
- Volleyball

So what new sport did you try? I picked tennis. I found a tennis court in a park nearby, and I've been practicing with my brother. At first, the balls we hit were flying all over the place, but now we're pretty good!

Whatever sport you pick, remember to play hard, play fair, and have fun!

WEBELOS WALKABOUT

My dad told me one time that there are 4 million miles of roads in America. That's a whole lot of pavement! But guess what? Some of the coolest places to visit are far from any road. In fact, the only way to get to the best campsites, fishing spots, and scenic overlooks is to hike to them.

Of course, there are also some cool places to explore closer to home, including city parks, old railroad beds that have been turned into trails, and even your own neighborhood. (You'll be amazed at how much more you can see when you walk instead of ride in a car.)

Hiking is what the Webelos Walkabout adventure is all about. With boots on your feet and a pack on your back, you never know where you can go!

SNAPSHOT OF ADVENTURE

Hiking is walking with a purpose. It is great exercise and a fun activity to do with your den or family. In the Webelos Walkabout adventure, you'll learn how to prepare for a hike, what you should bring along, and what you should do if there is an emergency. During your den hike, you'll also have the chance to do a service project.

REQUIREMENT

Do all of these: Approved by

1. Create a hike plan.   _____

2. Assemble a hiking first-aid kit.   _____

3. Describe and identify from photos any poisonous plants and dangerous animals and insects you might encounter on your hike.   _____

4. Before your hike, plan and prepare a nutritious lunch. Enjoy it on your hike, and clean up afterward.   _____

5. Recite the Outdoor Code and the Leave No Trace Principles for Kids from memory. Talk about how you can demonstrate them on your Webelos adventures.   _____

6. With your Webelos den or with a family member, hike 3 miles (in the country if possible).   _____

7. Complete a service project on or near the hike location.   _____

8. Perform one of the following leadership roles during your hike: trail leader, first-aid leader, lunch leader, or service project leader.   _____

REQUIREMENT 1 | Create a hike plan.

Before you take a hike, you need to have a plan. Where are you going? How far will you hike? How long will the hike take? What will you do along the trail?

How fast can you hike? On a 3-mile hike, most dens can expect to average about 1-2 miles an hour, including stops.

To create your hike plan, work with your den leader to decide the following information:

Hike location: _____

Hike distance: _____

Gathering place: _____

Gathering time: _____

Hike start time: _____

Hike finish time: _____

Other information: _____

_____

If you are planning to use an existing trail (at a state park, for example), try to get a copy of the trail map. Study it ahead of time to learn more about the trail. Is the trail easy or hard? Where can you get water and go to the bathroom? Is there a good place along the trail to eat lunch?

If you're making up your own route, work with your den leader to create a map.

REQUIREMENT 2 | Assemble a hiking first-aid kit.

When you're hiking, you have to take care of any minor emergencies that come up. The Scout motto is "Be Prepared." One way to be prepared is to carry a first-aid kit whenever you go hiking.

> The First Responder adventure describes how to perform first aid and what should go in a first-aid kit.

Make a list of minor emergencies you might encounter when on a hike:

_____   _____

_____   _____

_____   _____

_____   _____

What items should you take along to handle these emergencies? List the items here:

_____   _____

_____   _____

_____   _____

_____   _____

With your den leader, build an outdoor first-aid kit containing these items and take it on your hike.

A Scout is brave. If an emergency occurs on your hike, remember to stay calm and use your first-aid training. Panicking doesn't help anybody.

REQUIREMENT 3 | Describe and identify from photos any poisonous plants and dangerous animals and insects you might encounter on your hike.

Most plants are beautiful and harmless, and most animals are more afraid of you than you are of them. However, you should be aware of the poisonous plants and dangerous animals that you might see on the trail—even in a city park or neighborhood.

Poisonous Plants

Here are the most common poisonous plants. If you touch them, your skin may get red and itchy. You can prevent a reaction by washing with soap and water as soon as possible.

- **Poison ivy** grows throughout most of the continental United States as either a shrub or a vine. Look for leaves with three leaflets and maybe white berries.

- **Poison oak** grows as a low shrub in the eastern United States and as clumps or vines on the Pacific coast. Look for clusters of three leaves and possibly yellow-white berries.

- **Poison sumac** grows as a tall shrub or a small tree in wet areas in the northeastern, midwestern, and southeastern United States. Look for leaves with seven or more leaflets and possibly yellow-white berries.

Poison ivy   **Poison oak**   **Poison sumac**

To avoid poison ivy and poison oak, remember this rhyme: "Leaves of three, let it be; berries white, poisonous sight."

Venomous Reptiles

Snakes and other reptiles will usually get out of your way when they see you coming. But if you stumble over one, it may bite. Fortunately, most snakes and other reptiles don't have poison in their bites.

Here are the few that do.

- **Gila monster:** Found in parts of Nevada and Utah and down into Mexico

- **Eastern diamondback rattlesnake:** Found along the Atlantic coast from North Carolina to Florida and west to Louisiana

- **Western diamondback rattlesnake:** Found in the southwestern United States, from Missouri and east Texas to southern California

- **Timber rattlesnake:** Found from Maine to Texas

♦ **Prairie rattlesnake:** Found in the western half of the United States

♦ **Sidewinder or horned rattlesnake:** Found in the deserts of the Southwest

On coral snakes, the red and yellow bands touch; on other snakes, they don't. Remember this rhyme: "Red on yellow, kill a fellow; red on black, friend of Jack."

♦ **Coral snake:** Found in some Southeastern states and in southern New Mexico and Arizona

♦ **Water moccasin (cottonmouth):** Found in or near water from southeastern Virginia to Florida to east Texas and up through Arkansas and parts of nearby states

• **Copperhead:** Found in most Southern states, but also as far north as Massachusetts and as far west as Illinois and Texas

Dangerous Insects

• **Bees, hornets and wasps:** Most flying insects are just annoying, like mosquitos. A few of them can be dangerous for people with bad allergies. If someone gets stung by a bee, hornet, or wasp and has trouble breathing, it's important to seek medical help right away. People who know they are allergic to insect stings usually carry special medicine called epinephrine with them all the time. If you carry this medicine with you, be sure your leader knows about it!

• **Ticks:** Ticks are hard-shelled insects that like to bury their heads in your skin. (Yuck!) You should check yourself for ticks when you've been in the woods. If you find one, have an adult gently pull it out with tweezers. Wash the area with soap and water and put antiseptic medicine on it.

• **Chiggers:** Chiggers are too small to see, but they can cause big itches when they burrow into your skin. Don't scratch chigger bites; cover them with calamine lotion or special chigger medicine, such as 1 percent hydrocortisone ointment.

◆ **Spiders:** Some spiders, especially the black widow and brown recluse, can make you sick if they bite you. Symptoms can include redness and pain at the bite site and also fever, chills, nausea, vomiting, joint or muscle pain, and cramps. Anyone who has been bitten by a spider should see a doctor as soon as possible.

Black widow

Brown recluse

When the older guys in my Boy Scout troop went to Philmont Scout Ranch in New Mexico, they had to watch out for bears and mountain lions. In most of the country, you aren't likely to see any of those unless you hike to the zoo.

REQUIREMENT 4 | Before your hike, plan and prepare a nutritious lunch. Enjoy it on your hike, and clean up afterward.

Eating is fun—especially when you've been working hard. You don't want hunger to keep you from finishing your hike or having a great time with your den, so it's important to bring plenty of food on your trek.

Work with your den to plan a nutritious lunch that everyone can enjoy. First, be sure you know if any Scouts have food allergies. Next, brainstorm with your den what to make. Remember to think about food that will be filling and easy to carry. You'll be taking any trash with you when you leave, so simple foods are best.

One great thing about trail food is that you usually don't have dishes to wash. Just bag your trash and carry it out in your daypack.

SAMPLE TRAIL LUNCH

PB&J pita sandwiches:
Before the hike, spread peanut butter
and jelly in pita pockets and place them
in plastic bags. (Astronauts sometimes enjoy
PB&J sandwiches made with tortillas. They
don't create bread crumbs, which can be
a problem in a space station.)

Trail mix:
Before the hike, make your own mixture of
any of these items: raisins, granola clusters,
cereal, candy-coated chocolate, pretzels,
dried fruit, nuts, sunflower seeds

Beef jerky

Apple or orange

Water

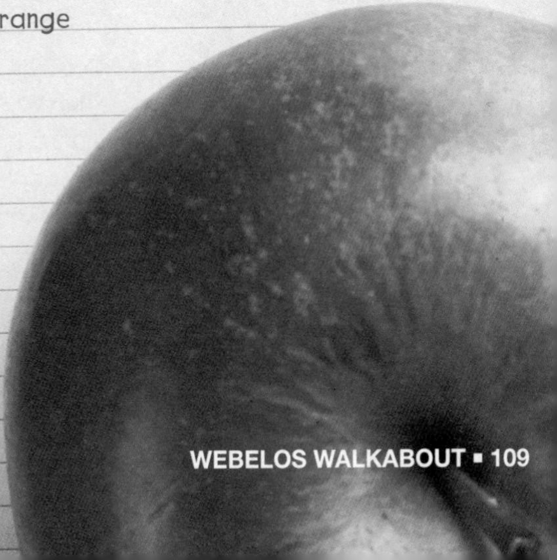

Now it's your turn. Make a plan so you know who is taking care of each part of the meal.

Meal Plan

Lunch menu:

_____

_____

_____

My job:

_____

_____

_____

When you're done eating and your den is ready to move on, do a check of the lunch area. Look for food scraps, wrappers, and any other waste that wasn't there when you arrived. (And if you did find trash when you got there, well, you're Cub Scouts—you know what to do!)

After your lunch, you'll be ready to climb the next steep hill or join in the next trail song. Onward, Scout!

There's nothing like a hike to remind Scouts of the importance of caring for the earth. And Scouts of all ages can make a big difference when they act responsibly in the outdoors. After all, there are millions of us out there!

Just think about the good that happens when that many people promise to do their best to protect nature and keep our country beautiful. That's what the Outdoor Code and the Leave No Trace Principles for Kids do—they remind us that even the little choices matter when it comes to nature.

As a Webelos Scout, you'll give extra attention to being conservation-minded, which means protecting natural resources. Two of the Leave No Trace Principles for Kids will help you do that: "Know Before You Go" and "Choose the Right Path." When you plan ahead, you'll be familiar with the area and prepared for your outing. When you stay on existing trails, you'll protect the land around them.

So, to be sure you'll have those words guiding you in this adventure (and in the many even greater adventures to come), take some time to memorize the Outdoor Code and the Leave No Trace Principles for Kids. You can find both in the back of your handbook.

When you've got both down, recite them for your den leader and discuss how you'll apply them on your hike.

Once you have a plan and are ready for emergencies, it's time to go hiking!

Unlike camping, hiking doesn't require a lot of equipment. There are some things you should always carry, however. You might have used the Cub Scout Six Essentials in the past. Since you're preparing to be Boy Scouts, you can use a new list that includes some additional essential items. They are called the Scout Basic Essentials.

The Scout Basic Essentials*

1. First-aid kit
2. Extra clothing
3. Rain gear
4. Filled water bottle
5. Pocketknife (if you've earned your Whittling Chip)
6. Flashlight
7. Trail food
8. Sun protection
9. Map and compass

* As a Boy Scout, you can earn your Firem'n Chit. That will allow you to carry matches and a fire starter.

What else should you take on your hike? A whistle isn't on the Scout Basic Essentials list, but it might be appropriate to bring one on a hike. You might also want insect repellent or another item. What should you leave at home?

When you go hiking, you have to take care of your feet. High-top shoes or boots are the best because they keep out rocks and sand and help protect your ankles. Your shoes should fit fairly tightly around your heel, but there should be room to wiggle your toes. If your shoes don't fit well, you can get blisters, and that's no fun!

When you get new boots or shoes, always break them in by wearing them part of every day for a week or more before you go hiking.

Socks are almost as important as shoes. They soak up moisture and cushion your feet. Hiking socks made of polypropylene or a wool/nylon blend work better than cotton socks. Take an extra pair on your hike and put them on at your lunch break. Your feet will thank you.

How to Hike

You may know how to walk, but hiking is different. Here are some things that make hiking easy and fun:

- **Look around.** Unless the trail is rocky or uneven, stop looking at your feet and start looking at the world around you. Spread out on the trail so you can see more than your buddy's back.

- **Take breaks.** Plan to stop for 10 minutes after every 30 minutes of hiking. Stretch your muscles and study the world around you. Make sure everyone gets to rest. If possible, take breaks after you climb big hills—not before—so the hiking will be easy when you start up again.

- **Stay on the trail.** Don't go around muddy spots or take shortcuts. That makes trails wider and damages the environment.

- **Walk in single file.** If you're hiking along a road, stay in single file on the left side. Wear white or reflective clothing or carry a flashlight.

- **Respect other hikers.** Don't be too noisy. If you meet other people, give them the right of way, especially if they are going uphill or are on horseback.

The trails you enjoy hiking on as a Webelos Scout didn't just magically appear. People who came before you worked hard to build them.

You can pay those people back by doing a service project. Your den leader will help you identify service project ideas. Maybe you'll repair trail damage. Maybe you'll pick up trash. Maybe you'll hang birdhouses. Whatever you do will make the environment nicer for future hikers.

A Scout is kind. Taking care of natural places shows kindness to animals and to other visitors.

Sometimes, service means reaching out directly to other people. Maybe you can ask some people from a retirement community to enjoy your hike with you. They might have stories to share of their own time as Scouts!

REQUIREMENT 8 | Perform one of the following leadership roles during your hike: trail leader, first-aid leader, lunch leader, or service project leader.

On your hike, you can help your den by serving as a leader. Here are some jobs you can do:

- ◆ **Trail leader:** Responsible for calling breaks, following the map, setting a comfortable pace, and pointing out hazards to other hikers

- ◆ **First-aid leader:** Responsible for carrying the first-aid kit (or assigning someone else to carry it) and helping to give first aid if needed

- ◆ **Lunch leader:** Responsible for assigning Scouts to carry food, identifying a lunch spot, and supervising cleanup

- ◆ **Service project leader:** Responsible for helping with service project assignments and carrying tools and other supplies

The best leaders lead by example. That means they show other people how to act instead of telling them what to do. They also work just as hard as the other members of the team. Nobody likes to be bossed around by somebody who's not working.

After the hike, discuss with your den how you did as a leader. Identify one or two things you could have done better.

A Scout is cheerful. He looks on the bright side when bad things happen and does chores without complaining. How can you be cheerful on hikes?

I don't know about you, but I love hiking. It's really cool to be able to go places most people have never been and to carry everything you need on your back.

And once you get to be good at hiking, you can try your hand—make that your feet—at backpacking. Our troop goes backpacking every spring to this forest where you can see for miles from the top of a mountain. The climb is tough, but the view makes it all worthwhile.

I hope you find something just as cool on your hiking adventures!

BUILDING A BETTER WORLD

A while back, my family went to this ceremony where people from all over the world became citizens of the United States. They were all waving little American flags, and a few were so happy as they repeated their citizenship oath that they were crying. Afterward we talked about some of their stories and how hard they had worked to become citizens.

That ceremony made me realize that being a citizen is a big deal. But citizenship is more than being. It's doing. In this adventure, you'll learn all about what citizens do.

SNAPSHOT OF ADVENTURE

This adventure is all about being a good citizen. You'll learn about the United States flag and about your rights and duties as an American. You'll meet with a city leader and discuss a problem facing your community. You'll learn that citizenship starts at home as you work to conserve energy and natural resources. Finally, you'll find out about Scouting in another country and what it means to be a citizen of the world.

REQUIREMENTS

Do all of these: **Approved by**

1. Explain the history of the United States flag. Show how to properly display the flag in public, and help lead a flag ceremony.   _____

2. Learn about and describe your rights and duties as a citizen, and explain what it means to be loyal to your country.   _____

3. Discuss in your Webelos den the term "rule of law," and talk about how it applies to you in your everyday life.   _____

4. Meet with a government leader, and learn about his or her role in your community. Discuss with the leader an important issue facing your community.   _____

5. Learn about your family's expenses, and help brainstorm ways to save money. Plan and manage a budget.   _____

6. Learn about energy use in your community and in other parts of our world.   _____

7. Identify one energy problem in your community, and find out what has caused it.   _____

8. With the assistance of your den leader or parent, participate in an event that would help lead others in recycling and conserving resources. _____

9. Show that you are an active leader by planning an activity without your den leader's help. _____

10. Do one of these:

   A. Learn about Scouting in another part of the world. With the help of your parent or your den leader, pick one country where Scouting exists, and research its Scouting program. _____

   B. Set up an exhibit at a pack meeting to share information about the World Friendship Fund. _____

   C. Find a brother Scout unit in another country. _____

   D. Under the supervision of your parent, guardian, or den leader, connect with a Scout in another country during an event such as Jamboree on the Air or Jamboree on the Internet or by other means. _____

The Flag of the United States of America

The United States flag is very familiar. We see it at Cub Scout meetings, in school, in front of government buildings, and at sporting events. You could probably draw it from memory without much trouble.

But the flag hasn't always looked like it does today. If a person from history such as George Washington saw today's flag, he would probably say there was something wrong with it!

Here are some of the flags that have flown over our country.

British Red Ensign. This ensign (another word for flag) flew over the American colonies before the American Revolution. It shows Great Britain's Union Flag of 1606, which combines the crosses of St. George (for England) and St. Andrew (for Scotland).

Grand Union Flag. George Washington flew this flag over his army headquarters near Boston, Massachusetts, in 1776, a year after the American Revolution began. This flag included 13 stripes representing the Thirteen Colonies.

Old Glory. This is the first official flag of the United States. On June 14, 1777, the Continental Congress decided that the flag should have 13 stripes like the Grand Union Flag, along with a union of "thirteen stars, white in a blue field, representing a new constellation." We celebrate June 14 as Flag Day each year.

Star-Spangled Banner. This flag includes 15 stripes and 15 stars because Vermont and Kentucky had joined the Union in the 1790s. It flew over Fort McHenry near Baltimore, Maryland, during the War of 1812 against Great Britain. Francis Scott Key watched it waving as the British bombarded the fort.

Then he wrote our national anthem, "The Star-Spangled Banner."

Flag of 1818. This flag has 20 stars but only 13 stripes. As more states joined the Union, people realized that the stripes were going to get too narrow. (Can you imagine 50 stripes on a flag?) Since 1818, all flags have included 13 stripes representing the Thirteen Colonies and one star for each state.

Today's Flag. Here's the flag we use today. The most recent stars were added in 1959 (for Alaska) and 1960 (for Hawaii). This version of the flag has been in use longer than any other version in our history.

Displaying the Flag

When the flag is displayed flat on a wall, the stars should always be up and to the left (the flag's right).

When the flag is on a stage, it should be on the speaker's right. When it is in the audience, it should be on the audience's right.

When the flag is displayed with other flags like state flags, it should be higher than them. When it is flown with flags of other nations, all the flags should be at the same height, but the United States flag should be on its own right.

Raising and Lowering the United States Flag

It takes two people to raise and lower the flag correctly. The first person holds the flag. The second person attaches it to the halyard (rope) and raises it, keeping it close to the pole by holding the halyard tight. He then fastens the halyard to the cleat on the pole. (Make sure it's snug so the flag stays at the top.)

The flag should be raised quickly in the morning and lowered slowly in the evening.

The guidelines for displaying the United States flag are part of something called the United States Code. You can learn more about it at your library or, with permission, online at **www.usflag.org**.

The president, a governor, or the mayor of the District of Columbia can order the flag to be flown at half-staff on certain occasions, such as when a national leader dies. In the morning, the flag should be raised to full-staff and then lowered to half-staff. In the evening, it should be raised to full-staff before it is lowered.

Despite what you may have heard, you don't have to retire a United States flag if it accidentally touches the ground. In fact, it's OK to clean or repair a flag that becomes dirty or torn.

Folding the United States Flag

The United States flag is folded in a special way until only the blue field shows. First, fold the flag lengthwise in half, then lengthwise again with the blue field on the outside. (It can help to have a third person support the middle of the flag.) Next, make tight triangular folds, starting from the striped end, until only the blue field is showing. Tuck in the loose end.

Have you ever made a paper football? The flag is folded the same way. Just don't play football with it!

Showing Respect to the United States Flag

There are many rules about the flag, but the most important one is simple: Show respect. The flag represents our country and all the men and women who worked to make it great, so don't treat it like an ordinary piece of cloth.

Two ways you can show respect to the flag are by saluting it and flying it.

Saluting the United States Flag

If you are in uniform, give the Cub Scout salute at these times:

- ◆ When the flag is being raised or lowered.
- ◆ When the flag passes by or when you pass the flag. In a parade, salute just before the flag passes and hold your salute until it has gone by.
- ◆ When you recite the Pledge of Allegiance or sing "The Star-Spangled Banner."

If you are not in uniform, greet the flag by taking off your hat and placing your right hand over your heart.

Flying the United States Flag

The flag is flown on public buildings every day when weather permits. You can fly it at your home every day, too.

A Scout is loyal. Showing respect for the flag is a way to show loyalty to your country.

Some special days to fly the flag are:

- ◆ New Year's Day, January 1
- ◆ Inauguration Day, January 20 in the year after a presidential election
- ◆ Martin Luther King Jr. Day, third Monday in January
- ◆ Lincoln's Birthday, February 12
- ◆ Washington's Birthday or Presidents Day, third Monday in February
- ◆ Armed Forces Day, third Saturday in May
- ◆ Memorial Day, last Monday in May (half-staff until noon, full-staff until sunset)
- ◆ Flag Day, June 14
- ◆ Independence Day, July 4
- ◆ Labor Day, first Monday in September
- ◆ Patriot Day, September 11
- ◆ Constitution Day, September 17
- ◆ Veterans Day, November 11

It is also flown on other days proclaimed by the president of the United States, on the birthdays of the states, and on state holidays.

Retiring the Flag

When a United States flag becomes worn beyond repair, it should be retired by burning it completely to ash. This should be done in a simple manner with dignity and respect. Your den or pack may do this as part of a ceremony, but your family could do this as well.

Be very careful when retiring a flag so you don't injure yourself, especially if the flag is made of synthetic material. Melting nylon can cause serious burns if you let it touch your skin.

REQUIREMENT 2 | Learn about and describe your rights and duties as a citizen, and explain what it means to be loyal to your country.

As a Webelos Scout, you are not old enough to vote or serve in the military or run for political office, but you still have duties as a citizen of the United States.

> In the Scout Oath, you promise to do your duty to your country. One way to do that is by obeying the law.

> Some people are citizens of other countries but live in our country. You may know somebody like that. People who are not American citizens have some of the same duties and basic rights as citizens. However, there are things they can't do, like vote and run for president.

Here are some things you and your family should do:

- ◆ Obey laws
- ◆ Respect the rights and property of others
- ◆ Help the police
- ◆ Take care of the environment by recycling and conserving natural resources
- ◆ Keep informed about what is going on around you
- ◆ Help change things that are not good

When you are an adult, you should also:

- ◆ Vote
- ◆ Pay taxes
- ◆ Serve on a jury when asked to do so

As a citizen you also have many rights as defined by the United States Constitution and other governing documents.

Here are some specific things you and your family can do:

- Worship how and where you like
- Say what you think
- Join other people in peaceful assemblies
- Petition the government if you think it is doing something wrong
- Own property and choose where to live
- Get a public school education through 12th grade
- Have a trial by jury if you are accused of a crime
- Vote (age 18 or older)

We are lucky to have many freedoms in the United States, but always remember that those freedoms come with responsibility. As President John Kennedy said, you should "ask not what your country can do for you, but ask what you can do for your country."

Being Loyal

All Scouts promise to be loyal—that's the second point of the Scout Law. You are loyal when you obey the laws of our country, your state, and your community. You are loyal when you try to make your community a better place to live. You are loyal when you stay informed about how government works. You are loyal when you support those who work to keep our country safe.

My Scoutmaster says Martin Luther King Jr. is a good example of somebody who was loyal to his country by pointing out what it was doing wrong. He used some of his rights, including freedom of speech and freedom of assembly, to fight against laws that were unfair to African Americans.

You are also loyal when you try to get things fixed that are wrong. If you think a law is unfair, you should obey it, but you should also work to get it changed.

> "My country, right or wrong; if right, to be kept right; and if wrong, to be set right."—U.S. Senator Carl Schurz

Have you ever watched a TV show or movie where a king made up laws on the spot or threw people in jail just because he felt like it? A few countries still operate like that, but most operate under what is called the "rule of law."

The rule of law means that:

♦ Laws apply to everyone, both government officials and private citizens.

♦ Laws are clear and fair and are evenly applied.

♦ Laws respect basic rights like people's security.

♦ The way laws are created is open and fair.

Talk with your den about how that idea affects you. How does following the Scout Oath and Scout Law serve as a "rule of law" to help us work together in Scouting?

REQUIREMENT 4 | Meet with a government leader and learn about his or her role in your community. Discuss with the leader an important issue facing your community.

Your community is made up of many leaders who work hard to keep it safe and running well. They probably include a mayor, city council members, judges, police and fire chiefs, and people who run various government departments.

With the help of your den leader, pick a local government leader and plan to meet with him or her. Before the meeting, decide on one or two questions you would like to ask.

Here are some possible questions:

♦ What is your most important responsibility?

♦ What background or education prepared you for this job?

♦ Why did you want to be a government leader?

♦ How can citizens help you be more effective?

♦ What is the biggest challenge facing our community?

Also before the meeting, watch a local news program or read a local newspaper and find an issue that you feel is important in your community. Be prepared to ask the government leader about this issue.

Many elected officials first held office in a Boy Scout troop or in student government at school. Ask the government leader you meet with about his or her early leadership experience.

REQUIREMENT 5 | Learn about your family's expenses, and help brainstorm ways to save money. Plan and manage a budget.

You've probably gone to the grocery store with your mom or dad and seen how much money it takes to feed your family for a week. But did you realize that food is just one expense your family has?

Although every family is different, all families have to pay for certain things.

Here are some of them:

- ✦ Food (groceries, restaurant meals, school lunches)
- ✦ Housing (rent or mortgage costs)
- ✦ Utilities (gas, electricity, water)
- ✦ Transportation (car payments, bus or subway fares, gas, maintenance)
- ✦ Clothing
- ✦ Doctor and dentist visits
- ✦ School supplies

If you have younger brothers and sisters, your family may have childcare costs. If you have a pet, your family pays for pet food and visits to the veterinarian. If you go to a private school, your family pays tuition.

Many of the fun things your family does also cost money, including:

- ✦ Family vacations
- ✦ Trips to the movie theater, a theme park, or a sporting event
- ✦ Shopping
- ✦ Playing on a sports team
- ✦ Movie and video-game rentals
- ✦ Scouting activities

Talk with your family about your month-to-month expenses. Find out which ones are the same each month and which ones can change. Talk about some ways that you could decrease your family's expenses.

 A Scout is thrifty. You can show that you are thrifty by helping your family find ways to save money.

Here are two examples to get you started:

♦ You can save on movie tickets by going to an afternoon matinee, or renting a DVD instead of going to the theater.

♦ You can save on transportation costs by combining errands into one trip or going places by bike.

Making a Budget

A budget is a document that helps you plan your finances. It shows how much money you will bring in (called income) and how much money you will spend (called expenses) for a certain period of time. Your family probably has a budget, even if it's not written down. Your school has a budget, and so does every business and government. The budget for the United States government is hundreds of pages long!

For this requirement, create a budget for yourself for a two-week period. Write it in the space shown on the next page.

MY BUDGET

Income

Allowance	$ _____
Gifts (like birthday money)	$ _____
Extra chores .	$ _____
Other _____	$ _____
Total income	$ _____

Expenses

Movie ticket	$ _____
Video-game or movie rental	$ _____
Snacks	$ _____
Clothes	$ _____
Music	$ _____
Other _____	$ _____
Total expenses	$ _____
Here's what I have left	$ _____

Add up all your income items and put the total on the line labeled Total income. Add up all your expenses and put the total on the line labeled Total expenses. Now, subtract the Total expenses number from the Total income number. That total is what you have left over. You could save that money for a future large purchase, like camping gear.

If the Total expenses number is bigger than the Total income number, you are planning to spend more money than you take in, which is not good! Go back and adjust your expenses so that you have enough money to pay for them.

Keep track of your income and expenses for two weeks to see how well you followed your budget. Afterward, share your results with your den leader and your fellow Webelos Scouts.

Part of building a better world is making sure you don't waste energy and other natural resources. This requirement will help you get started.

Saving Energy

To stay warm or cool, see at night, and go from place to place, we need energy. Your community uses many types of energy. So does your family. Find out what kinds of energy you use, and write them in this chart.

THE ENERGY I USE

To stay warm or cool in my home _____

To travel by car _____

To travel by bus or subway _____

To watch TV _____

To have warm showers _____

To see in my room when it's dark outside _____

_____

Some types of energy are renewable, which means you can never use them up. These include energy from solar panels, wind turbines, and hydroelectric dams. Other types of energy are finite, which means they will eventually run out. These include gasoline, natural gas, and coal.

Whether the energy we use is renewable or not, it is still important to conserve it. If your family wastes a lot of energy, your utility bills will be high and you won't have money to spend on other things. If too many people use their air conditioners on a very hot day, a city can temporarily run out of power, which is called a blackout.

Pick one of the types of energy your family uses and decide one way that you could use less of it. Practice this saving idea for one month, and ask your family to join you.

Here are some ways you can save electricity, for example:

◆ Set your thermostat a little warmer in the summer and a little cooler in the winter.

◆ Keep your blinds or curtains closed on hot days.

◆ Take shorter showers.

◆ Use ceiling fans to make rooms feel cooler.

◆ Don't open the refrigerator door more than you have to.

◆ Unplug electronic devices when you're not using them.

◆ Turn off the lights when you leave a room.

◆ Use energy-efficient light bulbs.

You can learn more about each type of light bulb in the Fix It adventure on page 384.

 With a parent's or guardian's permission, visit **http://energy.gov/energysaver/ articles/types-lighting** for additional information on saving energy at home.

Incandescent bulb   **Compact fluorescent (CFL) bulb**   **Light-emitting diode (LED) bulb**

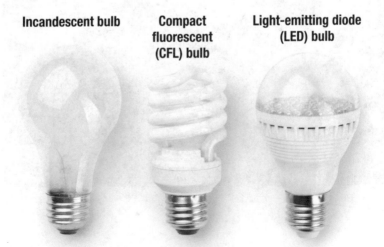

REQUIREMENT 7 | Identify one energy problem in your community, and find out what caused it.

With your den leader's help, find out about an energy problem that affects the people in your community. Learn what has created this problem. Prepare a den exhibit for a pack meeting to teach other pack families about the problem and how it could be solved.

You can help conserve resources by remembering three words: reduce, reuse, and recycle:

+ **Reduce.** Don't buy things you don't need. Take care of your clothes and toys so they will last longer. Look for products that use less packaging.

+ **Reuse.** Only buy things that can be reused (like refillable water bottles instead of bottled water). Find new ways to use old things (like turning old comic books into wrapping paper). Shop for clothes and books at thrift stores and give clothes you've outgrown to charity. Take cloth shopping bags to the grocery store instead of getting disposable bags.

+ **Recycle.** When things can't be reused, take them to your local recycling center so they can be recycled into new products.

> Our Scout camp has picnic tables made of recycled plastic. The camp ranger told us it takes 1,250 milk jugs to make one table. That's a lot of vitamin D!

Recycling is a great way to conserve natural resources. Your school or community probably has recycling stations set up, or you may be able to set out recyclable materials with your ordinary trash. Some stores have recycling bins for plastic bags and other recyclable materials.

> Some people drive cars that have been converted to run on used cooking oil. They smell like french fries when they go down the street!

The most common materials that are recycled are paper, glass, metal, and plastic. Other things can be recycled, too, like used motor oil, tires, and even computers. You can recycle food waste by composting it, which turns it into fertilizer you can use in a garden.

Plastic bottles, packages, and toys have numbered recycling symbols on them. The numbers tell what types of plastic they contain. Check with your local recycling center to see which types it accepts.

PLASTIC RECYCLING

If you don't recycle, now is a good time to start. If your family recycles, look for ways to do more. Keep a log of every item you recycle for one week, and share it at a den meeting. Will you be the best recycler in the den?

For this requirement, work with your den leader or parent to encourage others to recycle and conserve resources. What could you do?

Here are some ideas:

- Set up a conservation display at your chartered organization.
- Promote what can be recycled in your neighborhood.
- Hold a recycling drive for things like computers and batteries that can't be left in a recycling bin.
- Run a contest in your pack to see who can bring in the most recyclable materials.

REQUIREMENT 9 | Show that you are an active leader by planning an activity without your den leader's help.

While working on this adventure, you have met people who are leaders. These people see what needs to be done and make it happen.

Now, it's your turn. Work as a team with your den to plan and carry out an activity without your den leader's help. (Of course, he or she will need to be around to make sure everybody stays safe.) Your activity might be related to what you've learned about energy and resource management. It might be a fun activity for the younger boys in your pack. It might be a den field trip. Whatever it is, make sure you have a good plan and that you follow that plan to achieve your desired result.

Sometimes, it helps to write things down when you plan an activity. **If you can answer these questions, you are good to go:**

- ◆ Who is invited to take part in the activity? Who needs to give permission to take part in the activity?

- ◆ What are you going to do? What do you need to bring?

- ◆ When will the activity take place?

- ◆ Where will you go? How will you get there?

- ◆ How much does it cost?

REQUIREMENT 10 | Do one of these:

REQUIREMENT 10A | Learn about Scouting in another part of the world. With the help of your parent or your den leader, pick one country where Scouting exists, and research its Scouting program.

Scouting doesn't just happen in the United States. It happens in nearly every country around the world. Today, there are more than 30 million Scouts and leaders in more than 160 different countries!

Every country does Scouting its own way. The words of the Scout Oath and Law are different. The uniforms and badges are different. The membership requirements are different. Some countries even have girls in Cub Scouts.

If you have relatives in another country, ask them to send you information about the Scouting program there.

Today, it's easy to learn about Scouting in other countries. Most national Scout associations have websites, and even those where English is not spoken often have English translations available. With the help of your parent or den leader, pick a country where Scouting exists and learn more about their program for boys your age.

Try to find answer to these questions:

- What is the Scout Oath and Scout Law in that country?
- What badges do Scouts earn?
- What do their uniforms look like?
- What activities do they do?
- How is their program like Cub Scouting in America, and how is it different?

Share what you learned with your den. Then, set up an exhibit at a pack meeting to teach other pack families about that country's Scouting program.

 One good place to start looking for information about Scouts around the world is the World Scout Bureau's website, **www.scout.org**. Be sure you have your parent or guardian's permission to search the Internet.

One way you can show your connection with Scouts around the world is to wear the World Crest patch on your uniform. When you complete a service project that promotes world peace, you can add a Messengers of Peace ring patch around the World Crest.

REQUIREMENT 10B | Set up an exhibit at a pack meeting to share information about the World Friendship Fund.

Many countries do not have the financial resources that our country enjoys. In those countries, Scouts can find it hard to purchase uniforms and go on trips, and Scout leaders can find it hard to build camps and publish Scout handbooks.

The Boy Scouts of America created the World Friendship Fund at the end of World War II to help rebuild Scouting in countries that had been affected by the war. Now, it helps strengthen and expand Scouting wherever there is a need.

Here are a few things the Fund has done:

 ◆ Supported creation of Russia's first Scout handbooks since 1917
 ◆ Helped build the first Scout camp in Madagascar
 ◆ Paid for a bus to help Scouts in Nepal get to camp
 ◆ Provided scholarships to help Scouts from many countries attend the world Scout jamboree

Collections for the World Friendship Fund are often organized at camporees, summer camps, and training courses for Scout leaders. Your den might want to organize a collection at a pack meeting or blue and gold banquet. Your den leader can get World Friendship Fund brochures and other information from your local council service center.

REQUIREMENT 10C | Find a brother Scout unit in another country.

One of the best ways to learn about Scouting in another country is to connect with a den of Cub Scouts there. With the help of your parent or den leader, make contact with a den in another country. (Your council's international representative may be able to help, too.) Tell them about Scouting in our country and find out what Scouting is like in their country. Exchange photos and patches with your brother den, if possible.

A Scout is friendly. When you connect with Scouts around the world, you can create friendships and strengthen the bonds of Scouting.

Jamboree on the Air (JOTA) is a special event held on the third full weekend of October every year. During JOTA, Scouts work with amateur radio operators to contact Scouts in other parts of the world. Approximately 700,000 Scouts in 13,000 different locations participate each year!

Jamboree on the Internet (JOTI) happens at the same time as JOTA. During the weekend, Scouts from around the world connect with each other through email, chat programs, and websites. JOTI attracts Scouts from more than 140 countries. You can participate with the help of your parent or den leader.

When you participate in either JOTA or JOTI, you can receive a special patch. But the really cool thing is making friends with a Scout in another part of the world.

If you aren't able to participate in JOTA or JOTI, your den leader may be able to help you connect with a Scout in another country by other means.

I've always been interested in other parts of the world, so I loved the Building a Better World adventure. When I worked on it, I learned about Scouting in Australia. I found out that they earn "boomerang" badges and that, instead of having Tigers, they have Joey Scouts. (A joey is a baby kangaroo). This year, my Boy Scout troop participated in the Jamboree on the Internet, and I actually got to chat with a Scout from Melbourne, Australia. He said camping there is fun, although you have to watch out for the dingos (wild dogs) and crocodiles. Yikes! I hope you've enjoyed this adventure, too, and that you help make the world better. After all, that's what Scouting is all about.

CAMPER

Ah, camping! There's nothing better than living in the great outdoors. I love going to sleep to the sound of owls and other night birds and waking up to the smell of breakfast cooking (when it's not my turn to cook, of course). Camp is a great place to relax and hang out with your friends. Plus, when you're at camp, all sorts of adventures lie just down the trail.

My Boy Scout troop goes camping nearly every month, so I've done a lot of camping in the last year or so. But it all started when I was a Webelos Scout. The Camper adventure will get you ready for a lifetime of outdoor fun, too.

SNAPSHOT OF ADVENTURE

Camping is more than just sleeping outside! In this adventure, you will get the chance to plan and go on a campout that includes a campfire program and fun activities like geocaching and star study. You'll also learn what it means to leave no trace when you're camping.

REQUIREMENT

Do all of these: Approved by

1. With the help of your den leader or family, plan and conduct a campout. If your chartered organization does not permit Cub Scout camping, you may substitute a family campout or a daylong outdoor activity with your den or pack. _____

2. On arrival at the campout, with your den and den leader or family, determine where to set up your tent. Demonstrate knowledge of what makes a good tent site and what makes a bad one. Set up your tent without help from an adult. _____

3. Once your tents are set up, discuss with your den what actions you should take in the case of the following extreme weather events which could require you to evacuate:

   A. Severe rainstorm causing flooding _____

B. Severe thunderstorm with lightning or tornadoes _____

C. Fire, earthquake, or other disaster that will require evacuation. Discuss what you have done to minimize as much danger as possible. _____

4. On a pack campout, work with your den leader or another adult to plan a campfire program with the other dens. Your campfire program should include an impressive opening, songs, skits, a Cubmaster's minute, and an inspirational closing ceremony. _____

5. Show how to tie a bowline. Explain when this knot should be used and why. Teach it to another Scout who is not a Webelos Scout. _____

6. Go on a geocaching adventure with your den or family. Show how you used a GPS unit or a smartphone with a GPS application to locate a geocache. _____

7. Recite the Outdoor Code and the Leave No Trace Principles for Kids from memory. Talk about how you can demonstrate them while you are working on your Arrow of Light. After one outing, list the things you did to follow the Outdoor Code and Leave No Trace. _____

If you went camping when you were younger, your parents or other adults may have done all the planning. As a Webelos Scout, you get to help plan your own adventures.

Work with your den leader or another adult in charge of your campout to help plan it. Pick a location and dates, and make a list of activities that you could do on the campout.

Our Campout

Location _____

Departure Date and Time _____

Return Date and Time _____

Adult Leader in Charge _____

Activities _____

Special Equipment We Need _____

> On one of my Webelos campouts, we saw some deer grazing near a lake. After they left, our den leader showed us how to make plaster casts of their hoof prints. I still have the one I made!

> * If your chartered organization does not permit Cub Scout camping, you may substitute a family campout or a daylong outdoor activity with your den or pack.

Campout Ideas

What can you do on your campout? Here are some ideas.

- ◆ Take a hike.
- ◆ Complete a compass course or geocaching game.
- ◆ Play a wide game like capture the flag.
- ◆ Have a first-aid relay.
- ◆ Compete in a sports tournament.
- ◆ Have a special cooking contest.
- ◆ Go stargazing.
- ◆ Do nature crafts.
- ◆ Have a scavenger hunt.
- ◆ Complete a service project.
- ◆ Plan and participate in a campfire program.
- ◆ Conduct a flag ceremony or flag retirement.
- ◆ Plan and participate in an interfaith worship service.

Camping Gear

A big part of being prepared is taking the right equipment on camping trips. On the next page are things you should take on den and pack outings. This list is like the Cub Scout Six Essentials you might have used before, but you've got some new items as you get ready for Boy Scouts. You can borrow some items until you are ready to invest in new equipment.

The Scout Basic Essentials *
(Things You Should Take on Every Outing)

1. First-aid kit

2. Extra clothing

3. Rain gear

4. Filled water bottle

5. Pocketknife (if you've earned your Whittling Chip)

6. Flashlight

7. Trail food

8. Sun protection

9. Map and compass

* As a Boy Scout, you can earn your Firem'n Chit. That will allow you to carry matches and a fire starter.

Overnight Gear

- Tent or tarp, poles, and stakes
- Ground cloth
- Sleeping bag
- Pillow
- Air mattress or pad
- Warm jacket
- Sweatshirt (try to avoid cotton)
- Sweatpants (for sleeping, try to avoid cotton)
- Cup, bowl, knife, fork, spoon, mesh bag
- Insect repellent
- Extra clothing
- Toothpaste, toothbrush, soap, washcloth, towel, comb
- Webelos Scout uniform
- Durable shoes/boots (depending on weather)
- Hat or cap

Optional Items

- Camera
- Binoculars
- Whistle
- Sunglasses
- Fishing gear
- Notebook and pencil
- Nature books
- Swimsuit
- Bath towel
- Bible, testament, prayer book, or other book for your faith

There are many things you can do to make your camp home as nice as possible, even if your tent may not be quite as comfortable as your bed back home. When you get to your campsite, spend a few minutes finding the best possible spot for your tent.

Look for a tent site that is flat or almost flat. A grassy area or an area covered in leaves will be softer than bare dirt. If bare dirt is the only option, a sleeping pad or inflatable mattress is a good idea!

Look around to make sure the site is not in a natural drainage area or on a trail or path. Look up to make sure there are no dead tree limbs overhead that might fall in a storm. Leave some space between your tent and the next one for privacy.

Once you've picked your tent site, move aside any rocks, pine cones, or sticks that would be uncomfortable to sleep on. Do not remove bushes or small plants; instead, put your tent in a spot where you will have only a small impact on nature. After the campout, restore the site to the way it looked when you arrived; Scouts always leave places better than they found them.

Now, work with your tentmate or other Webelos Scouts to set up your tent. Put your gear inside and get ready to start your camping adventure.

A Scout is helpful. Setting up camp is easier and more fun when you work together as a team.

Taking Care of Your Tent

Your tent will last for years if you take care of it. (Remember that a Scout is thrifty.) Here are some tips:

♦ Always pitch it on a ground cloth, which is a sheet of plastic or tarp that protects the floor from dirt, sharp objects, and moisture. (Fold the corners of the tarp under the tent so the ground cloth is no bigger than the tent; otherwise, rain can get in between.)

♦ Don't wear your shoes inside.

♦ Keep tent vents open to let moisture escape.

♦ Keep all flames away from tents. Never use candles, matches, stoves, heaters, or lanterns in or near a tent. No tent is fireproof. All tents can burn or melt when exposed to heat.

♦ Let the tent dry in the sun before you take it down. If you have to pack it up wet, set it up again as soon as you get home or hang it indoors until it dries completely. That will prevent mildew from ruining the fabric—and making it stink.

A. Severe rainstorm causing flooding

B. Severe thunderstorm with lightning or tornadoes

C. Fire, earthquake, or other disaster that will require evacuation. Discuss what you have done to minimize as much danger as possible.

On most campouts, the worst weather you'll see is rain and annoying heat or cold. Sometimes, however, the weather can be dangerous. It's important to Be Prepared—that's the Scout motto—for bad situations.

Severe Rain and Flooding

Flash floods can occur when there is very heavy rain over several hours or steady rain over several days. Because flash floods can strike with little warning, you should never camp on low ground next to streams when rain is expected.

When you're camping in the mountains, be aware of the weather upstream from your campsite. Heavy rain miles away can turn into flash floods downstream.

If flooding occurs, move to higher ground immediately. Stay out of streams, ditches, and other flooded areas. Adults should never try to drive through flood waters, no matter how shallow they may seem. Just a few inches of water can carry off a car!

To get a rough idea of how far away a storm is, count the number of seconds between when you see lightning and hear thunder. Divide by five to get the number of miles.

Severe Thunderstorms, Lightning, and Tornadoes

Thunderstorms can be loud and scary. Sometimes they produce dangerous lightning and tornadoes.

Lightning can strike 10 miles from a thunderstorm, so you should take shelter in a building or vehicle as soon as you hear thunder—even if the sun is shining overhead. Make sure you're not the highest object in the area, and avoid water, open areas, isolated trees, picnic shelters, and metal objects. If you're caught in the open, spread out 100 feet apart and crouch down like you do when you play leapfrog.

Tornadoes are funnel clouds that can form in spring and summer thunderstorms. The best place to be if a tornado hits is indoors, either in a basement or closet or against an interior wall. If you're caught outside, get in a ditch and lie as flat as possible.

The National Weather Service issues *watches* when conditions are right for severe weather and *warnings* when severe weather is occurring. Your leader can carry a portable weather radio or use a mobile phone application to receive information about watches, warnings, and forecasts for your area.

Fires, Earthquakes, and Other Disasters

In very rare cases, such as if there's a forest fire, you may have to evacuate your campsite. Your leader will tell the den where to meet, take attendance, and move the group to safety.

Staying Found

Anyone can get lost, even adults. But you can do some things to avoid getting lost—and to stay safe if you do get lost.

◆ Always stay with a buddy.

◆ Let an adult know if you and your buddy need to leave the group, and tell where you are going.

◆ Carry a whistle to signal for help. Three blasts in a row is the universal distress call.

◆ If you think you are lost, remember to "STOP!" Stay where you are, and stay calm. Think about how you can help others searching for you. Observe your surroundings and watch for searchers. Plan how to stay warm and dry until help arrives.

| On a pack campout, work with your den leader or another adult to plan a campfire program with the other dens. Your campfire program should include an impressive opening, songs, skits, a Cubmaster's minute, and an inspirational closing ceremony.

A highlight of most campouts is a campfire program that combines songs, skits, cheers, and more. It's a great way to relax after dinner and reflect on the fun day you've had.

Your Webelos den can help plan a campfire program by working with your den leader or another adult to fill out the worksheet shown here. Use an extra page for more dens, if needed. Later, as a Boy Scout, your patrol will work with other patrols to plan campfire programs.

As you fill out the worksheet, you should put energetic skits and songs at the beginning and quieter things near the end. It's important to be respectful of other campers and not disturb people and wildlife late at night.

In my Boy Scout troop, our favorite song is "My Bonnie Lies Over the Ocean." Every time you sing a word beginning with the letter "B," you either stand up or sit down. It's a lot of fun to sing it faster and faster —and good exercise, too!

Pack Campout Campfire Plan

Fill in the name of each skit and song so two dens don't do the same thing. Review your plan with your den leader or another adult to be sure the songs and skits are Scout-appropriate.

Opening/Fire Lighting Leader _____

Song #1 (Noisy Song) Name _____ Den _____

Skit #1 Name _____ Den _____

Song #2 Name _____ Den _____

Skit #2 Name _____ Den _____

Song #3 (Quiet Song) Name _____ Den _____

Cubmaster's/Den
Leader's Minute Leader _____

Inspirational
Closing/Song Leader _____

A bowline is a very useful knot to learn. It makes a fixed loop in a rope that will not slip, unlike a taut-line hitch or two half hitches. The bowline can be used to anchor one end of a rope to a tree or other stationary object, or as the loop around the person's chest in a rescue situation—such as pulling a person out of a hole or off the side of a cliff.

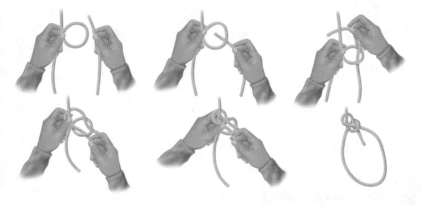

1. Make a small overhand loop in the standing part of the rope.

2. Bring the rope end up through the loop, around behind the standing part, and back down into the loop.

3. Tighten the bowline by pulling the standing part of the rope away from the loop.

Once you've mastered the bowline, teach it to a younger Cub Scout.

REQUIREMENT 6 | Go on a geocaching adventure with your den or family. Show how you used a GPS unit or a smartphone with a GPS application to locate a geocache.

Have you ever dreamed of searching for buried treasure? That's just what geocaching is all about. Geocaching lets anyone hunt for treasure with a few simple tools.

Instead of following a map with a big "X" on it, you use a Global Positioning System (GPS) unit (or a GPS app on a smartphone) to find geocaches, which are boxes hidden in public places like parks. Some geocaches are as big as a shoe box; others are as small as a pencil eraser. Some have trinkets in them that you can keep if you leave something else; others have logbooks where you can record your find.

To get started, go to **www.geocaching.com** (with your parent's permission) and get a list of geocaches in the area where you want to play. For each geocache, you'll find the map coordinates and a clue.

Here's an example from Philmont Scout Ranch:

Coordinates: N 36° 27.303 W 104° 57.219

Clue: Near the second rock pile

Enter the coordinates into your GPS device and start traveling toward the geocache. You may need to have a parent drive you for a while and then walk toward it from the road. When you get close, use the clue to help you find the geocache.

When you find the geocache, open it to see what's inside. You should find a logbook where you can record that you discovered it. If there's a trinket of some sort inside, you may take it with you as long as you leave something else behind for the next adventurer. Be sure to put the geocache back exactly where you found it so that other people can have the fun of finding it, too.

As you search for geocaches, look at the world around you, not just at your GPS unit. The fun of geocaching is in the search. Plus, you don't want to run into a tree or walk off a cliff! Never go onto private property without permission. Whenever possible, travel on durable surfaces. If you need to take a detour, the GPS unit will adjust automatically.

A Scout is trustworthy. When you find a geocache, keep the fun going for others by leaving an item if you remove one.

Getting Started With Geocaching

1. With your parent or den leader, create an account at Geocaching.com. (You have to be at least 13 years old to use the website without adult help.)

2. Visit the site's Hide & Seek a Cache page.

3. Search for geocaches by address, ZIP code, or state. There are more than 2 million active geocaches, so you can probably find one nearby.

4. Choose the geocaches you want to look for. Be sure to note the difficulty and terrain ratings.

GPS stands for Global Positioning System. That refers to a group of 24 satellites that circle the earth in very precise orbits and send location information to GPS units. GPS units are accurate to within about 50 feet!

Imagine arriving at a campsite and finding damaged trees, a smoldering campfire, and bags of trash that animals have torn into. Now imagine arriving at a campsite and feeling like you're the first group that's ever been there. Which campsite would you like more? The second one, of course.

The Outdoor Code is a promise all Scouts make to help care for the environment. It's important to even the youngest Cub Scouts and the most seasoned leaders. Now it's time to be sure you've learned it by heart.

Leave No Trace is a way of living in the outdoors that respects the environment and other people. By following Leave No Trace principles, we can take care of outdoor spaces and help preserve them for the Scouts of tomorrow. Are you ready to learn these principles, too?

Find the Outdoor Code and the Leave No Trace Principles for Kids in the back of your *Webelos Handbook*. Read them and say them aloud until you have them memorized. When you're ready, recite them to your den leader.

A Scout is thrifty. Being thrifty means not wasting things—including natural resources. Leave No Trace principles and the Outdoor Code help you to be thrifty in the outdoors.

What can you and your den do to demonstrate the Outdoor Code and the Leave No Trace principles to your pack while on your campout?

_____

_____

_____

_____

_____

_____

So what's your favorite part of camping?

I can't decide what I like best. I love the quiet of nature, but I also love hanging out with my friends and playing games. I love taking hikes, but I also love sitting around the campfire. I guess what I'm saying is that I love everything about camping. Even though I'm usually glad to get home to a soft bed and a hot shower, I can't wait to get back to camp again.

I hope you have as much fun camping as I do and get to go a lot more when you become a Boy Scout.

DUTY TO GOD
IN ACTION

The best way to show you're good at math is to solve math problems. The best way to show you can play soccer is to grab a ball and head for the field. And the best way to show you understand your duty to God is to put your faith into action. In fact, my faith leader told me that putting my faith into action shows others that I practice my belief in God.

Now that I'm in middle school, I'm starting to do my duty to God by working on service projects with my faith youth group. Recently, we collected more than 2,000 cans of food for people in need in our community. It was really cool to visit the food bank and learn about the families our project will help. As you work on the Duty to God in Action adventure, I hope you find similar ways to put your faith into action.

SNAPSHOT OF ADVENTURE

In this adventure, you will have the opportunity to further explore your faith and your duty to God in your own way. You can call on the past (your ancestors) and the present (you!) to get ideas about making faith an important part of your life.

REQUIREMENT

Do either requirement 1 OR requirement 2:   Approved by

1. Earn the religious emblem of your faith for Webelos Scouts, if you have not already done so.   _____

2. Do requirement 2a and any two from 2b–2e:

A. With your parent, guardian, or religious or spiritual leader, discuss and make a plan to do two things you think will help you better do your duty to God. Do these things for a month.   _____

B. Discuss with your family how the Scout Oath and Scout Law relate to your beliefs about duty to God.   _____

C. For at least a month, pray or reverently meditate each day as taught by your family or faith community.   _____

D. Read at least two accounts of people in history who have done their duty to God. (This can include family members and ancestors.) List their names and how they showed their duty to God.   _____

E. Under the direction of your parent, guardian, or religious or spiritual leader, do an act of service for someone in your family, neighborhood, or community. Talk about your service with your family and your Webelos den leader. Tell your family, den, or den leader how it related to doing your duty to God.   _____

REQUIREMENT 1 | Do either requirement 1 OR requirement 2.

REQUIREMENT 1 | Earn the religious emblem of your faith for Webelos Scouts, if you have not already done so.

Scouts can earn religious emblems sponsored by their respective faith groups. If you haven't already earned the one your faith offers for Webelos Scouts, you may do so now.

Did you know that many faith groups offer four different religious emblems? There's often one for Cub Scouts, one for Webelos Scouts, one for Boy Scouts, and one for older Boy Scouts or Venturers. You can continue your faith adventure once you become a Boy Scout by earning the religious emblems for Boy Scouts.

Duty to GOD

BOY SCOUTS OF AMERICA

@ With your parent's or guardian's permission, visit **www.praypub.org** or www.scouting.org/filestore/pdf/512-879_WB.pdf for more information.

REQUIREMENT 2 | Do requirement 2a and any two from requirements 2b–2e:

REQUIREMENT 2A | With your parent, guardian, or religious or spiritual leader, discuss and make a plan to do two things you think will help you better do your duty to God. Do these things for a month.

If you wanted to get closer to a new friend, you would talk with him and spend time with him. You would find out what he likes and dislikes. You might even throw a party for him on his birthday.

Getting closer to God is sort of like getting closer to a new friend. It's hard to know God if you don't spend time together, if you don't find out what God likes and dislikes, and if you don't honor God on special days. Talk with your parent, guardian, or your religious leaders about what it means to them to get closer to God.

Faith practices help you get closer to God. Talk with your religious leader or parent, and pick two practices you would like to try. Write them down, and do them for a month. At the end of the month, talk with your religious leader, guardian, or parent about how the practices helped you get closer to God.

Have you heard of Robert Baden-Powell? He invented Scouting a long time ago. He said Scouting and religion teach many similar values: "The whole of [Scouting] is based on religion, that is, on the realization and service of God."

For this requirement, see if you can figure out how the values your religion teaches are similar to the values in the Scout Oath and Scout Law.

Here are some ways you could do that:

- ◆ Play a matching game. Write the points of the Scout Law on 12 index cards and several of your religious beliefs on additional cards. Have players try to match a Scout Law card with a religious belief card. Talk about what the cards have in common.

- ◆ Write the parts of the Scout Oath on index cards. Think of a life experience that relates to each part of the Scout Oath. Act out what you should do based on the Scout Oath and based on your religious teachings.

- ◆ Teach your family a song with words that describe what you believe.

♦ Create a poem, story, or play that teaches about your religious beliefs using words from the Scout Oath or Scout Law.

♦ Find a story from a religious text that teaches about one of the points of the Scout Law. Tell the story to your family, or act it out for them. Explain how that point of the Scout Law relates to the story you chose.

Religious Belief	Character Trait	Scout Oath	Scout Law

Praying and meditating are important ways to connect with God. Your faith group may have a particular way of praying and meditating.

If you're not sure how to pray, try the five fingers prayer. In this prayer, each finger on your hand reminds you whom to pray for:

◆ **Thumb:** Your thumb is the closest to you. Pray for the people closest to you, such as family and friends.

◆ **Index finger.** This finger points the way. Pray for people who point the way, such as teachers, religious leaders, and Scout leaders.

◆ **Middle finger.** This finger stands the tallest. Pray for people in authority, such as government leaders.

◆ **Ring finger.** This finger is the weakest on your hand. Pray for those who are weak, sick, or needy.

◆ **Pinky.** This finger is the smallest of all. Pray for yourself and your own needs.

REQUIREMENT 2D | Read at least two accounts of people in history who have done their duty to God. (This can include family members and ancestors.) List their names and how they showed their duty to God.

Many religions are very old. Millions of people may have practiced your religion before you were born. You can learn to do your duty to God by finding out how people in history did their duty to God.

Pick at least two people from history who did their duty to God. They might be family members or famous people. They might be from your faith group or another religious group. They might have done one thing that was really special, or they might have done their duty to God throughout their lives. Find out what they did, and write on the chart. Then talk with your family or den leader about what you learned and how you could apply it to your own life.

Name	Action

A Scout is kind. Many people in history have done their duty to God by showing kindness toward others.

An important part of duty to God is helping other people. When there is a natural disaster like a hurricane, faith groups are among the first on the scene. If you look around your town or nearby cities, you will probably see schools, colleges, or hospitals that were founded by faith groups. Your faith group may support people who travel to other countries to help people who are in need.

But acts of service don't have to be big. As part of your duty to God, you can do them every day. Talk with your religious leader, and pick an act of service you will do. Afterward, talk with your family, den, or den leader about how it made you feel.

I always knew my granddad was a cool guy, but until I did this adventure, I didn't know that he had been doing service projects for 40 years in our faith community. His name even appears on a big plaque. Talk about doing your duty to God! I hope I can do something big like that someday. How about you?

SCOUTING ADVENTURE

When I became a Webelos Scout, I thought it was the best thing I'd ever done. And it was great! But then I became a Boy Scout and found out that it's even better. In Boy Scouting, you get to do a lot of the same stuff you've been doing, like camping and earning badges, but you get to do more stuff, too. Like electing your own leaders. And going on bigger adventures. And working to become Eagle Scouts, which is the coolest thing of all.

I've only been a Boy Scout for about a year, but I'm already planning to go on my first backpacking trip. I can't wait!

SNAPSHOT OF ADVENTURE

The Scouting Adventure is all about what happens when you leave your Webelos den and become a Boy Scout. In this adventure, you'll learn about things like the Scout slogan and the patrol method. You'll find out about merit badges and ranks, and then you'll visit a Boy Scout troop meeting. Best of all, you'll go along with a Boy Scout troop on one of their outdoor activities. By the time you finish this adventure, you'll be ready for the new adventures that await you in Boy Scouting.

REQUIREMENT

Do all of these: **Approved by**

1. Prepare yourself to become a Boy Scout by completing all of the items below:

   A. Repeat from memory the Scout Oath, Scout Law, Scout motto, and Scout slogan. In your own words, explain their meanings to your den leader, parent, or guardian. _____

   B. Explain what Scout spirit is. Describe for your den leader, parent, or guardian some ways you have shown Scout spirit by practicing the Scout Oath, Scout Law, Scout motto, and Scout slogan. _____

   C. Give the Boy Scout sign, salute, and handshake. Explain when they should be used. _____

   D. Describe the First Class Scout badge, and tell what each part stands for. Explain the significance of the First Class Scout badge. _____

   E. Repeat from memory the Outdoor Code. In your own words, explain what the Outdoor Code means to you. _____

2. Visit a Boy Scout troop meeting with your den members, leaders, and parent or guardian. After the meeting, do the following:

A. Describe how the Scouts in the troop provide its leadership. _____

B. Describe the four steps of Boy Scout advancement. _____

C. Describe ranks in Boy Scouting and how they are earned. _____

D. Describe what merit badges are and how they are earned. _____

3. Practice the patrol method in your den for one month by doing the following:

A. Explain the patrol method. Describe the types of patrols that might be part of a Boy Scout troop. _____

B. Hold an election to choose the patrol leader. _____

C. Develop a patrol name and emblem (if your den does not already have one), as well as a patrol flag and yell. Explain how a patrol name, emblem, flag, and yell create patrol spirit. _____

D. As a patrol, make plans to participate in a Boy Scout troop's campout or other outdoor activity. _____

4. With your Webelos den leader, parent, or guardian, participate in a Boy Scout troop's campout or other outdoor activity. Use the patrol method while on the outing. _____

5. Do the following:

A. Show how to tie a square knot, two half hitches, and a taut-line hitch. Explain how each knot is used. _____

B. Show the proper care of a rope by learning how to whip and fuse the ends of different kinds of rope. _____

6. Demonstrate your knowledge of the pocketknife safety rules and the pocketknife pledge. If you have not already done so, earn your Whittling Chip card. _____

A. Repeat from memory the Scout Oath, Scout Law, Scout motto, and Scout slogan. In your own words, explain their meanings to your den leader, parent, or guardian.

B. Explain what Scout spirit is. Describe for your den leader, parent, or guardian some ways you have shown Scout spirit by practicing the Scout Oath, Scout Law, Scout motto, and Scout slogan.

C. Give the Boy Scout sign, salute, and handshake. Explain when they should be used.

D. Describe the First Class Scout badge, and tell what each part stands for. Explain the significance of the First Class Scout badge.

E. Repeat from memory the Outdoor Code. In your own words, explain what the Outdoor Code means to you.

Scout Oath

On my honor I will do my best
To do my duty to God and my country
*   and to obey the Scout Law;*
To help other people at all times;
To keep myself physically strong,
*   mentally awake, and morally straight.*

If you've been in Cub Scouting very long, you have heard the Scout Oath. As a Boy Scout, however, it becomes more of a big deal. Have you ever made a "cross my heart" promise? The Scout Oath is sort of like that, but it's a lot more serious. When you become a Boy Scout, you promise to live by the Scout Oath. And if you're like most Boy Scouts, you'll keep living by the Scout Oath for the rest of your life. But what do the words really mean?

On my honor I will do my best. Your honor is your reputation, what you are deep inside. When you promise on your honor to do something, you're putting your whole self into that promise. But you don't have to be perfect; you just have to do your best.

To do my duty to God and my country and to obey the Scout Law. As a Boy Scout, your first job is to serve your Creator in the ways your parents and faith leaders have taught you. Next comes your country. Countless men and women have worked and fought and even died to make the United States a great country; you can help make it even greater. Like our country, Scouting has some rules to follow. Those rules are found in the Scout Law, which every Scout promises to obey.

To help other people at all times. You can make the world a better place by helping people in need. That means big things like working on service projects and little things like reaching out to classmates at school who are having trouble.

To keep myself physically strong, mentally awake, and morally straight. You can't do your duty and help other people if you aren't taking care of yourself. You stay physically strong when you exercise, eat right, and avoid things that can damage your body. You stay mentally awake when you study and learn and ask questions. You stay morally straight when you are honest in your actions, clean in your thoughts and speech, and faithful in your religious duties.

A Scout is loyal. When you say the Scout Oath, you make a promise to be loyal to your country and the people who are important to you.

Scout Law

A Scout is trustworthy, loyal, helpful, friendly, courteous, kind, obedient, cheerful, thrifty, brave, clean, and reverent.

Some groups have thick books of rules you have to follow. Scouting is different. The most important rules you need to follow are found in the Scout Law, which is so short that you can memorize it.

Trustworthy. A Scout tells the truth. He is honest, and he keeps his promises. People can depend on him.

Loyal. A Scout is true to his family, friends, Scout leaders, school, and country.

Helpful. A Scout cares about other people. He happily helps others without expecting a reward.

Friendly. A Scout is a friend to all and a brother to every other Scout. He offers friendship to people of all races and nations, and he respects people even if their beliefs and customs are different from his.

Courteous. A Scout is polite to everyone regardless of their age or position. He knows that using good manners makes it easier for people to get along.

Kind. A Scout knows there is strength in being gentle. He treats others the way he would like to be treated. He does not harm or kill any living thing without reason.

Obedient. A Scout follows the rules of his family, school, and troop. He obeys the laws of his community and country. If he thinks a rule or law is unfair, he tries to have it changed in an orderly manner instead of disobeying it.

Cheerful. A Scout looks on the bright side of life. He cheerfully does tasks that come his way. He tries to make other people happy.

Thrifty. A Scout works to pay his way and to help others. He saves for the future and uses time and property carefully. He protects and conserves natural resources.

Brave. A Scout can face danger even if he is afraid. He has the courage to stand for what he thinks is right even if others laugh at him or threaten him.

Clean. A Scout keeps his body and mind fit. He chooses friends who live by high standards. He keeps his home and community clean.

Reverent. A Scout is reverent toward God. He is faithful in his religious duties. He respects the beliefs of others.

Scout Motto

Be prepared.

What's a motto? It's a short phrase that describes a person or a group's guiding principle. The Scout motto is "Be prepared."

Somebody once asked Robert Baden-Powell, the founder of Scouting, exactly what Scouts should be prepared for. "Why, for any old thing!" B-P said.

That's the idea behind the Scout motto. It means you're ready to do your duty as a Scout at any time.

> Do your teachers ever give pop quizzes? My uncle says life is one big pop quiz. That's why you always need to be prepared!

Scout Slogan

Do a Good Turn Daily.

What's a slogan? It's a short statement of a goal you want to reach. The Scout slogan is "Do a Good Turn Daily."

A Good Turn is an act of kindness, something you do to help

another person. It doesn't have to be big, but it should be something beyond what's expected of you. (Doing your chores doesn't count as a Good Turn. Doing your little brother's chores does.)

Scout Spirit

Scout spirit is an attitude that sets Scouts apart from other people. It's hard to define Scout spirit, but it's easy to see it in action. When you live by the Scout Oath, Scout Law, Scout motto, and Scout slogan every day, you are showing Scout spirit.

Scout Sign

The Scout sign is a universal symbol of Scouts. To make it, hold up the three middle fingers of your right hand, and cover the nail of your little finger with your thumb. Hold your elbow at a right angle. And stand up straight; you're a Scout!

The Scout sign is used to get people's attention. When you see a leader holding up the Scout sign, get quiet and hold up the Scout sign, too. Pretty soon, everybody in the room will do the same.

Scout Salute

The Scout salute is used to salute the United States flag. You can also use it to salute other Scouts and leaders. To make the salute, form the Scout sign with your right hand, then bring your hand up, palm down, so your forefinger touches the brim of your hat or the tip of your right eyebrow.

If you are not in uniform, salute the flag by placing your right hand over your heart.

Scout Handshake

Unlike most people, Scouts shake hands with their left hands. The left hand is closer to the heart, so the Scout handshake symbolizes friendship. It's a special handshake shared by millions of Scouts around the world.

According to a story Baden-Powell told, some warriors he met in Africa shook with their left hands. To do that, they had to put down their shields, thus showing trust in the people they were greeting.

The First Class Scout Badge

The Scout badge is an important symbol of the Boy Scouts of America. Scouts in other countries have their own badges that look similar.

Fleur-de-lis. The basic shape of the Scout badge is the fleur-de-lis (the French word for an iris flower). Its center point is shaped like the north arrow on an old compass. The three main parts, like the three raised fingers of the Scout sign, stand for the three parts of the Scout Oath: duty to God and country, duty to others, and duty to self.

Eagle and shield. The Scout badge includes the emblem of the United States of America, representing freedom and a Scout's willingness to defend that freedom.

Two stars. The two stars symbolize truth and knowledge. They also represent Scouting's outdoor adventures.

Scroll. The scroll at the bottom displays the Scout motto. The ends are turned up like a smile as a reminder that Scouts smile as they do their duty.

Knot. The knot below the scroll is a reminder to do a Good Turn daily.

The Outdoor Code

As an American, I will do my best to
Be clean in my outdoor manners,
Be careful with fire,
Be considerate in the outdoors, and
Be conservation-minded.

The Scout Law talks about how you should live as a Scout at all times. The Outdoor Code explains how you should live in the outdoors.

Being clean in your outdoor manners means taking care of the places you camp and hike and cleaning up after those who make a mess. Being careful with fire means preventing forest fires. Being considerate in the outdoors means respecting the plants, animals, and humans you encounter in the woods. Being conservation-minded means not wasting natural resources.

As a Scout, you have a special responsibility to take care of the natural areas you enjoy. By living by the Outdoor Code, you can help make sure future Scouts can enjoy nature just as much as you do.

> The Camper adventure tells you more about how to take care of the environment.

A. Describe how the Scouts in the troop provide its leadership.

B. Describe the four steps of Boy Scout advancement.

C. Describe ranks in Boy Scouting and how they are earned.

D. Describe what merit badges are and how they are earned.

As part of this adventure, you will visit a Boy Scout troop meeting. You might even visit the meetings of more than one troop so you can see how they are different and which one you want to join.

The troop you visit may be chartered to the same organization as your Cub Scout pack and may even meet right down the hall from your den. If so, you'll see a lot of familiar faces. But you may visit a troop in a different part of town where you don't know anybody. That can be a little scary, but don't worry. Some of the Scouts you'll meet were Webelos Scouts not long ago.

Inside a Troop Meeting

Troop meetings are a lot different from the den and pack meetings you're used to attending, so you may not know exactly what's going on at first. In fact, you may not even think the Boy Scouts know what's going on! They really do, however.

So what *is* going on? Here's what a typical troop meeting looks like:

First, the senior patrol leader—he's the top elected leader—calls the troop to order using the Scout sign. One of the patrols—they're sort of like dens—leads a flag ceremony, and everybody recites the Pledge of Allegiance or Scout Oath and Scout Law.

Next, one of the older Scouts (or maybe an adult leader) teaches the group a skill like how to navigate using a compass. After the Scouts practice that skill for a while, they break up into patrols. One patrol might work on advancement requirements, another might decorate its patrol flag, and a third might make plans for an upcoming patrol hike. During this time (and really during the whole meeting) individual Scouts may be running around working on advancement, doing their troop jobs, or meeting with the Scoutmaster.

After the patrol meetings, everybody comes back together to play a game. This may be a game just for fun, or it may give the Scouts a chance to practice the skill they learned earlier. For example, they might navigate a compass course out in the parking lot.

Finally, the whole troop gets back together for the closing ceremony. The senior patrol leader makes a few announcements. The Scoutmaster gives some words of wisdom—called a Scoutmaster's Minute. The patrol that led the flag ceremony retrieves the colors. And just like that, the meeting's over.

A Scout is obedient. One way you can show obedience is by paying attention to your patrol leader and senior patrol leader.

If things are going well, about the only time an adult says anything during a troop meeting is when the Scoutmaster gives the Scoutmaster's Minute. Other than that, the meeting is run by the Scouts themselves. The same thing is true for hikes, campouts, service projects, and everything else.

Adult leaders are there, of course, but they're more like coaches. The Scoutmaster and assistant Scoutmasters train the youth leaders and then stand on the sidelines watching them in action.

Who Runs the Troop?

You can identify the youth leaders by the badges of office they wear on their left sleeves. Adult leaders also wear badges of office. When you visit a troop meeting, look for these leaders:

- **Senior patrol leader:** leads the troop
- **Assistant senior patrol leader:** supports the senior patrol leader
- **Troop guide:** helps a patrol of young Scouts, much like a den chief helps a Cub Scout den
- **Quartermaster:** takes care of the troop's equipment
- **Scribe:** takes care of the troop's records
- **Instructor:** teaches skills
- **Patrol leader:** leads a patrol
- **Assistant patrol leader:** assists the patrol leader
- **Scoutmaster:** coaches the senior patrol leader and other youth leaders
- **Assistant Scoutmaster:** supports the Scoutmaster

If you get a chance at the troop meeting, ask some youth and adult leaders what they do. Be on the lookout for other badges of office, and find out about those leadership roles, too.

How Boy Scout Advancement Works

There are four steps of advancement in Boy Scouting:

- ◆ You learn.
- ◆ You are tested.
- ◆ You are reviewed.
- ◆ You are recognized.

You learn.

Learning and practicing skills that lead to advancement happens all the time in a Boy Scout troop. All the skills you need to learn are outlined in the *Boy Scout Handbook*, so you can start learning them on your own. You can also learn new skills at every troop meeting, working on your own or with your patrol, and you can practice those skills daily and on every outing.

You are tested.

Once you feel you have learned an advancement requirement, you must demonstrate to a leader that you have mastered that skill. That leader might be an assistant Scoutmaster, the troop guide assigned to your patrol, the instructor, or even your patrol leader. After testing you, that leader signs off on the requirement in your book.

When you get your copy of the *Boy Scout Handbook,* it will be your personal record of your advancement. It is your responsibility to ask for and obtain the necessary signoffs when you are tested and to keep your handbook in good shape. If there is ever any question about your achieving a requirement, your handbook is the official record. So don't lose it!

THE SCOUTMASTER CONFERENCE

One requirement for every Boy Scout rank is the Scoutmaster conference. During this visit with your Scoutmaster, you talk about your progress in Scouting and how things are going at home and at school. The Scoutmaster can help you set goals for your next rank and answer any questions you have about Scouting. If you're having problems, the Scoutmaster can help you figure out how to solve them. You can ask for a Scoutmaster conference any time you want one, and your Scoutmaster will make every effort to schedule it as soon as possible after your request—maybe right then!

You are reviewed.

After you have completed all the requirements for a rank (described on page 194), you go before a board of review. This is a group of adults from the troop committee who talk with you about what you've learned and double-check that you've done all the requirements, but not re-test you. They will ask you how you are enjoying Scouting and what the troop can do to help you get more out of the program. They might even give you tips about completing the next rank.

You are recognized.

Now comes the fun part. Not long after you pass the board of review, you will receive your rank patch, which you can wear on the left pocket of your Boy Scout uniform shirt. Many troops will provide it to you the next week. Later, you'll be recognized again at a troop court of honor. This is a special awards ceremony

the troop holds every three or four months. It's a big deal; parents, grandparents, brothers, sisters, and troop members attend.

Ranks

The first rank you'll earn as a Boy Scout is the Scout rank, which you earn by completing the Boy Scout joining requirements. As you complete this adventure, you will be learning all of the requirements for earning your Scout rank.

After earning the Scout rank, you work through six other ranks: Tenderfoot, Second Class, First Class, Star, Life, and Eagle Scout. Only about five in every 100 Scouts become Eagle Scouts, so it's a really big deal!

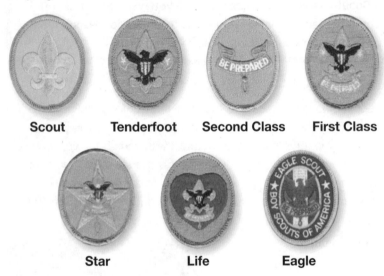

Scout　　**Tenderfoot**　　**Second Class**　　**First Class**

Star　　　　**Life**　　　　**Eagle**

To become an Eagle Scout, you have to:

- ◆ Master basic skills in camping, first aid, nature study, and more
- ◆ Earn 21 merit badges
- ◆ Serve your troop as a leader
- ◆ Serve your community through service projects, including a big one you plan and lead yourself

That's a lot of work, but you have your whole time as a Boy Scout to complete it. Many adults look back at earning their Eagle and realize that it set them on a path for success in life. You may find a lifelong hobby or career from your work toward earning your Eagle Scout Award.

In Cub Scouting, you've worked on most of your advancement requirements together as a den. In Boy Scouting, you work at your own pace, especially after the first year. Some Scouts earn the Eagle Scout Award earlier than others, but it must be earned by the Scout's 18th birthday. The choice is yours.

Merit Badges

Merit badges are awards you can earn as a Boy Scout for learning about a specific topic. There are more than 130 different merit badges, but most Scouts earn maybe 20 or 30. Once you become a First Class Scout, you must earn merit badges to advance in rank.

Search and Rescue   Chess   Camping   Pioneering

Lifesaving   Swimming   Canoeing   First Aid

Game Design   Hiking

I'm on the robotics team at my school, so I'm all over earning the Robotics merit badge!

Here are some examples:

- Scout skills merit badges: Camping, First Aid, Hiking
- Sports merit badges: Cycling, Skiing, Whitewater
- Hobby merit badges: Chess, Game Design, Geocaching
- Career merit badges: Fire Safety, Medicine, Programming
- Personal growth merit badges: Personal Fitness, Personal Management, Scholarship
- Citizenship merit badges: Citizenship in the World, Crime Prevention, Sustainability

To earn a merit badge, you meet with an adult expert in the field and work through a set of requirements. Depending on the badge, you might get to tour a factory, fly in an airplane, or go on an adventure. Along the way, you might discover a hobby or career you can pursue for your whole life.

To advance in rank beyond First Class, you have to earn a certain number of merit badges. For the Eagle Scout rank, you must earn a total of 21 merit badges: 13 from a list of Eagle-required merit badges and nine that you choose yourself. Some Scouts actually earn all the merit badges! Merit badges are worn on a merit badge sash, which is worn on special occasions.

A. Explain the patrol method. Describe the types of patrols that might be part of a Boy Scout troop.

B. Hold an election to choose the patrol leader.

C. Develop a patrol name and emblem (if your den does not already have one), as well as a patrol flag and yell. Explain how a patrol name, emblem, flag, and yell create patrol spirit.

D. As a patrol, make plans to participate in a Boy Scout troop's campout or other outdoor activity.

Your patrol is the basic team you will work with as a Boy Scout. Your patrol will work together, cook together, camp and hike together, and celebrate successes together. In fact, many patrols stay together from the time they join Boy Scouting until the members get too old to be in the troop any longer.

Your patrol will select its own name, make its own flag, come up with its own yell, and elect its own leader. That leader, the patrol leader, represents the patrol to a group called the patrol leaders' council (PLC). This is the group that plans the troop meetings and outings. If your patrol wants to learn about geocaching, for example, your patrol leader will take that idea to the PLC, which will vote on it.

Your patrol can also plan its own activities. Sometimes, these will be part of a bigger troop outing, like a day hike during a weekend campout. Sometimes, they will be just for your patrol.

A well-functioning patrol is what makes a Boy Scout troop work.

PATROL SPIRIT

Patrol spirit is the glue that holds the patrol together and keeps it going. Your patrol will develop spirit as you enjoy experiences together. Your name, flag, and yell help give your patrol a unique identify.

- ◆ **Patrol name.** Every patrol needs a good name, one that really describes what the patrol is all about. If your members like to swim, you might become the Sharks. If you're all into science fiction, you might become the Alien Patrol.

- ◆ **Patrol flag.** Your flag is your trademark. It shows your patrol name, emblem, troop number, and the names of your members. As you win competitions, you can hang ribbons from it as reminders of your accomplishments.

- ◆ **Patrol yell.** Your yell lets other patrols know you've arrived. It should be short and snappy and reflect your patrols' goals. Some patrols also have a patrol song. It's easy to make one up if you use a melody that everyone already knows.

What patrol am I in?
The Trekking T. rex Patrol. We call ourselves that because we all like to go hiking.

Types of Patrols

A Boy Scout troop can have different kinds of patrols, depending on how it's organized. Some troops will have one of each kind of patrol; some troops will have several.

New-Scout Patrol

A new-Scout patrol is for Scouts who have just joined the troop. An older Scout called a troop guide works with the Scouts. An assistant Scoutmaster supports the troop guide.

Scouts usually stay in a new-Scout patrol for their first year in the troop or until they reach First Class rank, whichever comes first. Sometimes, a new-Scout patrol will stay together as a traditional patrol for the rest of their time in Scouting.

Traditional Patrol

A traditional patrol includes Scouts who have similar interests and abilities and who like to spend time together. If the troop has new-Scout patrols, members of traditional patrols will usually be at least First Class in rank.

The real fun of Boy Scouting happens when the troop leaves its meeting place and heads "out there." For this requirement, your den gets to tag along and participate in a troop's activity.

During the activity, think about these questions:

♦ How did the Boy Scouts in charge of the activity show leadership?

♦ How did the activity help the Boy Scouts who participated advance in rank?

♦ What was the most fun thing you did?

When you visit the members of a troop, ask what some of their favorite campouts were. Most have probably been to summer camp, and some may have gone on a high-adventure trip. When you see one of the patches or logos shown here on an older Scout's uniform, you'll know he's been on a very special trip. Ask him about it!

A. Show how to tie a square knot, two half hitches, and a taut-line hitch. Explain how each knot is used.

B. Show the proper care of a rope by learning how to whip and fuse the ends of different kinds of rope.

Square Knot

The square knot has many uses, from securing packages and the sails of ships to tying the ends of bandages. It is called a joining knot because it joins together two ropes and because it is the knot you learn when you become a Boy Scout. You may also recognize it as part of the World Crest badge that you already wear on your uniform.

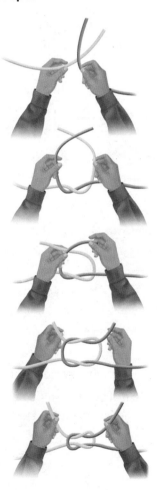

1. Hold a rope end in each hand.

2. Pass the right end over and under the rope in your left hand.

3. Pass the rope end now in your left hand over and under the one now in your right hand.

4. Pull the knot snug.

Remember "right over left, left over right." If you go right over left and then right over left again, you'll end up with a granny knot, which is not very secure.

Two Half Hitches

A hitch is a knot that ties a rope to something. Use two half hitches when you want to tie a rope (called a guy line) to a tent or dining fly. The knot will slide down easily to secure the rope.

1. Pass the end of the rope through the grommet or around the post.

2. Bring the end over and under the body of the rope (known as the standing part), then back through the loop that has formed. This makes a half hitch.

3. Take the end around the standing part a second time, and tie another half hitch.

4. Pull the knot snug.

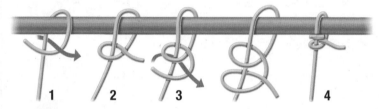

Taut-Line Hitch

A taut-line hitch is similar to two half hitches, but it creates a loop that doesn't slide. Use it to attach the guy line on your tent or dining fly to a stake in the ground. You can easily adjust it to tighten the rope. (Taut is another word for tight.)

1. Pass the end of the rope around the tent stake.

2. Bring the end under and over the standing part of the line to form a loop, then twice through the loop.

3. Again bring the rope end under, over, and through a loop, but this time farther up the standing part.

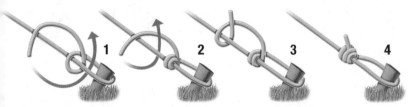

4. Work any slack out of the knot.

5. Slide the hitch to tighten or loosen the rope.

Whipping and Fusing Rope

As you use rope, the ends can become frayed. To make the ends more durable, you can whip them if the rope is made of natural fibers like sisal, or fuse them if they are made out of synthetic material like nylon.

Whipping Rope

Cut off the part of the rope that is already unraveled. Cut a piece of strong string, dental floss, or thin twine at least 8 to 10 inches long. Make a bight, or loop, and place it on one end of the rope.

Wrap the string tightly around the rope several times. When the whipping is as wide as the rope is thick, slip the end through the loop. Then pull both string ends hard, and cut them off.

Fusing Rope

Rope and cord made from plastic or nylon will melt when exposed to high heat. Cut away the frayed part of the rope. Then, working in a well-ventilated area, hold each end a few inches above a lighted match or candle to melt and fuse the strands together. Melted rope is hot and sticky, so don't touch the end until it is completely cool.

A pocketknife is a useful tool to take along on Scout outings. Like any tool, you must follow certain safety rules. Otherwise, you can damage your pocketknife and hurt yourself or other people.

The Whittling Chip

The Whittling Chip is a special card that gives you permission to use a pocketknife.

You can earn it by doing these things:

1. Know the safety rules for handling a knife.

2. Show that you know how to take care of and use a pocketknife.

3. Make a carving with a pocketknife. Work with your den leader or other adult when doing this.

4. Read, understand, and promise to abide by the "Knives Are Not Toys" guidelines.

5. Read, understand, and promise to abide by the "Pocketknife Pledge."

Later, when you become a Boy Scout, you can earn the Totin' Chip. It is similar to the Whittling Chip, but it also gives you permission to use axes and saws.

Safety Rules

- A knife is a tool, not a toy.
- Know how to sharpen a knife. A sharp knife is safer because it is less likely to slip and cut you.
- Keep the blade clean.

- Never carry an open pocketknife.

- When you are not using your knife, close it and put it away.

- Keep your knife dry.

- When you are using the cutting blade, do not try to make big shavings or chips. Easy does it.

- Make a safety circle: Before you pick up your knife to use it, stretch your arm out and turn in a circle. If you can't touch anyone else, it is safe to use your knife.

Knives Are Not Toys

- Close the blade with the palm of your hand.

- Never use a knife on something that will dull or break it.

- Be careful that you do not cut yourself or any person nearby.

- Never use a knife to strip the bark from a tree.

- Do not carve your initials into anything that does not belong to you.

POCKETKNIFE PLEDGE

In return for the privilege of carrying a pocketknife to designated Cub Scout functions, I agree to the following:

I will treat my pocketknife with the respect due a useful tool.

I will always close my pocketknife and put it away when not in use.

I will not use my pocketknife when it might injure someone near me.

I promise never to throw my pocketknife for any reason.

I will use my pocketknife in a safe manner at all times.

Signature _____

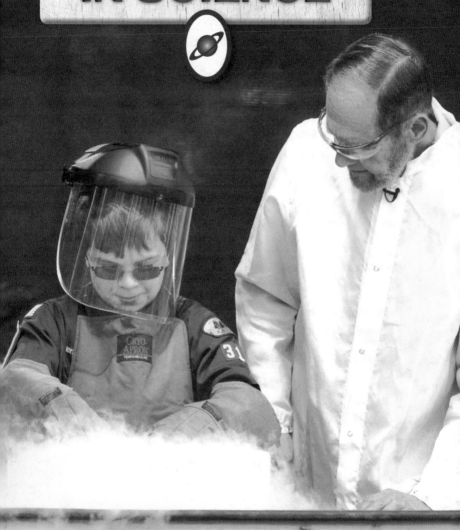

ADVENTURES
IN SCIENCE

SNAPSHOT OF ADVENTURE

Science is all about asking questions like "What is it?" "How does it work?" and "How did it come to be that way?" In Adventures in Science, you will discover how scientists answer those questions and what we can learn as we try to answer our own questions. Best of all, you'll get to do what real scientists do: design and perform experiments. Along the way, you'll learn about physics, chemistry, astronomy, plant science, and more. So grab your notebook, and let's get started!

REQUIREMENT

Do all of these: Approved by

1. An experiment is a "fair test" to compare possible explanations. Draw a picture of a fair test that shows what you need to do to test a fertilizer's effects on plant growth.   _____

2. Visit a museum, a college, a laboratory, an observatory, a zoo, an aquarium, or other facility that employs scientists. Prepare three questions ahead of time, and talk to a scientist about his or her work.   _____

3. Complete any four of the following:

   A. Carry out the experiment you designed for requirement 1, above. Report what you learned about the effect of fertilizer on the plants that you grew.   _____

   B. Carry out the experiment you designed for requirement 1, but change the independent variable. Report what you learned about the effect of changing the variable on the plants that you grew.   _____

C. Build a model solar system. Chart the distances between the planets so that the model is to scale. Use what you learn from this requirement to explain the value of making a model in science. _____

D. With adult supervision, build and launch a model rocket. Use the rocket to design a fair test to answer a question about force or motion. _____

E. Create two circuits of three light bulbs and a battery. Construct one as a series circuit and the other as a parallel circuit. _____

F. Study the night sky. Sketch the appearance of the North Star (Polaris) and the Big Dipper (part of the Ursa Major constellation) over at least six hours. Describe what you observed, and explain the meaning of your observations. _____

G. With adult assistance, explore safe chemical reactions with household materials. Using two substances, observe what happens when the amounts of the reactants are increased. _____

H. Explore properties of motion on a playground. How does the weight of a person affect how fast they slide down a slide or how fast a swing moves? Design a fair test to answer one of those questions. _____

I. Read a biography of a scientist. Tell your den leader or the other members of your den what the scientist is famous for and why his or her work is important. _____

Imagine that you're a medical researcher who wants to test three new medicines to see which one helps people who have a cold feel better. If you gave a sick person all three medicines and he got well, how would you know which medicine worked? You wouldn't!

But what if you started with three sick people and gave each one a different medicine? Then you would know which medicine (or medicines) worked.

When a scientist asks a question, he or she comes up with a fair test to answer that question. This is called an experiment. An experiment is designed to rule out possible explanations and, as much as possible, test only a single explanation.

In an experiment, scientists look at three things:

♦ What they will change—called the **independent variable**

♦ What they will keep the same—called the **control variable**, or **control**

♦ What difference they are looking for—called the **dependent variable**

In the medicine experiment, the independent variable is which medicine each person takes. The control is the fact that each person has a cold. The dependent variable is whether or not each person gets well.

For this requirement, you will draw a picture of an experiment to test fertilizers. First, think about what independent variables, controls, and dependent variables your experiment would use.

A scientist might start by creating a chart like the one below to help figure out what the important parts of the experiment could be. One of the biggest challenges in creating a fair test is to figure out what to keep the same, what to change, and how to find out if a meaningful result occurs.

Measuring the Impact of Fertilizer

Independent Variable	Controls	Dependent Variable
Fertilizer added vs. plain soil	Same type of plant Same amount of water Same type of soil Same amount of light Same temperature	How tall the plant grows

What would you add to the list of controls? What are some other ways to see whether the fertilizer made a difference? Measuring how tall the plant grows might not be the only dependent variable you could test for.

Draw a picture of your own fair test to compare fertilizers and label your drawing with all the variables that you would want to keep track of in your experiment. You might draw this as a comic strip to show the steps in your test and the changes over time.

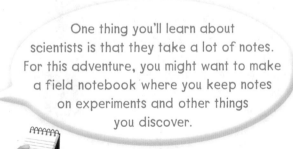

One thing you'll learn about scientists is that they take a lot of notes. For this adventure, you might want to make a field notebook where you keep notes on experiments and other things you discover.

Scientists work in many different places. When you visit a scientist in one of those places, you can better understand what he or she does and the tools he or she uses every day.

Just like you plan your investigations, you should plan your visit to a scientist. What would you like to learn? Write down your questions in your field notebook ahead of time.

Before your visit, try to guess how the scientist might answer your questions. Afterward, see how his or her answers compare with your guesses.

REQUIREMENT 3A | Carry out the experiment you designed for requirement 1, above. Report what you learned about the effect of fertilizer on the plants that you grew.

An important part of designing a fair test is deciding ahead of time what you expect the result to be. For your fair test, that means making a prediction about how the fertilizer will influence the way the plant grows. Write your prediction in your field notebook, and then carry out the experiment.

After the experiment ends, compare your prediction with what you actually observed. Did the plant grow as tall as you predicted? Did the plants grow in ways that you were not able to predict? How can you explain this result?

Draw a picture of what happened, and make a note in your field notebook about what you would like to do to learn more.

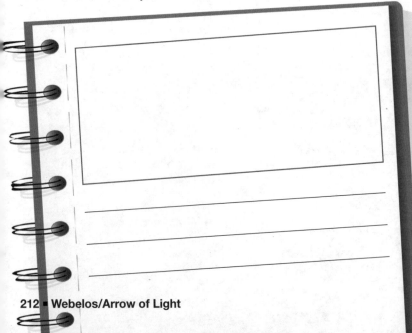

There are lots of different ways to carry out an investigation using the same materials and variables. Here are some other independent variables you could test in the plant experiment:

- Potting soil vs. sand
- Six hours of light per day vs. 24 hours of light per day
- Colored light vs. white light
- Fresh water vs. salty water
- 100 ml of water per day vs. 1,000 ml of water per day

Design another fair test and write down what you predict will happen. Remember to use only one independent variable in your experiment.

Now, carry out the new experiment. What did you find out? Did the result match your prediction? If not, how was it different? Draw a picture of what happened, and make a note in your field notebook about what you would like to do to learn more.

The more you carry out experiments like this, the more you will learn about the subject you are studying. For example, over time you might learn that a combination of factors—say, fertilizer plus plenty of sunlight—helps plants grow better than fertilizer alone. Or you might learn that a certain fertilizer works better on flowers than on vegetables.

Scientists also like to repeat the same experiments over and over. They even publish the details of their experiments so other scientists can reproduce them. Getting the same results many times proves that the results are accurate and not caused by some random event, like worms in the soil affecting plant growth.

REQUIREMENT 3C | Build a model solar system.
Chart the distances between the planets so that
the model is to scale. Use what you learn from this
requirement to explain the value of making a model
in science.

Our solar system is really, really big. It takes Earth one year to travel around the sun, but it takes Neptune, which is way out at the edge of the solar system, 165 years. Light travels at a speed of 238,000 miles every second, but it takes light from the sun more than seven minutes to reach Earth, which is 93 million miles away. Yes, the solar system is huge!

For this requirement, your challenge is to build a model solar system that has the same scale as the actual solar system. In other words, the relative distances between the planets in your model will be the same as they are between the real planets.

This chart shows each planet's approximate distance from the sun, along with scale distances in both inches and centimeters. It also shows Proxima Centauri, the nearest star to the sun.

Object	Approximate Distance to Sun (miles)	Scale Distance (1) 1 million miles = 1 inch	Scale Distance (2) 1 million miles = 1 cm
Sun	--	--	--
Mercury	36,000,000	36 in	36 cm
Venus	67,000,000	67 in	67 cm
Earth	93,000,000	93 in	93 cm
Mars	141,500,000	141.5 in	141.5 cm
Jupiter	483,300,000	483.3 in	483.3 cm
Saturn	886,200,000	886.2 in	886.2 cm
Uranus	1,782,900,000	1,782.9 in	1,782.9 cm
Neptune	2,792,600,000	2,792.6 in	2,792.6 cm
Proxima Centauri (nearest star to sun)	25,200,000,000,000	25,200,000 in	25,200,000 cm

To get started, make a series of signs, one for the sun and one for each planet. Label the signs and add pictures if you want to. Write on the planet signs how far away from the sun each one is.

Now, decide whether you will use inches or centimeters in your model. An inch is more than twice as long as a centimeter, so the scale model in inches would be larger than the scale model in centimeters. Will the sun and all of the planets fit in your home if you make the model in inches? What if you make it in centimeters? Get out a ruler and test your prediction.

Unless you live in an aircraft hangar, the model organized in inches won't fit in your home. The distance from the sun to Neptune is more than 230 feet—that's two-thirds of a football field! You will need to make your model solar system outside.

Use a measuring tape and an open space to lay out your model solar system. A school yard or a park would be a good spot if you have permission to build your model there. You will need a friend to help you lay out your solar system. In fact, this would be a fun project to do with your whole den. Every Webelos Scout could pick a planet and make his own sign.

In your field notebook, write down answers to these questions:

- ♦ What is the value of making a model for things that are so big, such as the solar system?
- ♦ How can models be useful in science?

REQUIREMENT 3D | With adult supervision, build and launch a model rocket. Use the rocket to design a fair test to answer a question about force or motion.

Building a model rocket is a great project to do with your den or with an adult. Rockets are lots of fun, and they are also a great tool for investigating ideas related to force and movement. As you did earlier, use the chart below to help you design a fair test to answer some questions about force and motion. Add anything else to this list that you believe is important.

Testing the Effect of Weight on a Rocket's Flight

Independent Variable	Controls	Dependent Variable
Heavy rocket vs. light rocket	Same rocket motor Same rocket size Same wind speed	How high will the rocket fly?

Part of being a scientist is being creative. Your rocket may fly hundreds of feet into the air. How can you measure how high it flies? Talk with friends in your den or your adult partner about how to measure the rocket's maximum height.

You might want to explore some other properties of a model rocket. Can you launch a raw egg and return it—uncracked—to the earth? Can you consistently predict where the rocket will land? What other experiments could you come up with to extend your knowledge of force and motion?

REQUIREMENT 3E | Create two circuits of three
light bulbs and a battery. Construct one as a series
circuit and the other as a parallel circuit.

How long does a battery last? If you've been on a campout and had a flashlight that didn't light up, you know that battery life can be a big problem. In this investigation, you will explore possible connections between the way an electrical circuit is put together and how long a battery will last.

An electrical circuit is like a big circle. The electricity comes out of the power source (the battery in this case), goes through the output device (the bulbs in this case), and cycles back to the power source. If you break the circuit, the electricity stops flowing.

Parallel Circuit

Series Circuit

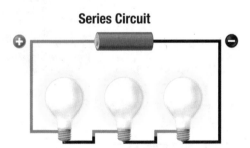

When you have more than one output device, you can create two types of circuits: series and parallel. In a series circuit, the electricity goes through each of the output devices in turn. In a parallel circuit, the electricity follows separate paths through each output device. The pictures on this page show the difference.

Here is a chart of possible variables and controls. Add anything else to this list that you believe is important.

Measuring Battery Life in Different Circuit Types

Independent Variable	Controls	Dependent Variable
Series circuit vs. parallel circuit	Same kind of bulb Same kind of batteries Batteries in the same condition Same kind of wire	Working life of battery (time)

To carry out this investigation, you will need flashlight bulbs, wire, several batteries, and a watch to time the life of the battery. Set up one series circuit and one parallel circuit using a battery and three bulbs. You can find bases for bulbs and batteries at some hardware and technology stores; your science teacher may also have some materials that you can borrow. The bases are handy to use, but you can simply fasten the wires to the batteries and bulbs with electrical or duct tape.

One of the challenges of this test is to figure out when the light bulbs go out. That will be your evidence that there is no longer enough energy in the battery to light the bulb. You will need to think creatively about how to measure when the light goes out.

After your investigation, think about these questions:

* In which circuit did the battery last longer? Is there a connection between the type of circuit and how long the battery works?

* What other differences do you observe?

* Is there a connection between the brightness of the bulbs and the way the circuit is hooked up?

* What other questions can you ask about the circuits you built?

If you end up with more questions in your field notebook than when you started, you are on track to being a talented scientist. More questions lead to more future adventures in science!

Making observations of the world around you is an important part of science. The things you observe help you form important questions and start to make predictions. Your predictions, whether or not they are correct, are important steps in helping you explain why things happen the way they do.

The stars and constellations of the northern hemisphere can help you understand changes in the night sky. For this investigation, sketch the appearance of the North Star and the Big Dipper, which is part of the Ursa Major constellation, over at least six hours. You will want to do this on a clear weekend night, when you can stay up late with your family's permission. (This would be a great activity to do on a Webelos den campout.)

As early in the evening as possible, make a sketch of the night sky. Draw it as precisely as you can, so that you can see which way the "pointer stars" on the side of the Big Dipper are oriented.

Return in three hours and make another sketch. Try to be precise as before, so that you can accurately record any motion that you observe.

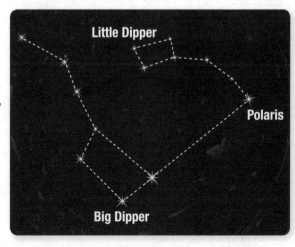

Return three hours later and record what you see. You might have to wake yourself up or get your parent to help. Again, make your sketch as accurate as possible.

Compare your three sketches and think about these questions:

◆ What are some ways to explain what you observed?

◆ Which is the best explanation: that the earth is moving or that the stars are moving?

◆ How long will it take for the Big Dipper to return to where it was when you first recorded it?

◆ How could you use what you observed to tell time? What are the advantages and disadvantages of a "star clock" that uses a constellation?

Chemical changes are an important area in the science of chemistry. When some substances are combined, they create a new substance that is different from the ones you started with. Sometimes, chemical reactions create changes in color or temperature or produce gases.

 Some chemical combinations, such as those involving household cleaners, can cause dangerous reactions. Check with a parent or guardian and consult a chemistry book before trying any experiments with household chemicals.

One choice for this investigation is to combine two simple chemicals from your family's kitchen in a zip-top bag: baking soda and vinegar. Both have chemical formulas that can be used to describe them. Baking soda is called sodium bicarbonate ($NaHCO_3$); vinegar is a weak acid called acetic acid ($C_2H_4O_2$).

When baking soda and vinegar are combined, a chemical reaction takes place and a gas is produced. Your challenge is to see if there are any patterns in how much gas is produced when baking soda and vinegar are combined in different proportions.

 For this and all other chemistry experiments, you should wear eye protection.

Measuring the Gas Produced in a Chemical Reaction

Here are the factors to consider in your investigation. Add anything else to this list that you believe is important.

Independent Variable	Controls	Dependent Variable
Amount of chemicals	Types of chemicals Tools to collect and measure products	How much bag expands

Think about these questions as you design your investigation:

◆ How can you combine the baking soda and vinegar in such a way that you capture all the gas that is produced?

◆ How can you accurately measure how much gas is produced?

◆ How can you make sure the bag you mix the chemicals in doesn't contain anything else that could affect the experiment?

◆ Can you use what you learned to make a prediction for how much a bag will expand with different combinations of baking soda and vinegar? If so, make a prediction and see how close your prediction comes to the actual expanded size of the bag.

| **Explore properties of motion on a playground. How does the weight of a person affect how fast they slide down a slide or how fast a swing moves? Design a fair test to answer one of those questions.**

Does a heavier person slide faster? Does a lighter person swing faster? These are questions that you can answer using playground equipment and some friends or family members who weigh different amounts.

Here are some factors to consider if you choose the slide investigation. Add anything else to this list that you believe is important.

Measuring the Effect of Weight on Slide Time

Independent Variable	Controls	Dependent Variable
Weight of person	Amount of friction: have everyone sit on a towel to keep it the same	Time to reach the bottom of the slide
	Consistent starting point: start the timer when the person begins to slide	
	Consistent ending point: stop the timer when the same part of the body reaches the same point at the bottom of the slide	

Set up an experiment where you time how fast different people go down a slide. Decide when and where to start your timer. What timer will you use? Smartphones and digital watches usually have a stopwatch function.

Consider these things as you plan your investigation:

♦ Before you do the investigation, create a chart to write down your data. This will help you think through the project in advance and ensure you record everything you need to make a good decision.

- Have everyone go down the slide several times and figure out an average for each person.

- Sitting on a towel can ensure that everyone touches the slide with the same kind of fabric. (If one person wore jeans and another wore slick pants, that would affect the results.) You could also use waxed paper from your kitchen.

- Be careful! Have a spotter at the bottom of the slide to keep people from hitting the ground.

After your investigation, think about these questions:

- What did you learn?

- Did the weight of the person on the slide have a big effect on how fast he or she moved down the slide?

- Was there a pattern?

Write down your conclusions in your field notebook. If you can think of better ways to do the experiment or if new questions come up, be sure to record them in your notebook as well.

Here are some factors to consider if you choose the swing investigation. Add anything else to this list that you believe is important.

Measuring the Effect of Weight on Swing Time

Independent Variable	Controls	Dependent Variable
Weight of person	Release everyone from the same height	Time for one swing
	Keep legs from swinging	
	Start timer at the same point in the swing	
	Stop timer at same point in the swing	

Consider these things as you plan your investigation:

- Before you do the investigation, create a chart to write down your data. This will help you think through the project in advance and ensure you record everything you need to make a good decision.

- Have everyone repeat the swing several times and figure out an average for each person.

- How do you make sure that everyone starts from the same point?

- How can you make sure everyone swings the same way? Because you are measuring the time for a swing, it will affect your findings if a person pumps his or her legs.

- Decide when and where to start your timer. What timer will you use? Smartphones and digital watches usually have a stopwatch function.

After your investigation, think about these questions:

- What did you learn?

- Did the weight of the person on the swing have a big effect on the time for a single swing?

- Was there a pattern?

Write down your conclusions in your field notebook. If you can think of better ways to do the experiment or if new questions come up, be sure to record them in your notebook as well.

A Scout is cheerful. When a science investigation doesn't work out as planned, focus on what you did learn and what you can try next.

REQUIREMENT 3I | Read a biography of a scientist. Tell your den leader or the other members of your den what the scientist is famous for and why his or her work is important.

Reading stories about scientists and what they have accomplished can be inspiring. It may even start you on the road to your own great scientific adventures!

Here are some scientists you could learn about:

Albert Einstein, physicist

Galileo Galilei, astronomer

George Washington Carver, botanist

Benjamin Franklin, researcher in many fields

Marie Curie, physicist and chemist

Paul Siple, weather researcher (and Eagle Scout)

Peter Agre, biologist (and Eagle Scout)

E.O. Wilson, biologist (and Eagle Scout)

Guion S. Bluford Jr., astronaut (and Eagle Scout)

Luis W. Alvarez, physicist

Lee Berger, archaeologist (and Eagle Scout)

Michael Manyak, expedition medicine pioneer (and Eagle Scout)

Who Will Be the Scientists of Tomorrow?

One day, you could become a NESA World Explorer. The National Eagle Scout Association started the program to reward Eagle Scouts who aspire to be explorers and field scientists. The Scouts who are chosen head off to the learning experience of a lifetime.

Here are some recent Eagle Scout Explorers:

Alex Overman
Eagle Scout Argonaut

C.B. Wren
Eagle Scout Argonaut

Tristan Bullard
Eagle Scout Astronomer

Alex Houston
Antarctic Sustainability Eagle Scout

AQUANAUT

SNAPSHOT OF ADVENTURE

Swimming and boating are great exercise and a whole lot of fun. They're also the only way you can explore the 70 percent of the earth that is covered in water. In this adventure, you'll discover how to enjoy swimming and boating safely and how to respond to water emergencies. You'll also learn some skills that will help you have even more exciting adventures after you become a Boy Scout. So grab your swim trunks and your buddy tag, and let's hit the water!

REQUIREMENT

Complete 1–5 and any two from 6–10:

Approved by

1. State the safety precautions you need to take before doing any water activity.

   _____

2. Recognize the purpose and the three classifications of swimming ability groups in Scouting.

   _____

3. Discuss the importance of learning the skills you need to know before going boating.

   _____

4. Explain the meaning of "order of rescue," and demonstrate the reach and throw rescue techniques from land.

   _____

5. Attempt the BSA swimmer test.

   _____

6. Demonstrate the precautions you must take before attempting to dive headfirst into the water, and attempt a front surface dive.

   _____

7. Learn and demonstrate two of the following strokes: crawl, sidestroke, breaststroke, or elementary backstroke. _____

8. Invite a member or former member of a lifeguard team, rescue squad, the U.S. Coast Guard, U.S. Navy, or other armed forces branch who has had swimming and rescue training to your den meeting. Find out what training and other experiences this person has had. _____

9. Demonstrate how to correctly fasten a life jacket that is the right size for you. Jump into water over your head. Show how the life jacket helps keep your head above water by swimming 25 feet. Get out of the water, remove the life jacket, and hang it where it will dry. _____

10. If you are a qualified swimmer, select a paddle of the proper size, and paddle a canoe with an adult's supervision. _____

While swimming and boating are lots of fun, they do require you to follow safety rules and to be alert for danger. In Scouting, we have two sets of rules we follow to be safe in and on the water: Safe Swim Defense and Safety Afloat. The adults who lead aquatic activities must be trained in these rules. Discuss the rules with your leader or a parent or guardian, and explain how you will follow safety guidelines.

 A Scout is obedient. During any water activity, follow the rules so everyone can be safe and have fun in the water.

Safe Swim Defense

Safe Swim Defense covers these eight points:

1. **Supervision.** A trained adult leads all swimming activities.

2. **Physical Fitness.** All participants submit a complete health history before swimming.

3. **Safe Swim Area.** Swimming only takes place in an area that is safe.

4. **Lifeguards.** At least two lifeguards—and one rescuer for every 10 participants—are on duty.

5. **Lookout.** Besides the lifeguards, someone monitors the swimmers at all times.

6. **Ability Groups.** All participants are classified as swimmers, beginners, or nonswimmers and stay in designated areas.

7. **Buddy System.** Each participant has a buddy. Buddies stay together, look out for each other, and get help if one of them needs assistance or goes missing.

8. **Discipline.** All participants know, understand, and follow the rules for the activity. Everyone obeys the activity's leader.

THE BUDDY SYSTEM

One of the most important ways you can ensure a safe swim is to follow the buddy system. You will be paired with another Scout and should always stay with him. Keep an eye on him, and call for help if he needs it. Always check into and out of the swimming area together.

Every 10 minutes or so, the lookout will call for a buddy check. As quickly as possible, get to your buddy and raise his hand. See if you can be the first buddy pair to do this!

The buddy system is also a good idea when you are hiking, cooking, or doing any other activity!

Safety Afloat

Safety Afloat is similar to Safe Swim Defense, but it applies to boating. It covers these nine points:

1. **Supervision.** A trained adult leads all boating activities. In Cub Scouting, there must be one trained adult for every five participants.

2. **Physical Fitness.** All participants submit a complete health history before boating.

3. **Swimming Ability.** As a Cub Scout, you may participate in boating on lakes and ponds. If you are not classified as a swimmer, you may operate a rowboat or pedal boat with a buddy who is a swimmer or ride in a canoe or other paddle craft with an adult who is a swimmer.

4. **Life Jackets.** All participants must wear properly fitted U.S. Coast Guard-approved life jackets at all times.

5. **Buddy System.** Each participant has a buddy. Buddies stay together, look out for each other, and get help if one of them needs assistance or goes missing.

6. **Know Your Boat.** All participants must know how to safely operate the water craft they are using.

7. **Planning.** The adults in charge of the activity make plans for the activity, including checking the weather and being prepared if an emergency arises or equipment malfunctions.

8. **Equipment.** All watercraft are suitable for the activity. Life jackets and paddles are sized to the participants. Emergency equipment is ready for use.

9. **Discipline.** All participants know, understand, and follow the rules for the activity. Everyone obeys the activity's leader.

Just about anyone can have fun in the water, even people who can't swim. But it wouldn't be very smart for kids who can't swim to get into water over their heads, would it?

To keep everybody safe in the water, Scouting puts everybody (both Scouts and adults) into three ability groups:

- ◆ Those who can swim well are called **swimmers**. They can go into water up to 12 feet deep.

- ◆ Those who can swim a little are called **beginners**. They can go into water where they can stand up to just over their heads.

- ◆ Those who can't swim yet are called **nonswimmers**. They can go into water up to chest-deep.

In swimming pools and lakes at Scout camps, ropes or piers separate the swimmer, beginner, and nonswimmer areas so everybody knows where they can swim and play safely.

BUDDY TAGS

After you take your swim test, you will receive a buddy tag with your name on it. If you are a swimmer, the red and blue parts will be colored in. If you are a beginner, the red part will be colored in. If you are a nonswimmer, nothing will be colored in—until you learn some skills and become a beginner or swimmer!

Before you start boating, there are some important things you should know:

* Always put on a life jacket before getting into the boat. Life jackets are required for all boating activities in Scouting.

* Step into the center of the boat when boarding or changing seats, and always stay low. Some boats, like canoes, can easily tip over if you are not careful.

* Balance your load. Divide weight evenly from side to side and from the bow (front) to the stern (back).

* Don't overload a boat. In a rowboat, one person per seat is a good rule.

* If your boat tips over or fills with water, hang on. Even a boat filled with water can still float. You can kick the boat to shore or drift in.

* Watch the weather, and stay on shore if there's bad weather nearby. If you're on the water and the weather gets bad, head for shore immediately. If you're caught on the water in bad weather, seat your passengers on the floor of the boat. Have everyone sit as low as possible. Head your boat into the waves.

* Sharp turns are dangerous, so take it easy.

* Keep a lookout for other boaters and for swimmers.

Rowing Strokes

When you row, you actually face the back of the boat. (Your buddy can help you steer.) Hold the oar handles firmly with your knuckles up and wrists and arms straight. Bend forward a little bit.

Each stroke has four parts:

◆ **Catch.** Lower the oar blades edgewise into the water behind you, not too deep.

◆ **Pull.** Lean backward, pulling on the oars and bending your arms until your elbows come in against your ribs.

◆ **Feather.** Lift the oars slightly out of the water, and turn your knuckles up toward your face so the blades are flat above the water's surface.

◆ **Recover.** Bend forward, and straighten your wrists and arms, ready to begin another stroke.

To do the backstroke, push on the oars instead of pulling. To turn, pull on one oar while you push on the other.

Catch

Pull

Feather

Recover

Canoeing Strokes

With canoeing, both people in the canoe paddle, usually on opposite sides and stroking at the same time. The person in the back steers and gives direction. The person in the front adds power and helps the canoe go straight.

Catch

Hold the paddle firmly with both hands—one hand on the top of the handle and the other hand just above the throat (where the paddle starts to get wide). Bend forward a little, and let your upper body rotate as you paddle.

Power

The forward stroke has four parts:

♦ **Catch.** Lower the paddle blade edgewise into the water in front of you, not too deep.

Feather and Recover

♦ **Power.** Pull backward to your hip, keeping the paddle straight up and down.

♦ **Feather.** Lift the paddle slightly out of the water with the blade flat above the water's surface.

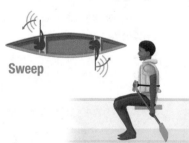
Sweep

♦ **Recover.** Rotate the paddle forward, and straighten your wrists and arms, ready to begin another stroke.

To do the backstroke, push on the paddle instead of pulling.

Use sweeps to turn a canoe. Reach out with the paddle and move it in a quarter circle, either forward or backward. Or use draw and pry strokes, pulling or pushing the paddle straight toward or away from the canoe.

If a swimmer or boater gets in trouble, trained rescuers know how to perform a rescue. To be as effective as possible and to protect themselves from becoming secondary victims, rescuers follow the order of rescue, doing the following actions in order:

+ **Reach** for the victim with whatever is available—a hand or foot, a tree branch, a canoe paddle, or a towel. Pools and waterfront areas usually have reach poles at least 10 feet long.

+ **Throw** or toss a line, buoy, or floating object (like a kickboard or even a drink cooler) to the victim to provide support. If the object is tied to a rope, the rescuer can pull the victim to safety. A trained rescuer can easily toss a ring buoy 25 feet or more.

+ **Row** means to use a boat (usually a rowboat) to go to the victim. The rescuer can then reach the victim and have him or her hold onto the back of the boat while the rescuer rows to safety. A rowing rescue should only be made by a trained rescuer who can handle a boat and is wearing a life jacket.

+ **Go** with support means to swim to the victim with a float, life jacket, or other support device. This is the most dangerous type of rescue and should only be attempted by a trained rescuer.

As a Webelos Scout, you are not expected to do the rescue work of a trained adult. However, you can perform a reach or throw rescue from shore or from a dock—even if you don't know how to swim. If someone falls in the water and no one else is around, you could save the person's life!

> **If you see someone in danger, first call for help from an adult. If no adult is present, you can try a reach or throw rescue.**

For this requirement, practice reach and throw rescues. You could do this in a pool or lake, but you could also do it on shore.

Here are some tips to make your rescues more effective:
Reach rescues

+ Lie down on the shore or pier so you are more stable and are closer to the victim's level.

+ Be sure to anchor yourself so you don't get pulled into the water. You could hold onto a ladder or post or have a friend stand behind you and hold onto you.

+ If you are using a reach pole, sweep it under the victim's arm from the side rather than poking at the victim straight on.

Throw rescues

+ Don't throw a ring buoy or float directly at your victim; you don't want to bonk him or her on the head!

+ If the object you're throwing is attached to a rope, throw it past the victim so the line falls across his or her shoulder. You can then reel it in so it's easy to grasp.

+ If you are throwing a rope (whether it's attached to an object or not), tie one end loosely around your wrist with a bowline so you won't accidently let it go.

> **In any water rescue, never put yourself in danger or at risk. If reaching and throwing don't work, get help!**

REQUIREMENT 5 | Attempt the BSA swimmer test.

If you are a swimmer, you will have more fun in the water and be safer, too. You will also be able to participate in more boating activities, like canoeing, kayaking, motorboating, and whitewater, when you become a Boy Scout.

To become a swimmer, you must pass this test:

♦ Jump feetfirst into water that's over your head in depth.

♦ Level off and swim 100 yards in one swim (without stops and including at least one sharp turn). The first 75 yards must be done in a strong manner using one or more of the following strokes: sidestroke, breaststroke, trudgen, or crawl; the last 25 yards must be done using an easy resting backstroke.

♦ After completing the swim, rest by floating.

Diving is a fun way to go deep underwater so you can explore the bottom of a lake or pool. It's also an important skill for trained rescuers.

However, diving can be dangerous if you don't know how deep the water is or what's beneath a cloudy surface. Always ask the lifeguard or adult in charge of a swimming activity whether it's OK to dive. Never dive in places where it's not allowed, including the shallow end of a pool.

A front surface dive is a dive that starts when you're already in the water. Here's how to do this dive:

◆ Float face down with your arms out ahead of you. Sweep your arms back toward your hips. At the same time, bend forward sharply at the hips. Aim the top part of your body toward the bottom of the pool or lake.

◆ Turn your palms down, and push them toward the bottom. Raise your legs above the surface as high as you can.

◆ Your head will now be pointing downward, and the weight of your legs above the water will drive you down. While you're underwater, try swimming a few strokes before you return to the surface.

There are many different swimming strokes you can use. Some help you go very fast but also require a lot of energy. Others are so easy and relaxing that you could use them to swim a whole mile.

Here are four strokes you should know:

Crawl

Float face down in the water with your arms and legs stretched out.

Move your legs up and down. Press down on the water with the top of your foot. This is called a flutter kick.

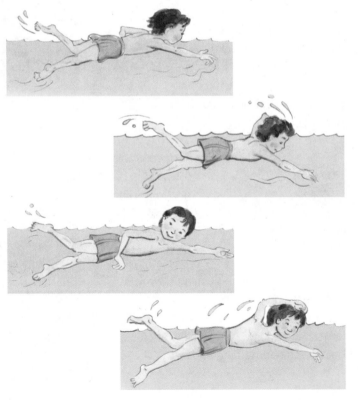

While still kicking, pull downward with your left arm. Breathe out through your nose and mouth while your face is in the water.

As your left-arm stroke ends, begin a stroke with your right arm. Raise your face by turning your head to the right so you can breathe in through your mouth.

Reach ahead again with your right arm. At the end of the right-arm stroke, begin a new one with the left arm. Turn your face under water again to breathe out.

Keep repeating the arm and leg motions, making them as smooth and even as possible.

When I was learning to swim, I had trouble doing the arm and leg motions together. It was like when you try to pat your head and rub your stomach at the same time. My teacher had me practice the motions separately before I put them together. That worked great!

Sidestroke

Lie on your side with one ear in the water. Stretch your bottom arm out ahead of you. Your top arm is at your side, along your leg.

Start with your feet together, and then bend your knees, pulling your heels toward your hips.

Cup your reaching hand a little. Sweep it down in front of your chest.

Move your feet apart by moving your top leg forward and your bottom leg backward.

Notice the hand and arm movement. As your lower hand sweeps water toward your feet, your upper hand moves toward your chest. They nearly meet.

When your legs are as far apart as possible, snap them together quickly the way you close a pair of scissors.

Your upper hand sweeps water toward your feet. Your lower hand reaches out ahead of you, returning to its starting position.

Stop your feet as they come together. Repeat the arm and leg movements.

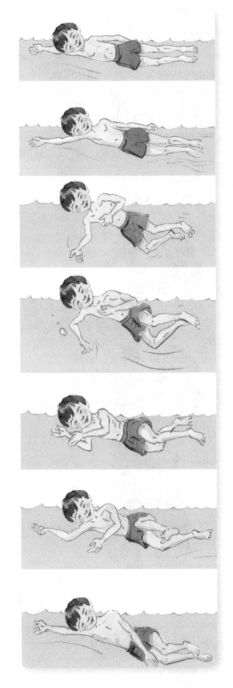

Breaststroke

Float face down in the water with your arms and legs stretched out.

Spread your arms out so they are diagonal from your body. Your elbows should be straight, and your palms should be facing slightly out.

Pull your elbows toward your sides and then bring your hands together in front of your chest as if you're trying to scoop the water toward you. Quickly push your hands back to where they started. (Your hands should trace the shape of an upside-down heart.)

As you start the arm stroke, bend your knees so your heels are close to your hips and your ankles are spread out. Make a quick circular motion outward and backward until your legs are fully extended.

Just before you push your hands forward and your legs backward, lift your head and upper chest out of the water and take a breath.

Glide for a second or two; then repeat the arm and leg movements.

Elementary Backstroke

Start by floating on your back, arms at your sides.

Bring your cupped hands up over your chest to your shoulders. At the same time, drop your heels downward. They should be beneath your knees.

Turn your toes outward and swing your feet outward in a circular motion without stopping. At the same time, reach your arms straight out. Then sweep them down to your sides as your legs come together in a straight-out position, with toes pointed. The arm pull and leg kick happen at the same time.

You should end up the same way you were at the start, and then glide before the next stroke.

Communities near large bodies of water have rescue squads that help swimmers or boaters who get into trouble. Rescue capabilities are also very important in the U.S. Coast Guard and U.S. Navy, America's maritime military services. In fact, the Coast Guard conducts dozens of search and rescue missions every day and saves thousands of people every year.

Members of these groups undergo extensive training on rescuing people while keeping themselves safe. Depending on where they serve, they often have specialized training in swift-water rescue and extraction by helicopter.

Your den leader can help you find a current or former member of a rescue squad or the military who has rescue training. When this person visits your den meeting, ask about his or her training and what sorts of rescues he or she has been involved with. Who knows? You might be inspired to join a rescue crew yourself when you get older.

When you go boating, one of your most important pieces of equipment is a life jacket. In fact, life jackets were not worn in more than 80 percent of fatal boating accidents.

A life jacket is designed to help you float if you fall in the water. The life jackets you are likely to find at Scout camp (Type II and Type III) will also help keep you in a face-up position.

For a life jacket to save your life, it must be the right size and must be worn snugly. If a friend can pull your life jacket over your head by tugging on the tops of the arm openings, it's too big, too loose, or both.

In an emergency, there's no time to grab your life jacket and put it on, so don't stow it under your seat. Everyone who is engaged in Scout boating activities must wear a properly fitted U.S. Coast Guard–approved life jacket at all times.

Canoeing is one of the most fun activities you can do on the water. As a Webelos Scout, you can paddle around lakes at district and council activities. Later, as a Boy Scout, you might get to canoe down rivers or explore the Boundary Waters Canoe Area Wilderness, part of the Northern Tier High Adventure program.

You'll have a lot more fun canoeing if your paddle is the right size. A good rule of thumb is to stand up and hold the paddle in front of you with the blade on the ground. If the grip is between your chin and your eyes, the paddle is probably about the right size. If the grip is only midway up your chest or is over your head, try another paddle.

ART EXPLOSION

SNAPSHOT OF ADVENTURE

Art is a powerful way to capture a moment in time, an idea, or an emotion. It's a lot of fun, too. You get to work with all sorts of gooey and gloppy materials, and you never have to worry about getting the right answer because everybody's art is different. Whether you're into drawing, painting, sculpture, computer illustration, or photography, you'll find something to love on this adventure.

REQUIREMENT

Do all of these: **Approved by**

1. Visit an art museum, gallery, or exhibit. Discuss with an adult the art you saw. What did you like? _____

2. Create two self-portraits using two different techniques, such as drawing, painting, printmaking, sculpture, and computer illustration. _____

3. Do two of the following:

   A. Draw or paint an original picture outdoors, using the art materials of your choice. _____

   B. Use clay to sculpt a simple form. _____

   C. Create an object using clay that can be fired, baked in the oven, or air-dried. _____

   D. Create a freestanding sculpture or mobile using wood, metal, papier-mâché, or found or recycled objects. _____

   E. Make a display of origami or kirigami projects. _____

   F. Use a computer illustration or painting program to create a work of art. _____

   G. Create an original logo or design. Transfer the design onto a T-shirt, hat, or other object. _____

H. Using a camera or other electronic device, take at least 10 photos of your family, a pet, or scenery. Use photo-editing software to crop, lighten or darken, and change some of the photos. _____

I. Create a comic strip with original characters. Include at least four panels to tell a story centered on one of the points of the Scout Law. Characters can be hand-drawn or computer-generated. _____

4. Choose one of the following methods to show your artwork:

A. Create a hard-copy or digital portfolio of your projects. Share it with your family and members of your den or pack. _____

B. Display your artwork in a pack, school, or community art show. _____

Art is everywhere! You might find posters, drawings, photographs, sculptures, and copies of famous paintings around your home, at school, on television, on the Internet, and at stores you visit. Many works of art have been turned into T-shirts, umbrellas, and greeting cards.

But to really enjoy and appreciate art, it helps to visit places that are designed just for displaying it. An art museum, of course, is a museum that focuses on art. In a museum, works of art will be grouped by artist, theme, or when they were created; and signs will help you understand what you're seeing. An art gallery is similar to a museum except that the art is for sale. An art exhibit takes art out of the museum or gallery into a place like a library or school so that more people can enjoy it.

One thing you'll discover is that artists have produced very different styles of art at different times in history. Here are some styles you may encounter:

- ◆ **Abstract art** uses color and shape to express emotion. You won't see subjects that you can recognize, but you may be able to sense what the artist was feeling when he or she created the art.

- ◆ **Expressionistic art** also expresses feeling. Here, the subjects are recognizable, but certain features are emphasized, like the scariness of a thunderstorm.

* **Impressionist art** is designed to show the artist's first impressions of looking at the subject. Impressionist paintings often show outdoor scenes and focus on how light and color appear.

* **Pop art** uses everyday objects and bright colors to communicate ideas. Some pop art looks like comic strips or collages.

* **Realist art** is designed to accurately record what the subject looks like—almost like taking a photograph. Realism was more popular before photography was invented because there was no other way to record how something looked.

* **Surrealist art** is often based on dreams or nightmares. The subjects may look recognizable, but something about them will be strange—sometimes very strange!

A self-portrait is a reflection of you—not just what you look like in a mirror but who you are, what you enjoy doing, what your favorite colors are, and how you think.

For this requirement, think about some things that define you, and then create self-portraits using two different techniques.

Ask yourself:

♦ How was the process different for each technique?

♦ Which technique did you enjoy most?

♦ What parts were challenging?

♦ What parts of yourself did you capture best in the portrait?

REQUIREMENT 3A | Draw or paint an original picture outdoors, using the art materials of your choice.

Drawing and painting are common ways to create art. You may have started drawing as soon as you could hold a crayon.

Picking Your Subject

To create a picture for this requirement, start by deciding what you want your picture to depict. Will it be your house? A scene in a nearby park? The playground at your school? (Be sure not to pick something like a dog that won't sit still!)

Decide where your picture will begin and end. Hold your hands up to form a frame, and move them around until you've enclosed just the parts of the scene you want to capture.

Picking Your Materials

You can create your picture using several different materials:

+ Pencil
+ Ink (black and other colors)
+ Crayon
+ Marker (fine or broad-tipped)
+ Paint

With pencil and ink, a fairly smooth paper gives you clean lines. With crayons and markers, you can use either smooth or rougher-textured paper for different effects. Paint is a little harder to use, but it lets you create a huge variety of effects.

Here are some good choices for paint that cleans up with soap and water:

- **Watercolor paint** comes as a set in a box. To use watercolor, you dab it with a wet brush. Watercolor paint won't hide a color you've already painted, but it lets the white of the paper show through, adding light to the color. You can paint on drawing paper or special watercolor paper.

- **Tempera paint** (poster color) is liquid and dries quickly. It comes in small bottles or large squeeze bottles. Use it on manila paper or heavy white drawing paper. With tempera and acrylic paint, you can paint over areas you want to change.

- **Acrylic paint** comes in large squeeze bottles or in tubes. Use acrylic paint on canvas board or heavy paper.

A Scout is thrifty. Some art supplies can be expensive, so look for alternatives. Save more costly supplies for den projects, where the costs can be shared.

For painting, you will need some other supplies:

- **Brushes.** Inexpensive brushes with synthetic bristles will work for tempera and acrylic paint. (For acrylic, you must have synthetic bristles because the paint will ruin natural-hair bristles.) Watercolor brushes are softer, and camel hair is the least expensive. It's helpful to have two sizes of brushes—one for larger areas and one for detail.

◆ **A mixing palette or tray.** You can use a large plastic lid from a food container for tube acrylics. For tempera, school acrylics, and watercolor, which are runny, use several jar lids, or buy an inexpensive plastic paint tray with wells for colors.

◆ **A palette knife.** You will need this flexible mixing tool if you are using tube acrylics. For other paints, mix colors with your brush.

◆ **A sturdy water container.** You will need to rinse paint from brushes before switching colors. Be sure to change the water often.

◆ **A sponge.** Use this to press excess water from your brush before dipping it in paint.

◆ **Cleanup supplies.** You'll need a rag for spills and soap and water to wash your brushes and other tools when you're done.

Paint can be messy! Work at a table with a washable surface, or cover the table with layers of newspaper to protect it. When you stop working, promptly wash your brushes and tools with soap and water. Store brushes with the bristles up in a jar, can, or mug.

Mixing Paint

A fun thing about painting is mixing paints to create different colors. From just a few basic colors, you can create just about any color for your paintings.

Look at the color wheel on this page. The primary colors are red, yellow, and blue. The secondary colors are orange, green, and violet. You can mix equal amounts of yellow and blue (primary colors) to make

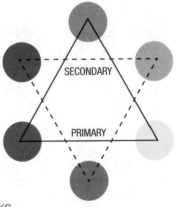

green (a secondary color). If you add more yellow, you will get a yellow-green; if you add more blue, you will get a blue-green.

To make a color lighter, add a small amount of white. To make it darker, add a little black.

If you're not sure about a color you've mixed, try it first on a piece of scrap paper. The more you paint, the more you'll learn about mixing colors.

Art supply stores sell paints in many colors. After working with the primary colors, you may decide to buy a few other colors to see what they are like.

Experiment!

You can use a brush in many different ways. A wet brush makes a different pattern than a mostly dry brush. If you lay the brush flat, it will leave brush marks on your paper or canvas. If you touch just the tip to the paper, it will leave dots.

You can also use tools other than brushes. A sponge dipped in paint adds texture. A string dragged through paint and pressed down on the paper or canvas leaves a line. Crumpled paper dipped in paper makes interesting patterns.

You can even mix different materials. For example, you could use crayons for the lines of a drawing and then brush on watercolor paint in some areas.

REQUIREMENT 3B | Use clay to sculpt a simple form.

When you have a piece of clay in your hands, what happens? You squeeze it, twist it, pull it, roll it, and shape it. And before you know it, you are sculpting!

What will you make? It could be the figure of a person or just his head and neck. It could be an animal or a fantastic creature no one has ever seen before. You could even sculpt your own design for a futuristic car. You decide.

Materials

You can sculpt with several different materials:

◆ **Plasteline**, a commercial modeling clay, is oily and plastic (which means you can shape it). It never dries out and is easy to work at room temperature. Plasteline costs more than natural clay, but you can save money in the long run because you can use it again and again.

◆ **Natural clay** comes from the earth. It can be worked easily when it's damp and is good for detail work. As it dries, it becomes stiffer. Because it does dry out, it must be kept covered when you are not working it; cover with a wet cloth or plastic bag. If the clay dries out too soon, you can soak it and knead it until it becomes soft again.

◆ **Self-hardening clay** is a prepared clay. It costs more than natural clay. It is easily worked as long as it is kept wet and soft. Once it dries, it becomes very hard and cannot be softened for reuse.

Tools

Your best tools for working clay are your fingers, but sometimes other tools can come in handy. Try these:

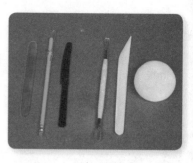

- Dull kitchen knife for cutting clay
- Tongue depressor or craft stick for detail work and smoothing
- Homemade modeling tool

MODELING TOOL

Make a modeling tool with a wooden dowel for a handle. Shape a hairpin or paper clip and attach it to the dowel by wrapping with thread. Coat the thread with model cement and let it dry.

Making a Clay Animal

A fun project to make is an animal like a dog or an elephant (or an animal that only exists in your mind). Here's how:

1. Find or sketch the animal you want to create.

2. Tear off a piece of clay and work it into the shape of the animal's body. Don't worry about making it perfect at this point.

3. Tear off small pieces of clay to form the legs. Work them into shape. Widen the ends to form feet. Again, your pieces don't have to be perfect yet.

4. Score the ends of the legs and the body where the parts will connect. To score the clay, make grooves with a knife or a toothpick dipped in water. This will help the parts stick together.

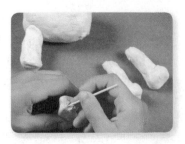

5. Attach the legs one at a time. Use your thumb or modeling tool to smooth the clay between the legs and the body. Check to see if the animal will stand on its own; if not, adjust the legs or widen the feet.

6. Repeat steps 3 through 5 to create the head and tail.

7. Repeat steps 3 through 5 to add ears and a nose or trunk to the head.

8. Adjust the sculpture so it looks the way you want it to. As you work, refer to your picture to make sure the animal's proportions are right. Keep working the clay until you're happy with the result.

9. With your knife or a needle, create the eyes, mouth, fur, and other features.

If you are using clay that dries out, you will need to hollow out your animal's body so it doesn't crack. Turn the animal over, and use your modeling tool to remove much of the clay inside. Then, close the hole and smooth it over.

REQUIREMENT 3C | Create an object using clay that can be fired, baked in the oven, or air-dried.

In addition to using store-bought clay, you can create your own modeling clay.

Ingredients:

- ♦ 4 cups of flour
- ♦ 1½ cups salt
- ♦ 2 tablespoons vegetable oil
- ♦ 1 cup warm water
- ♦ Food coloring (optional)

Directions:

1. Combine the flour and salt in a bowl.

2. Combine the oil and water in a second bowl. Add a few drops of food coloring if you want to make colored clay.

3. Stir the dry ingredients into the liquid ingredients.

4. Put the modeling clay on a floured surface. Knead until smooth.

This clay will last a long time if you store it in an airtight container in the refrigerator.

Once you've made your creation, bake it at 200 degrees for 30 to 45 minutes or until it sounds hollow when you tap on it. After your sculpture cools, you can paint it and then cover it with clear shellac to protect it.

REQUIREMENT 3D | Create a freestanding sculpture or mobile using wood, metal, papier-mâché, or found or recycled objects.

Sculptures and mobiles are a fun way to put a lot of small objects together to make a work of art. You can use all sorts of objects you find around your house or make out of simple materials.

Freestanding Sculpture

To make a freestanding sculpture, start by collecting odds and ends you'd like to combine. These might include scrap items, things you've saved, and things no one wants. Ideas include buttons, cloth, yarn, spools, craft sticks, toothpicks, bits of wood, string, plastic utensils, wire, chenille stems, old keys, bottle caps, egg cartons, pine cones, sticks, and seashells.

Next, create a good base for your sculpture. This could be a flat piece of wood, a lump of clay that you mold into shape, or a piece of floral foam. If you use wood, have an adult help you drill holes the right size for any sticks or wires you want to use as the sculpture's supports.

Finally, start building. Experiment with the placement of objects. Then, when you like how they look, tie or glue them into place.

Mobile

A mobile (MO-beel) is a hanging sculpture. It has many lightweight objects hanging from arms that move in the slightest breeze. To make a mobile, think of a design, create the parts, and balance them as you put your mobile together.

What will your mobile represent? It could be about your favorite sport. It could have butterflies or imaginary insects flying from it. It could show stars, planets, and spaceships. It could include curious shapes that no one can identify. You get to decide.

Draw a simple plan so you know how many hanging objects to make. They can be different sizes, but you will need to hang them so the mobile is balanced.

Create the objects for your mobile out of cardboard, foil, thin wood, or any lightweight material. Make a hole in the top of each one and attach a piece of string, heavy thread, or thin, flexible wire to it.

> To make sure you put the hole in the right spot, which is called the balance point, first push a pin through the top of the object and hold the object by the pin so it can swing freely. If the object hangs crookedly, move the pin. Keep doing this until you find the balance point.

Now, make the arms for your mobile. Put on safety glasses to protect your eyes. Using wire cutters, cut pieces of coat hanger wire, one per object. They can range from 12 to 24 inches in length. Straighten each piece by hammering it or pressing it into a vise. Then, bend it into a smooth, gentle arc. With pliers, bend up about one-half inch from each end, making a right angle.

Follow these steps to put your mobile together, starting from the bottom up:

1. Hang an object on each end of one wire arm.

2. Tie a thread or string to the center of the wire arm and slide it until the two objects balance. Make a loop at the other end of this thread. With flexible wire, make a small ring through this loop.

3. Slip the ring you just made over the end of a second wire arm. Fasten another object to the other end of this second wire.

4. Find the balance point of the second arm as you did for the first one by attaching a thread and sliding it. Again, make a thread loop at the other end of the thread, and add a wire ring to it.

5. Add the other wire arms and objects to the mobile. You may decide to move objects and rebalance arms. When you're happy with your mobile, bend the ends of the wire arms over to keep the objects in place.

6. Hang the mobile from the ceiling using fishing line or string.

Have you ever made a paper airplane? Have you ever made a snowflake by folding a piece of paper, snipping the sides with scissors, and then opening it up again? Then you have experienced the Japanese art forms called origami and kirigami. Origami is the art of folding paper to create sculptures. Kirigami is similar to origami but also involves cutting and gluing the paper.

For this requirement, make several origami or kirigami projects such as the ones shown below and on the next page. Your parent, guardian, or den leader can help you find additional patterns on the Internet.

ORIGAMI SAMURAI HELMET

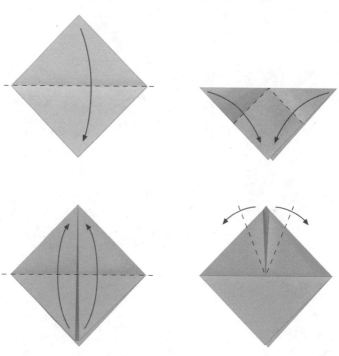

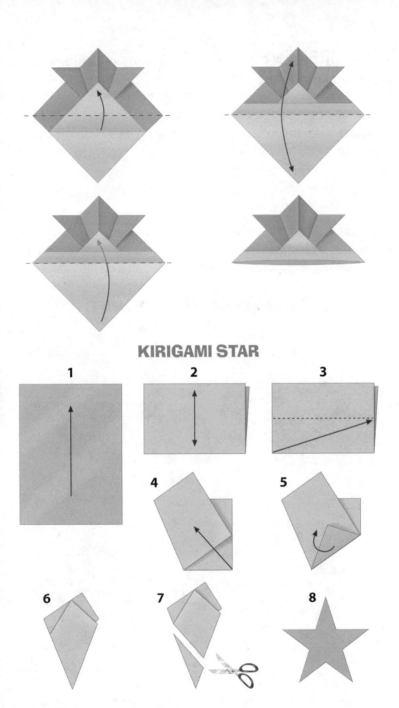

KIRIGAMI STAR

1

2

3

4

5

6

7

8

REQUIREMENT 3F | Use a computer illustration or painting program to create a work of art.

Just about every computer comes with an illustration or painting program. You can also find drawing apps for smartphones and tablets.

Most of these programs include tools that mimic what artists have been doing for thousands of years. You'll find a paint brush tool to paint shapes, a paint bucket tool to fill a space with color, and an eraser tool to undo mistakes. Some programs also include fun features: brushes that paint in patterns or tools that can create rainbows of color.

For this requirement, use a computer to create a work of art. You could start from scratch or modify a photo you've taken. The choice is yours!

REQUIREMENT 3G | Create an original logo or design. Transfer the design onto a T-shirt, hat, or other object.

Think about your favorite restaurant or sports team. Can you picture its logo in your head? What about your favorite computer program or smartphone app? Can you draw its icon from memory?

Logos, icons, and other designs are important symbols of the products, places, or organizations they represent. That's why they are protected by trademark laws and can only be used with permission of their owners.

For this requirement, create your own logo or design. It can represent you, your family, your Webelos den, or anything else you choose. Make it as eye-catching as possible, much like the logos and icons you see every day.

Once you've created your design, transfer it to a T-shirt, hat, or other object. One good way to do that is with iron-on transfer paper and an ink-jet printer. Simply print your computer image on the special paper and then have an adult help you iron it onto a T-shirt. You could also use silk screening, stenciling, or another method, if you prefer.

REQUIREMENT 3H | Using a camera or other electronic device, take at least 10 photos of your family, a pet, or scenery. Use photo-editing software to crop, lighten or darken, and change some of the photos.

Have you ever wondered why the photos you see in books and magazines look better than your family snapshots? One reason is that professional photographers use cameras that can be adjusted and have had a lot of practice! Another reason is that they use photo-editing software to improve the pictures they take.

You can do the same thing. Most computers include simple photo-editing software, and photo-editing apps are available for smartphones and tablets.

Here are some common tools to look for:

- ♦ **Crop tool.** This tool lets you remove parts of the photo you don't want.

- ♦ **Brightness tool.** This tool lets you make the overall photo lighter or darker.

- ♦ **Contrast tool.** This tool lets you separately adjust the difference between your photo's light and dark areas.

- ♦ **Red-eye reduction tool.** This tool fixes a problem where the camera flash makes a subject's eyes look bright red.

- ♦ **Effects tools and filters.** These tools add all sorts of special effects to your photo. Different tools can give your photo vibrant colors, make it look like a photo from a long time ago, or add a picture frame around it.

For this requirement, take at least 10 photos and change them using photo-editing software. Be sure to edit copies of your original photos in case you don't like the changes you make.

REQUIREMENT 3I | Create a comic strip with original characters. Include at least four panels to tell a story centered on one of the points of the Scout Law. Characters can be hand-drawn or computer-generated.

Comic strips are a great way to tell stories. With just a few pictures and a little dialog, you can communicate a surprising amount of information and many ideas.

For this requirement, create some original characters, and think of a story that involves one of the points of the Scout Law. Decide how to divide your story into panels, then create those panels on paper or on a computer.

REQUIREMENT 4 | Choose one of the following methods to show your artwork:

REQUIREMENT 4A | Create a hard-copy or digital portfolio of your projects. Share it with your family and members of your den or pack.

REQUIREMENT 4B | Display your artwork in a pack, school, or community art show.

Once you've created some works of art, you will undoubtedly want to share them with other people. You can do that in many ways:

♦ You can create a hard-copy portfolio by taking photos of your creations and putting them in a binder.

♦ You can create a digital portfolio by using software to turn photos of your creations into a slideshow or website.

♦ You can create an exhibit, similar to those you visited for requirement 1, at your school or at a pack meeting.

♦ You can enter pieces of art in a community art show or contest.

As people look at your creations, watch their reactions, and ask them what they like and don't like. You can use their feedback to make even better works of art in the future.

Last year for our pack's blue and gold banquet, my Scout buddies shared some cool art projects. Tom made a logo for our den's camping trip, and we made it into T-shirts. Matthew made a clay model of the Arrow of Light, and Alex made a forest out of origami. I shared photos I took of my family's favorite lake. We had our own art exhibit!

SNAPSHOT OF ADVENTURE

Everyone has differences, and everyone faces challenges. That's what makes us human. In this adventure, you will learn about the challenges other people face by looking at the world through their eyes. The more you understand, the more helpful you can be—and the more you can show your friends how to be nice to everyone, including people who are different. After all, we are all different in one way or another!

REQUIREMENT

Do all of these: **Approved by**

1. Develop an awareness of the challenges of the blind through participation in an activity that simulates blindness.   _____

2. Participate in an activity that simulates severe visual impairment, but not blindness.   _____

3. Participate in an activity that simulates the challenges of being deaf or hard of hearing.   _____

4. Engage in an activity that simulates mobility impairment.   _____

5. Take part in an activity that simulates dexterity impairment.   _____

6. With your den, participate in an activity that focuses on the acceptance of differences in general.   _____

7. Do two of the following:

   A. Do a Good Turn for residents at a skilled nursing facility or retirement community.   _____

   B. Invite an individual with a disability to visit your den, and discuss what activities he or she currently finds challenging or found challenging in the past.   _____

C. Attend a disabilities event such as a Special Olympics competition, an adaptive sports event, a performance with sign language interpretation, or an activity with service dogs. Tell your den what you thought about the experience. _____

D. Talk to someone who works with people who have disabilities. Ask what the person does and how he or she helps people with disabilities. _____

E. Using American Sign Language, sign the Scout Oath. _____

F. With the help of an adult, contact a service dog organization, and learn the entire process from pup training to assignment to a client. _____

G. Participate in a service project that focuses on a specific disability. _____

H. Participate in an activity with an organization whose members are disabled. _____

Vision is the ability to see with your eyes. Blindness is a lack of vision. Some people are totally blind, meaning they can't see anything at all. Others have partial blindness. They might see things as vague shadows, for example, or not be able to see at all after dark.

People who are totally blind must use their other senses to make up for their lack of vision. When a blind person crosses a street, he can't look and listen for cars like other people can; instead, he can only listen, which means he must listen very carefully. He also can't see the walk signs that sighted people rely on. That's why some communities have talking walk signs.

Many blind people use service dogs or canes to help them get around. They read books in Braille, which is a system that uses raised dots on the page to stand for letters, and they rely on computers that read Web pages out loud. They also rely on sighted friends to help them out from time to time, especially in unfamiliar surroundings.

You can simulate what it's like to be blind by putting on a blindfold and walking around your home. (Have a friend or family member serve as a spotter so you don't hurt yourself.) Try this activity: Walk to your kitchen, fix a snack, sit down at the table, and eat. Were you successful? That's something blind people do every day.

With your den or family, reflect on what you learned and how this activity made you feel.

REQUIREMENT 2 | Participate in an activity that simulates severe visual impairment, but not blindness.

Sometimes vision can be corrected with glasses or contact lenses. If you don't wear glasses or contact lenses yourself, you surely know people who do.

A good way to simulate partial blindness is to smear a thin layer of petroleum jelly on an old pair of safety glasses. You will be able to see through the glasses, but not very well. With the glasses on, try to put together a jigsaw puzzle or read the words on this page.

With your den or family, reflect on what you learned and how this activity made you feel.

REQUIREMENT 3 | Participate in an activity that simulates the challenges of being deaf or hard of hearing.

Like visual impairments, there are many degrees of hearing loss. Some people are totally deaf, meaning they can't hear anything. Others have trouble understanding what someone is saying when there is a lot of background noise. Some people are born deaf. Others lose all or part of their hearing as they age. In fact, everyone loses the ability to hear very high-pitched sounds when they get older. As a Webelos Scout, you can hear some sounds that your parents and den leader can't hear at all!

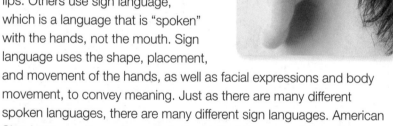

There are many ways to address hearing loss. Hearing aids are a great tool for people who have some hearing. These devices go in or behind the ear and make sounds louder or easier to hear.

Some deaf people learn to read lips. Others use sign language, which is a language that is "spoken" with the hands, not the mouth. Sign language uses the shape, placement, and movement of the hands, as well as facial expressions and body movement, to convey meaning. Just as there are many different spoken languages, there are many different sign languages. American Sign Language is used mostly in the United States and Canada.

A good way to experience what it's like to be deaf is to watch television with the sound turned off (or with the sound turned low and a radio blaring nearby). Watch a favorite show that you've seen before and try to read the lips of the actors. Can you follow the story? What happens when you can't see an actor's lips?

With your den or family, reflect on what you learned and how this activity made you feel.

REQUIREMENT 4 | Engage in an activity that simulates mobility impairment.

Mobility impairment means a reduced ability to get around on your legs. Some people are born with a mobility impairment because of conditions like spina bifida. Others lose the ability to walk due to age, illness, or accidents. Someone who breaks a leg and has to wear a cast for a few months has a temporary mobility impairment.

Like other disabilities, there are ways to compensate for mobility impairments. Many people use crutches, walkers, or wheelchairs to get around. People who have lost parts of their legs might even have prosthetic replacements that let them run, jump, and play sports.

> My den took turns shooting a basketball while sitting in a wheelchair. It was so hard!

A big obstacle for many people with mobility impairments is accessibility in homes and businesses. If you used a wheelchair, would you be able to get from the street to your bedroom? Are the doors in your home wide enough for a wheelchair to go through (at least 32 inches wide)?

If you are able to borrow a wheelchair or crutches, you can simulate a mobility impairment by trying to maneuver around your home or school. Or you could immobilize one of your legs by tying a long stick or splint to it both above and below your knee. See what it's like to walk when you can't bend your leg.

With your den or family, reflect on what you learned and how this activity made you feel.

REQUIREMENT 5 | Take part in an activity that simulates dexterity impairment.

Dexterity refers to the ability to use your hands and fingers to do everything from getting dressed to playing a musical instrument to shooting a basketball. Someone who breaks a finger or develops a condition like arthritis may find activities like fastening buttons or tying shoes a challenge.

To see what it's like to have a dexterity impairment, try to get dressed while wearing a pair of thick winter gloves. For an even harder challenge, tape a couple of the glove's fingers together.

With your den or family, reflect on what you learned and how this activity made you feel.

We are all different. Some of us wear glasses. Some of us have freckles or dimples. Some of us are really good at math or reading or sports, while others of us struggle in those areas.

Some people have disabilities that others can see, while other people might have disabilities that can't be seen. Those disabilities are often called "invisible" disabilities.

Learning about differences helps us understand each other. For this requirement do an activity with your den that focuses on accepting differences. Ask your den leader about the One Potato, My Potato game; it might be just what you are looking for. How did what you learned in requirements 1–5 help you understand differences among people?

With your den or family, reflect on what you learned and how this activity made you feel.

REQUIREMENT 7A | Do a Good Turn for residents at a skilled nursing facility or retirement community.

Some people who live in skilled nursing facilities and retirement communities have disabilities like you have learned about in this adventure. And all of them are different from you because they are the age of your grandparents or great-grandparents.

With the help of your parent or den leader, find a skilled nursing facility or retirement community and do a Good Turn there. If possible, spend some time with the residents. Ask them what life was like when they were your age. You may even find someone who was a Webelos Scout like you!

REQUIREMENT 7B | Invite an individual with a disability to visit your den, and discuss what activities he or she currently finds challenging or found challenging in the past.

It's one thing to ride in a wheelchair for 10 or 15 minutes. It's another thing entirely to use a wheelchair all day every day. Talk with someone who has a physical impairment and find out about the challenges he or she faces and the challenges he or she has overcome.

There are many organizations that work to make life easier and more fun for people with disabilities. Attend an event or activity sponsored by one of those organizations, and tell your den what you learned. Don't be surprised if you forget about the disabilities involved

and get caught up in the action. That's exactly what you should do: focus on people, not their disabilities!

All sorts of people work with those who have disabilities. Some have disabilities themselves; others just want to make the world a better place for everyone. Learn more about one of those people and what he or she does.

American Sign Language is a completely separate language. You have to learn it just like you might learn Spanish or Chinese. To get an idea of what it's like, learn the Scout Oath in American Sign Language.

Scout   Oath ("Promise")

(On my) honor ("Promise")   I   (will) do

(my) best   To

(tap fingers)

(do my) duty

(to) God

(and) my

country

(and) to

obey

(the) Scout

Law;

To

help ("people")

("help") (other) people

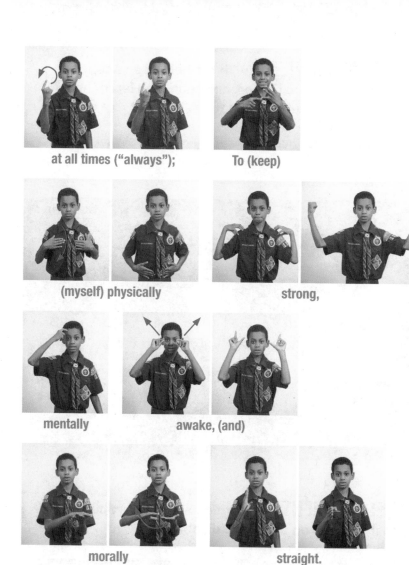

at all times ("always"); To (keep)

(myself) physically strong,

mentally awake, (and)

morally straight.

NOTE: Did you notice that some English words are not signed in American Sign Language? American Sign language is a conceptual language, which means that not every word of spoken English is signed. Some words are also signed in a different order. For example, the phrase "help other people at all times" can be signed as "people, help, always."

REQUIREMENT 7F | With the help of an adult, contact a service dog organization, and learn the entire process from pup training to assignment to a client.

Did you know that many families just like yours help train service dogs? Find an organization that provides service dogs, and learn about the training process.

REQUIREMENT 7G | Participate in a service project that focuses on a specific disability.

Organizations for people with disabilities always need help. Find an organization that focuses on a specific disability, and ask what you can do to help it or the people it serves.

REQUIREMENT 7H | Participate in an activity with an organization whose members are disabled.

For this requirement, find an organization for people with disabilities and participate in one of its activities.

Here are some ideas:

- Serve as a ball boy at a Special Olympics softball game.
- Attend a holiday party at a group home for people with developmental disabilities.
- Go on a campout with a pack of Cub Scouts who have special needs.
- Participate in a field trip with residents of a skilled nursing facility.

A Scout is friendly. Offer a smile to others at the event—you might make a new friend!

BUILD IT

SNAPSHOT OF ADVENTURE

If you visit a lumber store, you'll see rows and rows of all sorts of wood: boards, dowel rods, sheets of plywood, cedar shingles, and more. With some tools and time, a skilled craftsman can turn that wood into toys, bookcases, or even

an entire house. You won't build a house in this adventure, but you will build a smaller carpentry project. You'll also learn about the tools you could one day use to build just about anything you can dream up. So grab your tool belt, and let's get started.

REQUIREMENTS

Do all of these: Approved by

1. Learn about some basic tools and the proper use of each tool. Learn about and understand the need for safety when you work with tools.   _____

2. With the guidance of your Webelos leader, parent, or guardian, select a carpentry project and build it.   _____

3. List the tools that you use safely as you build your project; create a list of materials needed to build your project.   _____

4. Put a checkmark next to the tools on your list that you used for the first time.   _____

5. Learn about a construction career. With your Webelos den leader, parent, or guardian, visit a construction site and interview someone working in a construction career.   _____

The Boy Scouts of America does not authorize Webelos Scouts to use power tools as part of the Webelos program.

When you are building something, it is important to have the right tools. Imagine trying to cut a board in half with a pocketknife or pound in a nail with a rock. You might get the job done, but it would take a long time and you could easily hurt yourself. With the right tools, those jobs are much easier and safer to do.

Basic Tools and Their Uses

Skilled tradesmen, including carpenters, plumbers, electricians, and bricklayers, use tools that are designed for their specific trade. For carpenters, those tools include hammers, saws, screwdrivers, and more.

Hammer: A hammer drives and pulls nails. A common hammer weighs 12 to 16 ounces and has a curved claw for pulling nails.

Screwdrivers: Screwdrivers drive screws into wood. You'll probably need small, medium, and large screwdrivers for both slotted screws, which have straight slots on their heads, and Phillips screws, which have X-shaped slots.

Allen wrenches: Some screws have six-sided holes on top. To drive one of those screws, you need an L-shaped metal tool called an Allen wrench. Allen wrenches come in various sizes, and you have to use exactly the right size. Hardware stores sell Allen wrenches separately and in a tool that looks like a jackknife.

Chisel: A chisel looks somewhat like a flathead screwdriver. It has a sharper tip, however, and is used for shaving  away small amounts of wood. To use it, you hold it against the wood and hit the end of the handle with a mallet.

 **Awl:** An awl is a tool used for making small holes in wood and leather. It has a wooden handle and a thin, sharp metal point.

Pliers: Pliers are versatile tools that let you grip and twist things, bend and snip wire, and do other tasks that require strength. Pliers come in many types, including needle-nose pliers, standard/slip-joint pliers, locking pliers, and wire-cutter pliers. It's useful to have several sizes and types in your toolbox.

Hand saw: When you need to cut a board in half, a 14-inch rough-cut handsaw is handy to have. It will certainly do for cutting smaller pieces of wood. Since it fits into your toolbox, it will always be close at hand.

Coping saw: When you want to make detailed or curved cuts in wood, plastic, or foam, you will need a coping saw.

Sanding block: A sanding block is a tool that you attach sandpaper to. (You can also use soft foam sanding blocks that allow you to sand curved or contoured objects.) Sandpaper comes in various grit sizes. The smaller the number, the coarser the sandpaper. You might use 50-grit sandpaper to shape a piece of wood and then 150-grit sandpaper to smooth the wood before you paint it.

File: A file is a metal tool used for making wood or metal smooth. It can also be used to sharpen metal blades and tools.

Rasp: A rasp is a metal tool with a rough surface that is used to shape or remove excess material from wood or metal.

Tape measure: A tape measure lets you accurately measure pieces of wood up to several feet long. A 12- or 16-foot retractable tape measure will handle most jobs around the house. Most retract automatically and have a locking mechanism to keep the tape from recoiling (rolling up inside the case) until you want it to.

Carpenter's square: A carpenter's square helps you make perpendicular (right-angle) cuts. A 6-inch quick square will handle most small jobs.

Level: When you need to hang something, such as a picture, a level helps you make sure it doesn't tilt to one side. For most small jobs, a 9-inch torpedo level works fine.

Clamp: A clamp is used to hold pieces of wood together firmly for cutting or gluing. C clamps are common and come in many sizes. You will also find clamps that look somewhat like giant (and really strong) clothespins.

Vise: A vise does much the same job as a wood clamp. The main difference is that it is mounted to a workbench.

Toolbox or tool bag: Whether you have a few tools or a few dozen, it's important to keep them all together. A good place to store them is in a latching toolbox or tool bag that you can carry to wherever you are working.

Taking Care of Your Tools

Your tools will last longer if you take care of them. Here are some things you can do:

- When you are done working, wipe off your tools with a rag. You might also apply a little machine oil to prevent rusting.

- Dry your tools if they get wet.

- Use tools only for their intended purpose. For example, don't use a screwdriver as a chisel or pry bar.

- Put your tools back in your toolbox or tool bag when you are done with each one. That way, you won't lose your tools, and they won't be in your way as you continue working.

Tool Safety

You already know that certain tools, such as saws, can be dangerous, but you can actually hurt yourself with any tool if you aren't careful. One way to keep yourself safe is to use protective gear.

Here's some important gear to use:

+ **Hand protection:** Wear gloves when handling lumber, carrying boxes of nails, and using saws. Even with gloves on, always know where all your fingers are when you are cutting and hammering.

+ **Head protection:** Always wear a hardhat when you are working in an area that may have falling items or debris.

+ **Ear protection:** Your hearing can be damaged very easily. Be certain to wear good quality ear protection when you are in an area that may have construction noise.

+ **Eye protection:** Safety glasses are a must on every project. If you wear prescription glasses, you can get safety glasses that fit over your glasses or you can buy side shields that slip onto the earpiece of your glasses. Safety glasses prevent debris and dust from entering your eyes.

- **Foot protection:** Wear good quality leather shoes with thick soles, if possible. This type of shoe will protect your foot if something falls on it and will prevent a puncture if you step on a nail. Never wear sandals, flip-flops, or open-toed shoes when working with tools.

- **Lung protection:** Cutting, drilling, and especially sanding create small dust particles that can irritate your lungs if you breathe them in. You can protect yourself by wearing a dust mask (preferred) or by tying a bandanna or neckerchief around the lower part of your face.

How you use and care for your tools is also important:

- Tools that cut—such as saws, knives, and shears—should be kept sharp. If they are dull, you will have to use too much force, and they may slip and cut you.

- Keep your hands away from saw teeth and knife blades so that if the tool slips, you won't get hurt.

- When using a saw, make sure that the item you are cutting is held securely. If it slips while you are cutting it, you could accidentally cut yourself.

- Be careful when you are hammering. If you miss the nail head, you don't want to hit your thumb. Ouch!

- Practice using your tools with an adult partner until you know how to handle them well.

Practicing good safety skills with hand tools as a Webelos Scout will help prepare you for the greater challenge of using power tools when you are a Boy Scout.

REQUIREMENT 2 | With the guidance of your Webelos den leader, parent, or guardian, select a carpentry project and build it.

REQUIREMENT 3 | List the tools that you use safely as you build your project; create a list of materials needed to build your project.

REQUIREMENT 4 | Put a checkmark next to the tools on your list that you used for the first time.

The best way to learn how to use tools is to actually use them on a project. For this requirement, pick a carpentry project and build it. When you are finished, update the list on the next page to include all the tools you used. Put a checkmark next to those that you used safely and those that you used for the first time.

MY TOOL LIST

Tool	Used Safely	Used for the First Time
Hammer		
Chisel		
Allen wrench		
Pliers		
Hand saw		
Coping saw		
Awl		
Sanding block or sanding sponge		
File		
Rasp		
Carpenter's square		
Level		
Clamp		
Vise		

The next few pages show three projects you can build. You can find many more ideas in books or, with your parent's help, on the Internet. Your Webelos den leader can give you some ideas, too.

You can also try making your own plans. Think about what you want to make, and then draw a simple picture of each separate piece, as well as of the completed project. Decide how big the pieces should be and write the dimensions on your drawing. Review your drawing with an adult to be certain your measuring is accurate, then go to work!

Building a project can sometimes be expensive. If possible, reuse wood from construction sites or previous projects. (Be sure to get an adult's permission before visiting a construction site.) Your parent or den leader can help you find the materials you need.

Step Stool

Materials:

- A piece of wood that is 12 inches wide and 36 inches long, cut from a 1-inch x 12-inch board or ¾-inch plywood
- Finishing nails
- Wood putty
- Sandpaper
- Rag
- Paint or stain
- Paintbrush

> **Measure carefully so you don't waste any of the wood. Always remember to measure twice and cut once!**

Instructions:

1. Cut a piece of wood 18 inches long for the top of the stool.
2. Cut two 8-inch × 8-inch pieces for the legs. Clamp the two leg pieces together, and mark where you will cut the notches shown in the picture.

3. Saw the notches out while the legs are clamped together. This will make the legs exactly the same.

4. Cut two ¾-inch × 2-inch × 14-inch pieces for the side braces.

5. Using finishing nails, nail the legs to the top piece 2 inches from each end. Measure carefully before you drive the nails to be sure they go into the legs.

6. Countersink each nail. To do this, place another nail on top of the nail you've already driven, then tap it with your hammer until the first nail is completely below the surface of the wood. Fill the nail holes with wood putty.

7. Nail the side braces to the legs. Fit them just under the top of the stool and inside the legs. The braces will keep your stool stable. Countersink the nails, and fill the nail holes with putty.

8. Sand the stool all over. Use a damp rag to clean any grit from the stool before applying the finish.

9. Stain the stool to match other furniture, or paint it any color you like.

Paper Towel Holder

Materials:

+ Round or square base
+ Dowel rod that measures 1 ¼ inches in diameter
+ Screw
+ Felt or pieces of cork, if desired
+ Glue
+ Decorative piece for the top of the dowel rod, if desired
+ Paint or stain
+ Paintbrush

Instructions:

1. Cut the dowel rod to 14 inches.

2. Sand the dowel rod and base.

3. Using a measuring tape, find and mark the exact center of the base on both the top and the bottom.

4. Stand the dowel rod up and place the base on top of it. Make sure the dowel rod is in the center of the base.

5. Drive a screw through the center mark on the base into the dowel rod. This will be easier to do if an adult first drills a pilot hole with a power drill. (A pilot hole is a hole that is smaller than the screw.)

6. If desired, glue a decorative knob on the top of the dowel rod. Look for a knob that has a hole the same circumference as your dowel rod so it will slide onto the end.

7. If desired, glue a square of felt or pieces of cork to the bottom of the towel holder. This will protect the countertop and keep the towel holder from sliding.

8. Paint or stain the towel holder as desired.

Wall Shelf

Materials:

- ◆ 8-inch piece of 1-inch x 4-inch board
- ◆ 6-inch piece of 1-inch x 4-inch board
- ◆ Glue
- ◆ Finishing nails
- ◆ 1-inch angle brackets, screws, and wall anchors
- ◆ Paint or stain
- ◆ Paintbrush

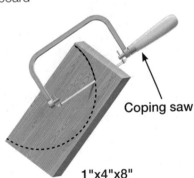

Protractor

Coping saw

1"x4"x8"

Instructions:

1. Using a protractor or a cooking pot as a guide, draw a half-circle on the 8-inch board. Make the shelf by carefully cutting along the line with a coping saw.

2. Draw a diagonal line on the 6-inch board. Make the brace by carefully cutting along the line with a coping saw.

3. Sand all the edges smooth.

4. Paint or stain the shelf and brace as desired.

1"x4"x6"
Cut diagonally

5. Use glue and finishing nails to attach the brace to the bottom of the shelf.

6. Screw angle brackets to the bottom of the shelf at the back edge. With an adult's help, use wall fasteners to attach your shelf to the wall. (You will need hollow-wall anchors to attach the shelf securely to wallboard.)

Glue 4-inch edge of this piece.

Nails

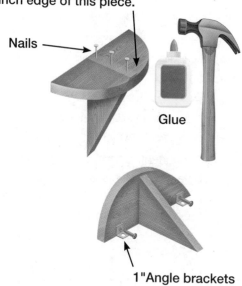

Glue

1"Angle brackets

A construction site is an exciting place to visit. You'll see workers moving all over the place, carrying materials, using tools, and reading blueprints. The work may look disorganized, but it's all carefully planned.

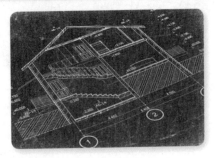

Every construction project starts with a set of blueprints that shows exactly how all the pieces should go together and in what order. First, workers lay the foundation, frame the building, and add the roof and walls. Electrical wiring and plumbing come next, along with doors, windows, and light fixtures. Near the end of the process, workers add siding, cabinetry, wallboard, paint, and floor coverings. Once the building has been inspected, it's ready to be occupied.

Some of the workers on a construction site do a lot of different jobs, including framing the building, putting in doors and windows, and hanging cabinets. Others handle specialized jobs such as roofing or plumbing.

Construction workers use their hands, but they also use their brains. A lot of measuring is involved, and good math skills are a must.

Teamwork is also very important. Construction workers have to cooperate with other people who do the same thing as them, as well as other teams that are part of the construction process. Look for examples of teamwork when you visit a construction site.

When you interview a construction worker, ask questions like these:

- What parts of the building do you work on?
- How did you acquire the skills you use? Did you go to trade school, learn on the job, or both?
- What's your favorite part of working in construction?
- What's the most fun building project you've ever worked on?

When I visited a construction site last year, I talked with a man who was laying bricks. He said it's very important to put each brick in just the right place. If a brick on the bottom row is out of place, that error will affect all the other rows. I guess life is like that, too. What you do as a Webelos Scout prepares you to be a good Boy Scout.

BUILD MY OWN HERO

SNAPSHOT OF ADVENTURE

Heroes are all around us, sometimes in uniform and sometimes in disguise. The Build My Own Hero adventure lets you discover what it means to be a hero. You'll learn about heroes in your community and other parts of the world and find out how you can be a hero, too!

REQUIREMENT

Do all of these: **Approved by**

1. Discover what it means to be a hero. Invite a local hero to meet with your den.   _____

2. Identify how citizens can be heroes in their communities.   _____

3. Recognize a hero in your community by presenting him or her with a "My Hero Award."   _____

4. Learn about a real-life hero from another part of the world who has helped make the world a better place.   _____

5. Learn about a Scout hero.   _____

6. Create your own superhero.   _____

PACK 387
Welcomes
our Veterans!

REQUIREMENT 1 | Discover what it means to be a hero. Invite a local hero to meet with your den.

A hero is a person who does extra-special things to help other people. Some people do heroic things as part of their jobs, such as soldiers and police officers. Other people do heroic things because they know how to act in an emergency, such as Scouts or American Red Cross volunteers. Some heroes are famous and win awards for their service. Other people are known as heroes only to the people they helped.

Talk with your den about people who live in your community who are heroes because of their jobs. Invite one of them to come to a den meeting and share his or her story with you. If a hero cannot attend a den meeting, you may go meet with him or her and later share what you learned with your den.

INVITING GUESTS TO YOUR DEN MEETING

♦ When you call to invite a guest, be sure to give your name, and clearly explain what you are asking for. Tell the guest when and where your den meets and how much time he or she should take.

♦ Leave your phone number in case your guest has questions later.

♦ Follow up your call with an email or postcard reminder.

♦ On the day of the meeting, arrange to meet your guest at the front door, and guide him or her to your meeting room.

♦ After the visit, send your guest a thank-you note from the den.

Before you meet with your hero, decide on a list of questions you will ask. It's a good idea to ask how the 12 points of the Scout Law relate to the hero's job and the decisions he or she must make each day.

REQUIREMENT 2 | Identify how citizens can be heroes in their communities.

Many heroes surround you in your everyday life. Think about family members, friends, a teacher, someone from your place of worship, your bus driver, and others.

EVERYDAY HEROISM

Here are the kinds of things you might see:

- Your teacher worked late at night to plan a school event.
- Your mom or dad tutored at a youth center.
- Your family helped at a food bank.
- Your neighbor picked up litter after a community picnic.
- Your grandparent volunteered at a local homeless shelter.
- Your friend shared her lunch with a student who forgot his.
- Your bus driver stopped older kids from picking on a younger kid.

Choose three of these people, and observe their activities for one week. Record what you see in a notebook. At the end of the week, review your notes, and identify the many small things people do every day that make them heroes.

A Scout is brave. Think about the ways people can be brave every day, such as by standing up for someone or doing what is right.

REQUIREMENT 3 | Recognize a hero in your community by presenting him or her with a "My Hero Award."

When you do something nice for someone else, you like to be thanked. Heroes do too! They aren't trying to earn awards or recognition, but they still like it when someone says thank you.

For this requirement, create a hero award and present it to a hero in your community—maybe even the hero who visits your den.

Here's how:

♦ Decide on three or four rules for selecting your hero. Should it be someone who is a hero because of his or her job, or should it be someone who did something heroic outside his job? Should it be someone who helped your den or who helped your whole community? Should it be someone well known in your community or someone only a few people know?

♦ Select the hero you want to recognize. If you can't decide on just one person, it's OK to give more than one award.

♦ Decide what the award will look like. Will it be a certificate or a trophy? Will it be a leather thong with beads or a small woodworking item?

♦ Contact your recipient and present the award. You could present it at a den or pack meeting, or you could go to the hero's workplace. If the hero is part of a faith community or a service club, perhaps you could present it in front of that group.

Just as we have heroes in our everyday life, many people around the world contribute their time and efforts to making our world a better place.

With the help of the Internet (with an adult's permission), the local or school library, a teacher, or your den leader or parent, learn about someone in another part of the world who is a real-life hero.

Find out:

+ Who the hero is
+ What the hero did
+ When the hero did this
+ Where the hero did this
+ Why the hero did this
+ How the hero did this

Share what you learned at a den meeting. You could tell the hero's story, make a poster, or even create a video about the hero.

Nelson Mandela was a hero from South Africa. He was honored by Scouts in his country.

REQUIREMENT 5 | Learn about a Scout hero.

Thanks to their special training, many Scouts become heroes. In *Boys' Life* magazine or on the *Boys' Life* website, read about a Scout who earned an award for heroism or special service. The "Scouts in Action" feature is a great place to start. Talk with your den about the story you read. Discuss how you might have acted in a similar situation.

SCOUTING HEROISM AWARDS

◆ **Honor Medal With Crossed Palms:** Presented to Scouts and adult leaders who demonstrate heroism by saving or attempting to save a life at extreme risk to self.

◆ **Honor Medal:** (at right) Presented to Scouts and adult leaders who demonstrate heroism by saving or attempting to save a life at considerable risk to self.

◆ **Medal of Merit:** Presented to Scouts and adult leaders who perform rare and exceptional acts of service.

◆ **National Certificate of Merit:** Presented to Scouts and adult leaders who perform acts of service deserving of special national recognition.

Everybody loves superheroes! You've probably watched movies about superheroes or read about them in comic books or graphic novels. Now it's your turn to create your own.

Make a drawing of your superhero, and decide what special powers he or she has. Talk about how your superhero achieved those powers and how he or she uses them to help people.

You might want to write a story or create a comic strip that uses your superhero as the main character. (If you create a comic strip, you

could model it after the "Scouts in Action" feature in *Boys' Life*.) How many points of the Scout Law do you see within your story? How does your superhero compare with the real-life heroes you learned about in this adventure?

My superhero puts out forest fires. He flies around finding fires and puts them out by spraying water from his wrists. What does your superhero do?

CASTAWAY

SNAPSHOT OF ADVENTURE

Lost on a desert island! Separated from your group in the middle of a jungle! Trapped on the side of a cliff that you can't climb! What do you do? How can you survive?

To survive in the wilderness, you need to learn survival skills long before you have to use them. This adventure will help you learn some of these important skills in case you ever get lost. Learning these skills will make you a better Scout and increase your chances of survival in an emergency.

REQUIREMENT

Approved by

1. Do two of these:

   A. With the help of an adult, demonstrate one way to light a fire without using matches. _____

   B. On a campout with your den or family, cook two different recipes that do not require pots and pans. If your chartered organization does not permit Cub Scout camping, you may substitute a family campout or a daylong outdoor activity with your den or pack. _____

   C. Using tree limbs or branches that have already fallen or been cut, build a shelter that will protect you overnight. _____

2. Do ALL of these:

   A. Learn what items should be in an outdoor survival kit that you can carry in a small bag or box in a daypack. Assemble your own small survival kit, and explain to your den leader why the items you chose are important for survival. _____

B. Show you can live "off the grid" by minimizing your use of electricity for one week. Keep a log of what you did. Discuss with your den members how you adjusted to this lifestyle. _____

C. With your den, invent a game that can be played without using electricity and using minimal equipment or simple items. _____

D. Name your game, write down the rules once you have decided on them, then play the game at two different den meetings or outings. _____

E. Teach your game to the members of your pack or other Scouts. _____

F. With your den, demonstrate two ways to treat drinking water to remove impurities. _____

G. Discuss what to do if you become lost in the woods. Tell what the letters "S-T-O-P" stand for. Tell what the universal emergency signal is. Describe three ways to signal for help. Demonstrate one of them. Describe what you can do to help rescuers find you. _____

H. Make a list of four qualities you think a leader should have in an emergency and why they are important to have. Pick two of them, and act them out for your den. Describe how each relates to a point of the Scout Law. Describe how working on this adventure gave you a better understanding of the Boy Scout motto. _____

REQUIREMENT 1 | Do two of these:

REQUIREMENT 1A | With the help of an adult, demonstrate one way to light a fire without using matches.

In an emergency, a fire can keep you warm. It can let you cook food so you don't go hungry. And it can help rescuers find you if you are lost. As a Webelos Scout, you have probably learned how to start a fire using matches. In an emergency, you might need to start a fire *without* matches. Yes, you can do it!

Lighting a fire without matches is a special skill. As with all special skills, you must use it carefully and responsibly. Live up to the trust your leader is giving you by only using this skill in a safe environment under the supervision of an adult.

For any kind of fire, you need these materials close at hand:

* **Tinder** is fine, dry material that will burst into flame at the touch of a match. Pine needles, the inner bark of dead branches, weed fluff, dry grasses, and slivers shaved with a knife from a dry stick are all good sources of tinder. Gather a double handful.

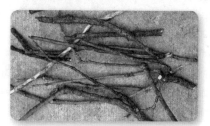

* **Kindling** is material that will burn with a little help. Twigs no thicker than a pencil are best — and the drier, the better. Gather an armload.

◆ **Fuel** is dead or downed wood no bigger than your wrist that will keep your fire burning. Keep it dry and away from your fire until you need it.

To start a fire without matches, your tinder must be extra fine and dry. The inner bark of dead branches will work if you shred it. So will an old bird's nest. If you plan ahead, you can carry some dryer lint with you in a plastic bag.

Once you've gathered your material, you have to generate enough heat to make your very fine tinder burn. Three ways to do that are by using a magnifying glass, using flint and steel, and using friction.

Magnifying Glass

The sun is very powerful. With a curved lens like a magnifying glass, you can focus the sun's rays to produce a very small point of heat. Here's how.

Protect your tinder from any breezes. Focus the light directly on your tinder and watch for smoke. Once you see it, gently blow on the ember to get the fire to spread to more of your tinder. As the fire spreads, add some kindling and then fuel to sustain the fire.

Flint and Steel

Another way to create sparks is by striking one hard object against another. You could use a rock and a knife blade, but the best thing to use is a special flint-and-steel set. This set includes a piece of flint (a kind of very hard rock) and a piece of steel.

Strike the flint sharply against the steel to produce brief sparks. Direct your sparks down into your tinder. Watch for smoke and gently blow on your ember so it will spread. Add kindling and fuel as the fire builds.

Friction

Friction is the energy created when you rub things together. (Rub your hand on your pants leg for 10 seconds or so, and you will feel heat. That heat came from friction.)

A fire-by-friction set uses friction to create burning embers, which you can use to ignite your tinder. The kit includes these pieces:

- Head board
- Spindle (pointed at the top, rounded at the bottom)
- Bow
- Fire board

Slide a leaf or piece of bark under one of the holes in the fire board. Put the bottom of the spindle in that hole and the head board on top of the spindle. Loop the bow string around the spindle, then tighten 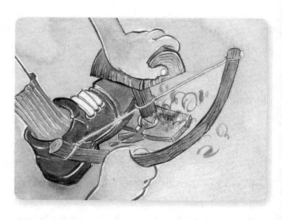 it. Move the bow back and forth to turn the spindle. Make slow, steady strokes for about 20 seconds; then go faster.

Soon, embers should fall from the hole in the fire board onto the leaf or bark. Blow gently on the embers to keep them burning, then move the leaf or bark away from the fire board and add tinder to it. Once the tinder lights, gradually add kindling and then fuel.

Whichever method you use, it is important to be ready with all the materials you need close at hand. You may not have time to go find more, so gather more than you think you need.

If you know what you are doing, you can cook just about anything in the woods that you can cook at home. In fact, you can cook many things without pots and pans. That means less cleanup and more time for fun.

Here are some easy recipes that produce great-tasting food. Ask your den leader for more ideas. Enjoy!

Bacon and Eggs in a Bag

Ingredients (for one Scout):

- 2 thick slices of bacon
- 1 egg
- 1 brown paper lunch bag
- 1 stick

Cut both slices of bacon in two. Lay the slices in the bottom of the bag to cover the paper as much as possible. Crack the egg onto the bacon. Roll the top of the bag down three times. Push the stick through the folded portion so that the bag is hanging from the stick. Hold the stick over a bed of coals for about 10 to 15 minutes. The bacon grease will protect the bag and help cook your meal.

> Eating undercooked eggs and meat can make you sick. Ask an adult to help you determine when your food is fully cooked.

Don't get in a hurry the way my den did when we went camping. Let your fire burn down until there are just hot coals. Otherwise, you'll burn your bag and everything will fall into the fire.

Campfire Cake in an Orange Shell

Ingredients (for six Scouts):

- 6 large oranges
- 18 oz. box of cake mix (plus required ingredients)
- Water
- Heavy-duty aluminum foil

Cut the oranges in half, and remove the fruit with a spoon. Be careful not to puncture the rind. Prepare the cake mix in a zippered plastic bag, following the instructions on the box. Fill each orange shell half full of cake mix. Replace the top, and wrap in foil. Bake in hot coals or on a grill for about 20 minutes, turning often. The cake will bake in the orange shell.

Mud Burgers

Ingredients:

- 1 potato per Scout
- Ground beef
- Chopped onion
- Salt and pepper

Cut the potato in half, and scoop out most of the insides. Mix the ground beef and onion together, and season the mixture with salt and pepper to taste. Put the beef mixture inside the potato, and close the potato up. Coat the potato with thick mud, and place it in the coals. Cook for about an hour.

You can eat the cooked meat and potato, but dispose of the mud-covered skin—unless you really like mud pies!

Be sure to clean up any food scraps or other trash and dispose of them properly.

If you get lost in the woods, shelter is very important. It protects you from the sun, wind, and rain, and it helps your body stay at a comfortable temperature.

But saving energy is also important if you are lost. If you use up most of your energy running around building a shelter, you'll have less energy for keeping warm at night.

You'll have to decide how much shelter you can build with the materials at hand. You'll want a shelter that will do the job but that also takes as little energy as possible to set up.

1. Start by looking around for places that offer some natural protection. The mouth of a cave would be great, but you might also find a sheltered area under a bushy tree or at the base of a cliff.

3. Now, think about how to build a roof over your head. If you have some loose, bare branches, pile them up, leaving a space underneath where you can crawl in. Cover the pile with more of the insulating material you used for your floor. If you can tell which way the wind is coming from, pile more material on that side of your structure to block the wind.

2. A good shelter starts with a floor. You can lose a lot of body heat through direct contact with the ground. Insulate your floor by piling up evergreen branches, pine needles, or dry leaves to form a ground bed.

KEEPING COOL (OR WARM)

Your body's core is your temperature regulator. It does all it can to keep you cool in hot weather and warm in cold weather. If you get too hot, you may suffer from heat exhaustion or heatstroke. If you get too cold, hypothermia can set in. When your body temperature changes more than a few degrees from normal, you can have a hard time thinking or functioning well. In extreme cases, heatstroke and hypothermia can lead to unconsciousness and even death.

You may have some items in your backpack that can make your shelter even better. A tarp or plastic sheet over the top of your shelter can help keep wind and rain out. A sleeping bag or pad can insulate the floor.

In order to be found, you need to be seen, so make sure your shelter is visible from as far away as possible. Many survival kits include an emergency blanket, which is a lightweight blanket made of shiny gold or silver material that can be easily seen from an airplane.

When you are finished with your shelter, put the materials you used back where you got them. Remember that a Scout leaves an area better than he found it.

If you have a trash bag, you can turn it into an emergency poncho by cutting holes for your head and arms. Wear it while you're building your shelter, then put it over the top of the shelter to block the wind and rain. Try not to work up a sweat, which will cool you down. Do your best to maintain a constant body temperature while you are working.

REQUIREMENT 2A | Learn what items should be in an outdoor survival kit that you can carry in a small bag or box in a daypack. Assemble your own small survival kit, and explain to your den leader why the items you chose are important for survival.

If you were trapped in your home, you would have a lot of things on hand that could help you survive, such as extra food and clothing. If you were lost in the woods, you would only have the things in your backpack and things you could find around you.

> The Scout motto is "Be Prepared." You can be prepared by making a survival kit and carrying it with you on outings.

Of course, you can't take everything from your house in your backpack, so you have to plan carefully. What should you take?

It's a good idea to start with the Scout Basic Essentials*:

- First-aid kit
- Extra clothing
- Rain gear
- Pocketknife (if you've earned your Whittling Chip)
- Flashlight
- Trail food
- Sun protection
- Map and compass

Scouts should have these items with them whenever they are camping or hiking.

- ***Matches and fire starters.** A fire can keep you warm and attract the attention of rescuers. As a Boy Scout, you can earn your Firem'n Chit to be allowed to carry matches.

Here are some other helpful items:

◆ **Duct tape.** Wrap a length around a plastic water bottle or a pencil.

◆ **Signal mirror.** A metal signal mirror can be slipped into your first aid kit or side pocket of your pack. Keep it in a case or a sock to protect it and keep it shiny.

◆ **Thin wire.** A few feet can come in handy for many uses.

◆ **Garbage bag.** A large, heavy-duty bag, preferably brightly colored, can be used as a shelter, poncho, or firewood cover.

◆ **Fishing line and hooks.** 50 feet of fishing line can come in handy for repairs and, of course, for fishing.

Choosing which items to stock in a survival kit will depend a lot on where you will be traveling. If you're in a hot, desert-like area, fishhooks might not be very useful. If you are traveling in the winter, you might include things that can keep you warm, such as hand warmers.

What would you take for a day hike on an easy trail? How about a hike through a dense forest?

As Americans, we use a lot of electricity and other forms of energy. Sometimes, it seems we can't take a walk around the neighborhood without using energy. We check the weather forecast on a website, grab an LED flashlight, track our route on a GPS unit, and carry along a personal music player to listen to our favorite songs or a camera or smartphone to take pictures. Then, when we get home, we soak up some air-conditioning and grab a cold drink from the refrigerator.

In a survival situation, you won't be able to use devices like these that rely on energy. For example, if the power in your house went out because of a storm, you might have to use candles for light and blankets to keep you warm. You would have to find other ways to entertain yourself and get important information like the weather forecast.

To get an idea what this would be like, avoid using any electronic devices for a week (except those you need for schoolwork or personal safety). That includes computers, tablets, telephones, televisions, video games, and anything else with a plug or batteries. Keep a log of what you did. Discuss with your den members how you adjusted to this lifestyle.

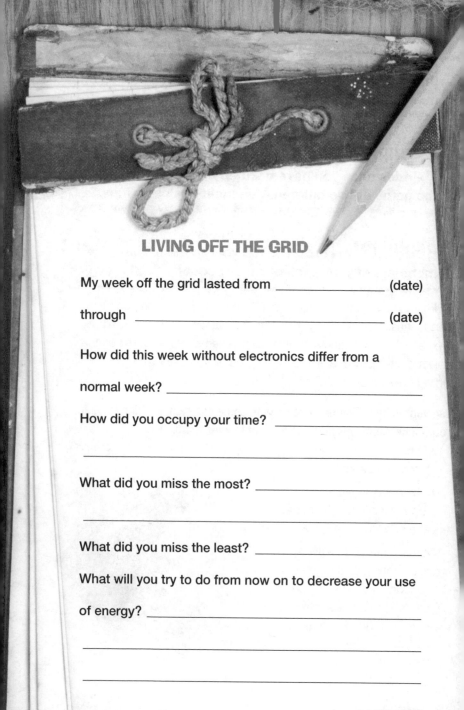

LIVING OFF THE GRID

My week off the grid lasted from _____ (date)

through _____ (date)

How did this week without electronics differ from a

normal week? _____

How did you occupy your time? _____

_____

What did you miss the most? _____

_____

What did you miss the least? _____

What will you try to do from now on to decrease your use

of energy? _____

_____

_____

REQUIREMENT 2C | With your den, invent a game that can be played without using electricity and using minimal equipment or simple items.

REQUIREMENT 2D | Name your game, write down the rules once you have decided on them, then play the game at two different den meetings or outings.

REQUIREMENT 2E | Teach your game to the members of your pack or other Scouts.

Imagine that you have a pair of hiking socks, a tree branch, some bandannas, a bell, and a water bottle. What kind of game could you create with those objects or other simple items? What would be the object of the game? Would the game be played between teams or individuals? What would the rules be?

Use your imagination to come up with some different, exciting rules for your game. Some possible rules might include things like:

- Everyone has to hop on one leg when "Red!" is yelled by someone holding a bandanna.

- The opposing team has to roll over twice if your team gets all the bandannas.

Name your game, write down the rules, then play the game at two different den meetings. Once you are happy with the game's rules, teach it to another group of Scouts.

Have fun!

OUR DEN GAME

Name of our game: _____

Some of our best rules:

_____

_____

_____

_____

Clean, healthy drinking water is very important for life. While humans can live for several days without food, water is a more critical need to keep our bodies running properly.

> Here's a good word to know: potable. If a water source is potable, that means the water is safe to drink.

But water can also make you sick if it has not been treated to remove bacteria and other microorganisms. The water you drink at home and school has probably been treated and tested to make sure it is safe. That's not true of water that comes from lakes, streams, and wells. You should always treat any water that does not come from a reliable source.

If you've ever watched a movie about the Old West, you may have seen cowboys stop near a river, dip their hands in, and scoop up a big drink of refreshing water. What you probably didn't see is how drinking that water upset their stomachs later. It's better to be safe than sorry—and sick!

Three ways to make water safe for drinking are boiling it, treating it, and filtering it.

Boiling

Boiling water is probably the easiest and least expensive method of water purification. Bringing water to a rolling boil for a full 10 minutes will kill most microorganisms. (A rolling boil means the top of the water is moving around in the pan.)

If the water is muddy, filter it through a bandanna first. That won't remove any microorganisms, but it will make the water look better when you boil it.

Chemical Treatment

Water treatment tablets are sold in small bottles and packets and are relatively inexpensive. To treat water, follow the instructions on the packaging. Most treatment tablets call for you to drop one or two tablets into a quart of water and then wait 30 minutes before drinking it. If you are treating water in a water bottle, loosen the lid slightly and slosh some treated water around on the threads of the lid.

Treatment tablets can lose their strength over time, so be sure to check the expiration date on the bottle. Use only fresh tablets.

Filtering

Water treatment filters made for hikers are quick and easy to use. They pump water through filter pores that are small enough to strain out bacteria and parasites. Filtering is the most expensive way to treat water, but it is also the most effective for all types of contaminants.

Carefully follow the instructions that come with the filter. A filter can become clogged if the water has a lot of dirt or sand in it, so you may want to strain the water through a bandanna before filtering it.

After you've tried two different types of treatment, taste the water. Which water tastes better? Which method was easier to use?

A very important part of survival is getting found. You can help rescuers find you by doing certain things.

STOP

First, remember to STOP:

S (Stop): Stay put. The worst thing you can do when you're lost is panic and leave your current location. Take a deep breath, calm yourself, and sit down. Drink some water, or eat a little food. If you're cold, put on your jacket.

T (Think): Once you've calmed down, think about your situation. Think about how you got where you are. You may discover that you're not as lost as you thought.

O (Observe): Look around. Listen for other Scouts. Check your supplies and the area around you for things that can help you survive.

P (Plan): Finally, make a plan for dealing with your situation. If you are absolutely sure you know the way back to your group, follow it carefully. Mark your way with broken branches or piles of stones so you can come back to your starting point if you need to. If you don't know the way back to your group, stay where you are. Decide what your priorities are, and take care of them one at a time.

Signaling

In a movie or TV show, you may have seen someone write "Help!" in the sand on a beach. That's a good idea—if you're on a beach.

Here are some signaling methods that will work everywhere:

- **Whistle.** A whistle can be heard much farther away than your voice. Blow three times in a row and keep repeating.

- **Signal mirror.** A signal mirror can reflect the sun's rays and draw the attention of low-flying aircraft. Some signal mirrors have a hole in them to let you see that you are aiming in the right direction.

- **Bright colors.** You can also attract attention by spreading brightly colored materials like tarps or emergency blankets in an open area.

- **Fire.** A large fire will attract attention at night. During the day, a smoky fire will do the same thing. Live vegetation, moss, and green leaves make a fire smoky. Be sure you build your fire in a safe place so it doesn't spread.

The universal emergency signal is anything that appears in a series of three. That could be three whistle blasts, three fires, or three large Xs formed with logs in an open field.

> **Don't practice signaling techniques in a place where other people might be concerned you are really in trouble, and don't practice building a fire without adult supervision.**

Make a list of four qualities you think a leader should have in an emergency and why they are important to have. Pick two of them, and act them out for your den. Describe how each relates to a point of the Scout Law. Describe how working on this adventure gave you a better understanding of the Boy Scout motto.

Leaders have many skills, and most of them are useful in emergencies. For example, a leader knows how to listen to other group members' ideas and give everyone a chance to speak. This example is one way a Scout is courteous.

Write down the qualities you think a leader should have in an emergency. Develop a skit that shows Scouts demonstrating those qualities and being leaders.

_____

_____

_____

_____

_____

_____

_____

BADEN-POWELL AT MAFEKING

Before he invented Scouting, Robert Baden-Powell was a soldier in the British Army. In 1899, he was in charge of the town of Mafeking in South Africa when enemy troops besieged it. For the next 217 days, he kept the town safe, even though he had only one-fourth as many troops as the enemy. He moved guns around the town to make it appear his troops were better armed than they were, he enlisted boys to serve as messengers, and he even arranged theatrical performances and sporting events to improve morale. The town survived the siege, and Baden-Powell became a national hero.

EARTH ROCKS!

SNAPSHOT OF ADVENTURE

Rocks and minerals are more than just things that lie in the ground. Yes, they help form our planet, but people also use them to create things that make our lives easier. In this adventure, you'll dig into the world of rocks and minerals and discover some surprises about the science of geology—like how the ground beneath your feet is constantly on the move.

REQUIREMENT

Do all of these: **Approved by**

1. Do the following:

   A. Explain the meaning of the word "geology."   _____

   B. Explain why this kind of science is an important part of your world.   _____

   C. Share with your family or with your den what you learned about the meaning of geology.   _____

2. Look for different kinds of rocks or minerals while on a rock hunt with your family or your den.   _____

3. Do the following:

   A. Identify the rocks you see on your rock hunt. Use the information in your handbook to determine which types of rocks you have collected.   _____

   B. With a magnifying glass, take a closer look at your collection. Determine any differences between your specimens.   _____

   C. Share what you see with your family or den.   _____

4. Do the following:

A. With your family or den, make a mineral test kit, and test rocks according to the Mohs scale of mineral hardness. _____

B. Record the results in your handbook. _____

5. With your family or den, identify on a road map of your state some geological features in your area. _____

6. Do the following:

A. Identify some of the geological building materials used in building your home. _____

B. Identify some of the geological materials used around your community. _____

C. Record the items you find. _____

7. Do either 7a or 7b:

A. Go on an outing with your family or den to one of the nearby locations you discovered on your state map, and record what you see as you look at the geographical surroundings. Share with your family or den while on this outing what you notice that might change this location in the future (wind, water, ice, drought, erosion). _____

B. Do the following:

i. With your family or your den, visit with a geologist or earth scientist and discover the many career fields that are included in the science of geology. _____

ii. Ask the geologist or earth scientist about the importance of fossils that are found. _____

iii. Ask the geologist or earth scientist what you can do to help preserve our natural resources. _____

8. Do at least one earth science demonstration or investigation with your den or with adult supervision, and explore geology in action. _____

REQUIREMENT 1A | Explain the meaning of the word "geology."

REQUIREMENT 1B | Explain why this kind of science is an important part of your world.

REQUIREMENT 1C | Share with your family or den what you learned about the meaning of geology.

Geology is the study of the earth, including the materials it is made of, the structure of those materials, and the processes that act on them. An important part of geology is studying how the earth changes over time. While the earth might not seem to change much, it is actually always changing. Wind and rain wear down mountains, earthquakes shake the ground, and volcanoes spew melted rock into the air. Even the continents are moving. North America is actually moving to the west-southwest about an inch a year!

Horseshoe Bend, Arizona

A geologist is a scientist who studies the earth. Some geologists study how the earth was formed and how it changes. Other geologists study earthquakes and volcanoes and try to reduce the damage they cause by learning how to predict them. Still others work to improve our lives by using rocks and minerals to supply many of the things we use every day.

Petroleum geologists study the earth's natural resources of oil and gas. Engineering geologists and structural geologists work on building projects. Hydrogeologists work with our water resources. Environmental geologists study the effects we humans have on our planet Earth. What type of geologist would you like to be?

REQUIREMENT 2 | Look for different kinds of rocks or minerals while on a rock hunt with your family or your den.

Everywhere you look there are rocks and minerals. They are part of your world every day. Some rocks are small pebbles, and some are gigantic mountains. Your own backyard and neighborhood are good places to begin collecting rocks. Think about how these rocks were formed and how they ended up where you found them.

Collecting Specimens

One way to begin a collection of geologic specimens is to visit a business that sells building stone or makes gravestones. These businesses might have small scraps of marble, granite, sandstone, limestone, pumice, shale, or slate they will give you. A nearby science museum might also have rock specimens for sale.

You can also go on a field trip. If possible, go with a rock hound, a collector who knows a lot about rocks. A rock hound will know which rocks contain useful materials. Look for minerals in gravel or sand pits, road cuts, diggings, mountains, hills, and stream banks. Keep your rock samples small. Small ones are easier to carry and easier to care for.

Safety is very important when on a rock hunt. Always have an adult with you. Stay away from dangerous areas like cliffs, quarries, mines, and mine dump heaps. Be careful when climbing on rocks. And watch out for snakes. They may live under rocks, so always poke around a rock with a long stick before reaching under it.

> Collecting rocks is not allowed in national parks and in many state parks. Ask permission before you collect anywhere. If you aren't permitted to collect rock samples, take pictures of your findings to use in a display.

Geologist's Equipment

- ♦ Written or verbal permission to collect rocks
- ♦ Safety glasses to protect your eyes
- ♦ A pocket magnifier for seeing things up close
- ♦ A geologist's hammer for pulling rocks out of hillsides and breaking them open
- ♦ A cold chisel, half an inch to 1 inch wide, for chipping stone with a hammer and for digging things loose
- ♦ Clear plastic food storage bags; write the number of the rock sample on paper and slip it into the bag with the rock sample
- ♦ A small notebook and pencil for recording where and when you found a sample; number each sample in the notebook
- ♦ Heavy gloves for rough work
- ♦ A small day pack for carrying equipment and rocks

Your Collection

You can display your rock collection by putting your rocks in egg cartons, or you can make dividers for shoeboxes. On each rock specimen, paint a spot of quick-drying white enamel. When it is dry, write a number on the

spot with a dark felt-tip pen. For each specimen, keep a card with that number. The card is where you will record what the specimen is and where and when you found it.

REQUIREMENT 3A | Identify the rocks you saw on your rock hunt. Use the information in your handbook to determine which types of rocks you have collected.

REQUIREMENT 3B | With a magnifying glass, take a closer look at your collection. Determine any differences between your specimens.

REQUIREMENT 3C | Share what you see with your family or den.

Using a guide to rocks and minerals, identify what you have collected or taken pictures of. With a magnifying glass, take a closer look at your collection. Do you see anything different when looking up close? Share what you see with your family or den.

Geologists use the following tests to identify minerals.

♦ **Color test:** Scratch the specimen on a plate of unglazed porcelain or the back of a piece of tile. The color that appears helps to identify it.

♦ **Luster test:** How does the specimen look when light is reflected from it? Is it shiny, dull, or greasy?

♦ **Cleavage test:** How does it split or break up? Does it turn into powder or split in layers? If it breaks into crystals, how many sides does a crystal have?

♦ **Chemical test:** Does it contain limestone? If a drop of vinegar bubbles on it, the answer is yes.

♦ **Hardness test:** How hard is it? See the hardness scale in requirement 4.

KINDS OF ROCKS

All rocks belong to one of the three main groups that make up the Earth's crust. They are igneous, sedimentary, and metamorphic rocks.

Igneous Rock

Igneous rock is any rock made by cooling magma (hot, molten material that flows under the Earth's surface) or lava (molten rock that comes out of a volcano). Examples of igneous rock include basalt, granite, and obsidian.

Igneous Rocks

Basalt   Gabbro   Granite   Obsidian   Pumice

Sedimentary Rock

Sediment is gravel, sand, clay, or soil that settles and hardens out of water in riverbeds, ponds, lakes, and oceans. Sediment may contain shells and skeletons. Sedimentary rock is formed in layers, like a giant cake, after sediment has been under great pressure for millions of years. If the sediment was originally sand, it becomes sandstone. Clay turns into shale. Shells and skeletons make limestone. Small pebbles and sand form conglomerate.

Sedimentary Rocks

Breccia   Conglomerate   Limestone   Sandstone   Shale

Metamorphic Rock

Metamorphic rock has been through a process much like baking. (*Meta* means changed, and *morphic* means form.) The change is caused by intense heat and great pressure deep in the earth.

Under these conditions, sedimentary limestone becomes marble. Sedimentary sandstone turns into quartzite. Igneous granite changes into gneiss (pronounced "nice").

Metamorphic Rocks

| Slate | Metaquartzite | Green schist | Marble | Gneiss |

USEFUL MINERALS

The Earth contains many useful minerals. Some, like silica (sand), are easy to see and collect. Others, like iron and zinc, are found in rocks. They must be removed from the rock by a process called smelting or refining.

There are three categories of useful minerals: metals, nonmetallic minerals, and fuels.

Examples of Minerals

Metals	Nonmetallic Minerals		Fuel
	Used in building materials and supplies	Precious and semiprecious stones	
Iron	Gypsum	Turquoise	Coal
Tin	Potash	Topaz	Natural gas
Platinum	Limestone	Garnet	Petroleum
Zinc	Sand	Tourmaline	
Mercury	Borax	Diamond	
Aluminum	Talc	Zircon	
Lead	Quartz	Sapphire	
Gold		Ruby	
Uranium			
Copper			
Silver			
Magnesium			

I used to think stones like diamonds and rubies were just used in jewelry. But I learned they are also used in other ways. Diamonds are so hard that they are used in cutting and grinding tools, and rubies help focus the light in some lasers used by scientists.

CRYSTALS

A crystal is a group of atoms that come together in a certain way to form a molecule. Each kind of crystal has special and unique characteristics and shapes. For example, sugar crystals are oval-shaped and slanted at the ends, while salt crystals are in the shape of little cubes. Crystals can be used in many ways: for eating, like sugar and salt, or as jewelry! Diamonds, rubies, sapphires, and emeralds are all different kinds of crystals, formed by different elements and atoms.

THE WEATHERING AND EROSION OF ROCKS

Weathering is what happens when rocks and minerals break apart because of water, ice, wind, heat, or cold. Erosion is what happens when the pieces caused by weathering are carried away. Weathering and erosion are important parts of geology.

Ice Erosion

Ice is another strong force that causes large amounts of physical erosion. In mountainous locations in the world, the rock and soil are commonly frozen together. Ice grows in the cracks of the rocks and pushes the rock particles apart. When the

water melts and freezes again, it moves the particles away from each other and the process repeats itself. When water flows down a hillside, it can cause erosion similar to wrinkles in the soil. Glaciers, which are huge pieces of ice, move slowly down a mountain with the force of gravity. The weight of the glacier presses into the ground, forcing it apart and separating rocks. During the movement of glaciers, some of the ice also melts and refreezes as it moves, continuing to pick up rock pieces, dragging them across other rocks in the glacier's path, and breaking them into even smaller pieces.

Wind Erosion

The movement of the wind erodes and creates different landforms. Wind is an invisible force that includes small pieces of rocks and minerals. This kind of erosion is not very strong because it takes a lot of energy to transport sand and dust. This type of erosion is known for smoothing the earth around us. Every time there is wind, the erosion impact can break off smaller pieces of larger rock. Sometimes the little rock pieces break into even smaller pieces. These smaller pieces can stay where the wind carries them until water washes them to another location, waiting for wind erosion to carry them away again.

Water Erosion

Have you ever noticed that rocks in riverbeds and on lake and ocean shores are small and smooth? That's because of water erosion. Water causes a great deal of physical erosion. When rain falls heavily, flooding can happen, changing everything that the fast-moving waters carry with it. Rushing water can also cause mudslides. The force of the rushing water causes sharp edges of rocks to knock loose, which creates smoothness. Water erosion has caused geological landforms such as canyons and rivers. The Grand Canyon, which is a mile deep and 277 miles long, was formed by water erosion.

FOSSILS

You may find fossils while you are looking for rock specimens. A fossil is a trace of animal or plant life from millions of years ago that has hardened in rock. A fossil may be a print of a shell or the skeleton of a fish or bird. It may be a dinosaur's track or a leaf or flower print.

Would you believe that fossils from the sea can be found in a desert? It's true! This means that the spot where they were found was once an ocean floor. Certain plants and animals live in hot climates, but their fossils have been found in cold countries. This means that these areas were not always cold.

Wind and water erosion have changed the earth's landscape and helped to move fossils and other geological items over time. Fossils have even been discovered on top of mountains.

Sedimentary rock usually contains fossils. Geologists study the rock layer in which the fossils were found. Then they can tell when the country was warm and for how long. Fossils show us what plants and trees lived millions of years ago and where. They show the changes that have happened through the years. You probably can find fossils in your own neighborhood. Look in diggings, road cuts, or stream banks— wherever cuts have been made through layers of sedimentary rock.

REQUIREMENT 4A | With your family or den, make a mineral test kit, and test rocks according to the Mohs scale of mineral hardness.

REQUIREMENT 4B | Record the results in your handbook.

A long time ago, a geologist named Friedrich Mohs figured out that you can test the hardness of rocks and minerals by seeing whether they can scratch other materials or whether other materials can scratch them. He created a scale that gives different rocks and minerals hardness values from 1 to 10.

Mohs Hardness Scale

Scale No.	Mineral Example	Scratch Test
1	Talc	Scratches easily with fingernail
2	Gypsum	Barely scratches with fingernail
3	Calcite	Barely scratches with copper penny
4	Fluorite	Scratches easily with file or knife blade
5	Apatite	Barely scratches with file or knife blade
6	Feldspar	Doesn't scratch with file or knife blade; scratches easily with glass
7	Quartz	Easily marks steel and hard glass
8	Topaz	Is harder than common minerals
9	Corundum	Scratches topaz
10	Diamond	Scratches corundum; hardest mineral

Many experienced rock collectors carry a mineral testing kit on their rock-hunting trips to test hardness and other mineral characteristics. Knowing the hardness of a mineral will not always tell you its identity, but it will help rule out some possibilities.

You can buy a mineral testing kit, but it's more fun to make one yourself using materials you can find around the house or buy cheaply.

Here's what you need:
+ Penny
+ Small piece of glass
+ Piece of unglazed tile
+ File or pocket knife
+ Small bottle of vinegar
+ Eyedropper
+ Rocks

Here's how to use your kit:
Step 1. Scratch the tile with your rock to determine the "streak" of the mineral. The streak is the color of the resulting powder. It's usually a more consistent color than the apparent color of the mineral. You can refer to a mineral identification chart to find out what minerals have this streak.

Step 2. Use the eyedropper to put a drop of vinegar on the mineral. If the vinegar fizzes, that means the mineral contains calcium carbonate.

Step 3. Test the hardness of the mineral by trying to scratch it, in order, with your fingernail, the penny, and the file or knife. Then, try to scratch the file or knife and the glass with the mineral. Refer to the chart to determine the mineral's hardness. For example, if you can scratch the mineral with your fingernail, it measures 1 or 2 on the scale. If the mineral can scratch the file or knife, it measures at least 7 on the scale.

Hardness tests

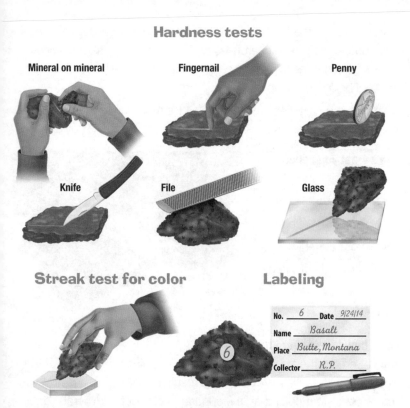

Mineral on mineral

Fingernail

Penny

Knife

File

Glass

Streak test for color

Labeling

No. _6_ Date _9/24/14_
Name _Basalt_
Place _Butte, Montana_
Collector _R.P._

Rock and Mineral Types	Description	Scratch Test	Scale No.

Geological features are all around us. Mountains, plains, lakes, rivers, swamps, and caves are just some of the natural features that may be found near where you live. And there may be man-made features like dams, quarries, mines, canals, and channelized streams.

Mark some of those features on a map of your area. Try to imagine what forces created them. Imagine going back in time to see how those features were created.

While you're exploring the past, see if you can discover how your area has changed over thousands and even millions of years. (A good place to start is a local science or natural history museum.)

You may discover things like this:

◆ During the Devonian Period (408 million to 360 million years ago), a shallow sea covered much of eastern North America from New York through Kentucky to Texas.

◆ The Colorado River has been forming the Grand Canyon for the past 17 million years.

◆ During the Wisconsin Glacial Episode (85,000 to 11,000 years ago), glaciers covered Canada, New England, the Upper Midwest, and parts of Idaho, Montana, and Washington.

◆ In the 20th century, the U.S. government built dams on many rivers to control flooding and generate hydroelectric power. One of the most famous, the Hoover Dam, impounds Lake Meade in Nevada and Arizona.

REQUIREMENT 6A | Identify some of the geological building materials used in building your home.

REQUIREMENT 6B | Identify some of the geological materials used around your community.

REQUIREMENT 6C | Record the items you find.

Although your home may be made mostly of wood products, plenty of geological building materials went into it as well. The chart shows some common geological materials used in construction. Can you add others?

The Lincoln Memorial is made of marble.

Geological Materials in Construction

Ore	Metal	Use
Hematite Limonite Magnetite	Iron	Beams, girders, posts, nails, machines, screws
Azurite Malachite Chalcocite	Copper	Electric wiring, gutters, roofing, pipes
Sphalerite	Zinc	Galvanized pipe, sheet metal
Bauxite	Aluminum	Siding, windows, doors, roofs
Quartz	Silicon	Glass
Kernite Borax	Boron	Glass
Limestone	Calcium	Cement, building stone

Here are a few places to look for some types of rocks in the city:

♦ **Granite.** This strong igneous rock is used often in city buildings. Look for it on the outside of buildings. It can be gray, pink, or a deeper rose color. It has a speckled pattern. The darkest flecks are mica crystals, and the glasslike areas are quartz crystals. You can find both rough and polished granite in buildings.

♦ **Sandstone.** In eastern cities, many older homes called brownstones were built of brick and then covered with brown sandstone blocks.

♦ **Slate.** This metamorphic rock, changed by heat and pressure, was once clay. It can be split into slabs. You might find an old sidewalk made of gray slate. Chalkboards in schools used to

The Washington National Cathedral is made of limestone.

be made of smooth black slate. Some roofs are made of slate.

♦ **Marble.** Look for marble in the lobbies of office buildings and banks. A streaky, swirling pattern of mixed color and a smooth, shiny surface will be the main clues. Marble comes in many different colors. The main color might be black, gray, green, pink, or white. You can find marble in museums and parks, too. Pure white marble is often used for sculptures, statues, and monuments.

Geological Building Materials Found	Used For

REQUIREMENT 7 | Do either 7a or 7b:

REQUIREMENT 7A | Go on an outing with your family or den to one of the nearby locations you discovered on your state map, and record what you see as you look at the geographical surroundings. Share with your family or den while on this outing what you notice that might change this location in the future (wind, water, ice, drought, erosion).

REQUIREMENT 7B | Do the following:

i. With your family or your den, visit with a geologist or earth scientist and discover the many career fields that are included in the science of geology.

ii. Ask the geologist or earth scientist about the importance of fossils that are found.

iii. Ask the geologist or earth scientist what you can do to help preserve our natural resources.

Taking a Geological Field Trip

Natural forces like wind, water, and earthquakes helped create the geological features you see around where you live. And those and other forces continue to change the environment.

Visit one of the locations you discovered in requirement 5. Try to imagine how the location could change in the future and what forces might cause those changes. Tell your family or den what you discovered.

My state _____

Geological features found in my state_____

_____

_____

_____

_____

I visited _____

_____

Geological forces that may change this location in the future

_____

_____

_____

_____

Visiting With a Geologist

One of the best ways to learn about geology is to meet with a geologist.

At your meeting, ask questions like these:

♦ What field of geology do you work in?

♦ What other kinds of geologists do you work with?

♦ What education is required to be a geologist?

♦ How can Webelos Scouts help preserve our natural resources?

REQUIREMENT 8 | Do at least one earth science demonstration or investigation with your den or with adult supervision, and explore geology in action.

Geologists learn important facts by conducting experiments. You can do the same thing by conducting demonstrations and investigations like these.

 Be sure to wear safety glasses when conducting any science investigations.

Sedimentary Layer Simulation

Use this simulation to learn how sedimentary layers are formed and what they look like.

Materials:

- Shoebox
- Aluminum foil
- String
- Sand

- Pebbles
- Powdered clay
- Cement
- Safety glasses

- Plaster of paris
- Shells
- Water

Line the box with aluminum foil and tie string around the sides so the box won't break or bulge when you fill it. Fill the box halfway with water. Put in a half-inch-deep mixture of sand and cement and let it settle. Then put in half-inch layers of plaster of paris and clay. Let each layer  settle. Mix pebbles and shells with a small amount of cement and make a layer of each. When the box is filled, let the "rock" harden for a few days. Cut away the box and you'll have a fair approximation of sedimentary layers.

Crystal Garden

Materials:

- 6 tablespoons of water
- 1 tablespoon of ammonia
- 6 tablespoons of laundry bluing
- 6 teaspoons of salt
- 6 pieces of charcoal (the kind used for outdoor cooking)

Mix the water, ammonia, bluing, and salt in a bowl. Put the charcoal in a pie pan. Pour the liquid over the pieces of charcoal. Put the pie pan in a warm place where the water will evaporate quickly. When the water has evaporated, a "garden" of crystals will have grown.

Impact of Water Investigation

Materials:

- Sedimentary rocks (like limestone or sandstone)
- Igneous rocks (like granite or pumice)
- Metamorphic rocks (like marble or slate)
- Water bottles
- Water

Put each kind of rock in a separate water bottle. Label each bottle with the rock type. Fill each bottle about half full with water (enough water so the rocks are covered). Freeze the bottles in a freezer, then take them out and let them thaw. Repeat the freezing/thawing process four or five more times. Take out the rocks and observe which rocks were damaged the most.

ENGINEER

SNAPSHOT OF ADVENTURE

Lots of people have great ideas: flying to the moon, tunneling under rivers, building robots that walk and talk, making triple-loop rollercoasters. Engineers turn those ideas into reality. They use science, math, and creative thinking to improve people's lives. In this adventure, you will learn what engineers do. Even better, you will do some engineering projects of your own. So put on your thinking cap, and get ready to think like an engineer!

REQUIREMENT

Do all of these: Approved by

1. Pick one type of engineer. With the help of the Internet, your local library, or a local engineer you may know or locate, discover and record in your book three things that describe what that engineer does. (Be sure to have your Webelos den leader, parent, or guardian's permission to use the Internet.) Share your findings with your Webelos den.   _____

2. Learn to follow engineering design principles by doing the following:

   A. Examine a set of blueprints. Using these as a model, construct your own set of blueprints or plans to design a project.   _____

   B. Using the blueprints or plans from your own design, construct your project. Your project may be something useful or something fun.   _____

   C. Share your project with your Webelos den and your pack by displaying the project at a pack meeting.   _____

3. Explore other fields of engineering and how they have helped form our past, present, and future.   _____

4. Pick and do two projects using the engineering skills you have learned. Share your projects with your den, and also exhibit them at a pack meeting.   _____

Engineers design everything from tiny materials you can only see through a microscope to spacecraft powerful enough to escape the earth's gravity. Most engineers work in an area (called a discipline) that focuses on a specific type of project.

There are dozens of different disciplines and subdisciplines.

Here are a few types of engineers whose work we can see and use every day:

* **Chemical engineer:** uses principles of chemistry to turn raw materials into products such as medicine, plastic, and fuel

* **Civil engineer:** designs projects such as roads, bridges, tunnels, and buildings

* **Electrical engineer:** uses electrical and electronic principles to create everything from power transmission systems to computers

* **Mechanical engineer:** designs mechanical products such as engines, bicycles, and the parts and materials that go into them

* **Structural engineer:** makes sure structures can support weight and resist forces like earthquakes and wind

* **Aerospace engineer:** designs aircraft, spacecraft, and satellites

* **Computer engineer:** designs computer hardware and software

Engineers from different disciplines work together on many projects. For example, if you were building a spaceship, you would need aerospace engineers, computer engineers, electrical engineers, mechanical engineers, and several other types of engineers that aren't listed here.

Choose one type of engineer, and learn more about what he or she does. Write what you learned on this page.

My Engineer

My engineer is a _____ engineer.

Two places where this engineer may work:

_____

_____

Three activities this engineer does as part of his or her job:

_____

_____

_____

Two school subjects you need to study to become an engineer:

_____

_____

Share your findings with your Webelos den. You could tell your story by drawing a picture of this sort of engineer at work, making a video, or doing some other form of presentation.

REQUIREMENT 2 | **Learn to follow engineering design principles by doing the following:**

REQUIREMENT 2A | Examine a set of blueprints. Using these as a model, construct your own set of blueprints or plans to design a project.

REQUIREMENT 2B | Using the blueprints or plans from your own design, construct your project. Your project may be something useful or something fun.

REQUIREMENT 2C | Share your project with your Webelos den and your pack by displaying the project at a pack meeting.

Blueprints

A written and/or picture design of a project is called a blueprint. Structural, civil, and electrical engineers are a few of the engineers who use blueprints to assist them with their projects.

Why are blueprints called blueprints? When they were first introduced in the 19th century, they were made with a process that resulted in white lines on a blue background.

Before you design your own project, look at a set of blueprints. You may use your local library, the Internet, or an individual you know who is an engineer or works in the construction field to find blueprints. House plans are good examples because many of the pictures they contain will be familiar to you.

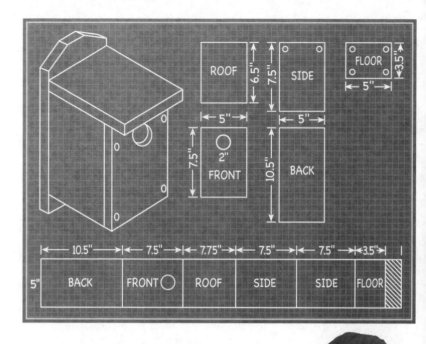

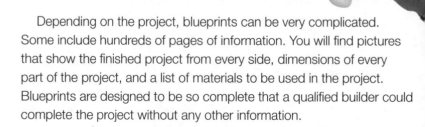

My dad's friend is a builder. He took our den through a partially completed house and showed us how things looked on the blueprints and in real life. It was cool to be able to see inside the walls and under the floors.

Depending on the project, blueprints can be very complicated. Some include hundreds of pages of information. You will find pictures that show the finished project from every side, dimensions of every part of the project, and a list of materials to be used in the project. Blueprints are designed to be so complete that a qualified builder could complete the project without any other information.

Testing and evaluation are also important parts of the engineering process. On major projects, engineers build models and run computer simulations before starting actual construction. These steps can save time and money if the design needs to be changed.

The Engineering Process

To understand how an engineer might approach a project, let's look at the engineering process. After an engineer becomes aware of a need, he or she gathers information, and then makes a design. The building phase begins after that.

Here's how you might use that process to construct a small item for your bedroom:

1. **Determine your need.** Let's say you don't have anything next to your bed to set your books and alarm clock on. You need a small table.

2. **Gather information.** Of course, tables come in all sorts of shapes and styles. You could ask questions like these to refine your idea:

    ♦ What will I put on the table? How much do the items weigh? (You need to know how sturdy your table needs to be.)

    ♦ What building materials should I use? (Now that you know your weight requirements, you can pick materials that will be strong enough to handle the weight of the items.)

    ♦ Will the materials be expensive if I have to purchase them? Can I recycle materials I already have? (Engineers have to make sure their designs are cost-effective.)

- ♦ What is the best design I can use? Should it have two, three, or four legs? Should it have a square, round, or rectangular top? How tall should it be? (These questions will guide you to the right design based on your table's location and use.)

- ♦ Will it help if I draw pictures of the design before I begin? These drawings can help start your blueprint!

3. **Prepare instructions.** The information you gathered should help you better understand the planning process and your needs. Now you can create a plan for building your table. Because of the process you followed, you will be able to build a better table than if you just started nailing boards together without a plan.

   By drawing your blueprint on graph paper, you can easily keep the drawing to scale. For example, one grid on the paper could equal 1 inch on the finished product.

   Be sure to make notes on your drawing about all dimensions and materials. Remember that another person should be able to create your project from the blueprint you have made.

   You might also want to make a small scale model of your project. Heavy cardboard, toothpicks, craft sticks, and tape are some materials you could use.

4. **Build your project.** Once you have prepared your design and your blueprint, you are ready to build your table. Here you will discover if your design ideas will work and if your blueprints have clear instructions and good information. It's a good idea to take notes and pictures as you go along so you remember what worked and what didn't.

5. **Evaluate your project.** After you build your table, you should test it to make sure it meets your needs. You can also ask yourself questions like these:

   ◆ Did the project turn out as I expected?

   ◆ How much did it cost to build the project?

   ◆ What would I do differently next time?

   ◆ What three things did I learn when I designed and built my project?

   ◆ What am I most proud of about my project?

   Share your project with your Webelos den and your pack by displaying the project at a pack meeting.

REQUIREMENT 3 | Explore other fields of engineering and how they have helped form our past, present, and future.

The next few pages introduce you to several engineering disciplines and show you projects you could do in each of those areas. Pick two of the projects, and complete them by using the same design process you used in requirement 2. Be sure to keep notes as you go. That way, if you decide to redo a project to achieve a different outcome, you will have information to refer back to.

DEFENSE ENGINEERING

Defense engineers develop items that assist in protecting our country. Around 400 BC, defense engineers in Greece developed catapults to shoot projectiles long distances.

Craft Stick Launcher

You can build a simple machine with craft sticks to launch marshmallows and other soft projectiles.

Materials:

- 9 craft sticks
- Rubber bands
- Plastic spoon
- Marshmallows

Instructions:

1. Stack seven craft sticks together. Secure them at each end with a rubber band.

2. Stack two craft sticks together. Secure one end with a rubber band and leave the other end open.

3. Wedge the large stack of craft sticks in between the other two craft sticks as shown in the picture.

4. Attach the plastic spoon to the top craft stick with a rubber band.

5. To use the launcher, put a marshmallow on the spoon, pull the spoon down as far as you can, and then release it.

Evaluation questions:

◆ How far can you make the marshmallows go?

◆ Can you aim them to hit targets?

◆ What would happen if you launched something heavier?

◆ Is your machine accurate? Can you send the marshmallow into a container?

◆ How could you change the project to make it work better?

AEROSPACE ENGINEERING

Aerospace engineers design aircraft and spacecraft. Among the challenges they face is making vehicles that are light enough to take off but also safe enough to carry humans.

Paper Airplanes

To explore how wings create lift and keep airplanes flying, construct three different paper airplanes. Find multiple designs at the library or on the Internet (with your parent's permission), or you can design your own. Fly all three planes, and evaluate how well they performed.

Evaluation questions:

◆ Which design flew the farthest?

◆ Which design flew the straightest?

◆ Which design flew the highest?

◆ What would happen if you used heavier or lighter paper?

◆ Which style performed the best?

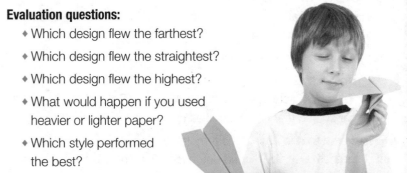

Stomp Rocket

A stomp rocket is a fun way to test aerodynamics, which is the study of the effects of air on items in motion.

Rocket materials:

- A 12-inch-long piece of half-inch PVC pipe
- A center-stapled magazine or catalog with the staples removed
- The fin and nose cone templates
- Transparent tape
- Scissors

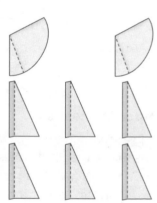

Instructions:

1. Lay three sheets of paper from the magazine or catalog on a table. Carefully roll the paper into a long tube around the pipe. Tape your roll in a few places to hold it.

2. Remove the pipe, being careful not to smash the roll.

3. Use another sheet of paper to cut a circle the same diameter as the tube. Tape this circle over one end of the tube. Be sure to completely seal that end so that no air can leak out.

4. Enlarge the fin and nose cone templates. Copy them onto cardstock and cut them out. You'll need one nose cone and three fins.

5. Fold the fins along the lines shown, and tape them to the tube near the open end.

6. Roll the nose cone so the paper overlaps to the dotted line shown on the template. Tape the nose cone onto the closed end of the tube.

Materials for rocket launcher:

- 1 10-foot length of half-inch PVC pipe
- 1 90-degree elbow of half-inch PVC pipe
- 1 socket cross of half-inch PVC pipe
- 2 socket caps of half-inch PVC pipe
- Empty 2-liter soft drink bottle
- PVC cement
- Hack saw
- Duct tape
- Sandpaper

Side view

Top view

Instructions (you'll need an adult to help):

1. From the 10-foot length of PVC pipe, cut three 1-foot pieces and one 4-inch piece. With the sandpaper, smooth all rough edges from the cut ends.

2. Insert the remaining long piece of pipe into one opening in the cross fitting and the 4-inch piece in the opposite opening. Insert a 1-foot piece of pipe in each of the other holes. Put socket caps over the open ends of the 1-foot pipes. (These 1-foot pieces will stabilize the launcher assembly.)

3. Attach the elbow to the end of the 4-inch pipe so the other hole in the elbow points straight up. Insert the final 1-foot piece of pipe into the elbow.

4. Once you are sure that the launcher is assembled correctly, disassemble each joint, spread PVC cement around the end of the pipe, and reinsert it in the fitting. PVC cement sets quickly, so just work on one joint at a time.

5. Securely tape the 2-liter bottle to the end of the long piece of pipe with duct tape.

6. To use the launcher, place your rocket over the vertical pipe and stomp on the 2-liter bottle. The air displaced from the bottle will pass through the tubing and send the rocket into the air.

 Stomp rockets are fun, but be careful! Never point the rocket at a person or anywhere but straight up. Keep spectators away from the launcher, and only launch under adult supervision.

Evaluation questions:

♦ Can you determine how high your rocket went? Did it go higher than your trees or house?

♦ Was the flight path straight up, in an arc, or sideways?

♦ What was the outside environment like (windy, calm, hot, cold)? Did the environment affect the flight of your rocket?

♦ Did your rocket survive its first flight? Can it be used again?

♦ Could you have used different materials in the construction and achieved a different outcome?

♦ How would a different launcher design affect the rocket's flight?

ARCHITECTURAL ENGINEERING

Architectural engineers design amazing buildings and other structures—some reach a half-mile high!

Ancient engineers built amazing structures, too, without using modern machines. The Great Pyramid of Giza in Egypt contains 2.3 million stones weighing 2 to 30 tons each! The builders used a block and tackle to lift very heavy objects that would otherwise not be movable.

Block and Tackle

One type of block and tackle works by using two pulleys to lift a weight. You thread a rope through the pulleys, and attach a weight to the bottom. You then pull on the other end of the rope. Because of the pulleys, you can lift a weight of 100 pounds by exerting just 25 pounds of force.

With the help of your parent or adult leader, construct a simple block and tackle with pulleys. After completion, lift several items with the block and tackle.

Materials:

- ◆ 2 two-sheave pulleys (pulleys that have two wheels side by side)
- ◆ 50 feet of five-eighth-inch rope
- ◆ Heavy object

Instructions:

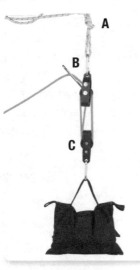

1. Hang one pulley from a bar that is at a comfortable height for you to reach (attachment point A).

2. Pass the rope through the left sheave of the top pulley.

3. Bring the rope down and through the left sheave of the lower pulley, which you can leave on the ground for now.

4. Pass the rope through the right sheave of the top pulley, so that both sheaves are full of rope.

5. Bring the rope down and through the bottom side of the right sheave on the lower pulley. Pull on the rope to draw the two pulleys close together.

6. Tie the end of the rope to the bottom eye of the top pulley (attachment point B).

7. Attach the object you want to lift to the bottom eye of the bottom pulley (attachment point C).

8. You've now completed your block and tackle. If you'd like, you can remove it from attachment point A and move it to a different location.

9. Now, use the block and tackle to lift some items. Be sure you ask your parent or den leader to help.

Evaluation questions:

- Were you surprised at how easily you could lift a heavy item?

- What was the weight of the heaviest item? How high did you lift it?

- Can you see how this tool would make building a tall structure faster and easier?

- How could you improve your block and tackle design?

CIVIL ENGINEERING

Civil engineers design bridges, roads, tunnels, and other structures. Part of their job is planning for the different forces that will affect what they build. These forces include torsion (the twisting that happens when wind hits a building) and load (such as the weight of cars and trucks crossing a bridge). Sometimes they account for these forces by making a structure flexible. Sometimes they account for these forces by transferring them to other parts of the structure.

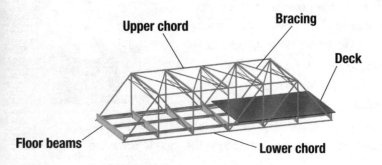

Spaghetti Bridge

A truss bridge is a very common bridge design. It is built with trusses, rigid frameworks made up of a series of triangles. The picture on the previous page shows a truss bridge and some of the bracing that makes it strong.

You can practice civil engineering principles by building a truss bridge out of spaghetti and school glue. Then you can experiment to see how much weight it can support.

Note: Let each section dry completely before moving it or attaching it.

Materials:

- Spaghetti
- School glue
- Waxed paper
- Corrugated cardboard
- Graph paper
- Straight pins

Instructions:

1. Lay a piece of graph paper on top of corrugated cardboard. On the graph paper, sketch your truss. Lay waxed paper on top of the graph paper so the glue you'll use in the next step won't stick to the graph paper.

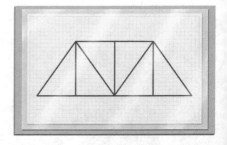

2. Break pieces of spaghetti to the lengths you need, and lay them on your truss drawing. Hold them in place with pins, and glue them together.

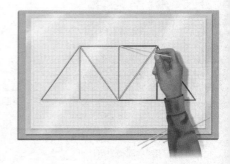

3. Repeat steps 1 and 2 to make a second truss.

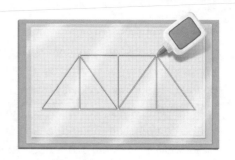

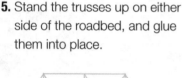

4. Build a roadbed out of spaghetti by gluing pieces of spaghetti together to make two long stringers. Then glue pieces across the stringers to create the deck.

5. Stand the trusses up on either side of the roadbed, and glue them into place.

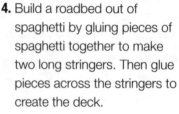

6. Connect the tops of the trusses with pieces of spaghetti. If you have a kitchen scale, weigh the bridge.

7. Set the bridge up between two boxes and hang a lightweight container underneath. Add light objects such as pennies to the container, one at a time, until the bridge collapses.

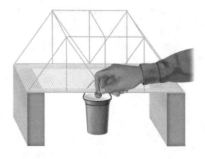

Evaluation questions:

- ♦ How much weight was the bridge able to bear before it collapsed?
- ♦ How did that compare with the weight of the bridge?
- ♦ What could you have done to make the bridge stronger?

ELECTRICAL ENGINEERING

Electrical engineers design, maintain, and improve products that are powered by or produce electricity. They will often design, assemble, and test new devices. Although some of the devices they work on are very complex, these devices are all based on simple electrical circuits.

Telegraph Machine

Long before telephones and computers, people communicated using telegraph. This machine transmitted a clicking sound each time the operator pressed a switch and closed an electrical circuit. You can  make a telegraph out of simple materials (although it won't transmit a signal to someone on the other side of the country!).

Materials:

- ♦ 2 pieces of wood
- ♦ 1 battery (a lantern battery works well)
- ♦ 2 metal strips cut from a can such as a soup can
- ♦ 3 screws
- ♦ 2 nails
- ♦ 2 wires
- ♦ Tinsnips
- ♦ Screwdriver

Instructions:

1. Cut metal strips from a can, and bend in the shapes shown for the "sounder" (the Z shape) and the key. (Make sure you remove sharp edges with a file or emery paper.) Screw them to the blocks of wood.

2. Put one screw underneath the key, with a quarter inch of clearance to the key.

3. Hammer in the nails for the receiver. (There should be one-sixteenth- to one-eighth-inch clearance between the nail heads and the sounder.)

4. Wire as shown. In wrapping the wire around the nails, start at the top of one nail and work down. Then, go across to the other nail and work up. Have at least eight turns on each nail.

5. When you push down on the key and make contact with the screw underneath it, the electric current is completed and passes through the wire. This magnetizes the wrapped nails, which then pull the sounder down to make a clicking sound.

Evaluation questions:

   ◆ How did this project demonstrate how an electrical circuit works?

   ◆ How many places in your home demonstrate this principle?

   ◆ How does this project compare with "real" telegraph machines? (You might have to do some research to find out.)

CHEMICAL ENGINEERING

Chemical engineers apply their understanding of chemistry and chemical processes to tackle all sorts of problems ranging from fuel production to the purification of drinking water. Sometimes their work involves creating chemical reactions; sometimes it involves preventing chemical reactions from happening.

Changing a Penny's Color

You can experiment with chemical reactions by using a penny and some vinegar.

Materials:
- ◆ 4 shiny pennies
- ◆ Vinegar
- ◆ A paper towel
- ◆ Cooking oil
- ◆ Nail polish
- ◆ Paint

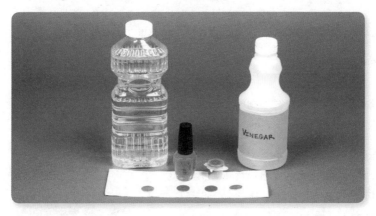

Instructions:

1. Cover one penny in cooking oil, cover one penny with nail polish, and cover one penny with paint. (Leave the fourth penny alone.) Allow time for the pennies to dry.

2. Soak the paper towel in vinegar and set it on a surface that will not be damaged by the vinegar.

3. Place the four pennies on the paper towel and leave them for several hours.

4. Check the pennies after one, three, and five hours, and note any changes in color.

Evaluation questions:

- ◆ What were the results?
- ◆ Which coatings (if any) protected the pennies?
- ◆ How else could you have protected the pennies?
- ◆ What did this experiment teach you about chemical reactions?

MECHANICAL ENGINEERING

Mechanical engineers touch almost every aspect of technology. They create machines, products, and technological systems that benefit society in many ways. Anything that has moving parts was designed with help from a mechanical engineer.

Weather Vane

A weather vane is a simple machine that shows which way the wind is blowing. It's a good example of a machine with moving parts.

Materials:

- Wooden block
- Spool
- Glue
- Coat-hanger wire
- Plastic straw
- Plastic bottle
- Tape

Instructions:

1. On the wooden block, mark compass directions (north, northeast, east, etc.).

2. Glue the spool in the center of the block.

3. Cut a triangle from a flat area of the plastic bottle, and tape it to the middle of the straw.

4. Place the straw in the hole in the spool. Stick a straight piece of coat-hanger wire through the straw and into the spool. The wire should be long enough to stick out the top of the straw.

5. Place the weather vane outdoors with the "north" mark on the base facing north.

6. Create a chart to show the wind direction at the same time every day. Remember that the wind direction is where the wind is blowing *from*.

Evaluation questions:

- How accurate is your weather vane? How could you make it more accurate?

- Are the moving parts likely to wear out? If so, how could you protect them?

- What other problems might happen with the weather vane? How could you prevent them?
- How does your weather vane compare with "real" weather vanes and windsocks?

Pinewood Derby Experiments

You've probably built and raced pinewood derby cars as a Cub Scout or Webelos Scout. You can also use pinewood derby cars to learn about principles of mechanical engineering.

> Some of these modifications will disqualify your car from an actual pinewood derby race!

Build a pinewood derby car (or use one from a previous race).

Make modifications like these, and test the car to see how the modifications change its speed:

- Add weight to the car or reduce the car's weight.
- Move the center of gravity from the back to the front.
- Carve the car's body to make it more aerodynamic.
- Add graphite to the wheels to reduce friction.
- Move the axles farther apart or closer together.
- Sand down the wheels so less of their surface touches the track.

Evaluation questions:

- Which changes made the most difference? Which ones didn't make much difference at all?
- How else could you modify the car to make it go faster?
- How do the principles you learned apply to actual cars and trucks?

FIX IT

SNAPSHOT OF ADVENTURE

As a Webelos Scout, you are old enough to help out around the house. Besides doing everyday tasks like picking up after yourself, you can help your family in many other ways. In the Fix It adventure, you will learn how things around your house work—and how you can make them better. Then,  the next time your lights go out, your sink clogs, or your bike tire goes flat, you'll be able to say, "I can fix it!"

REQUIREMENT

Do all of these:

Approved by

1. Put a Fix It Toolbox together. Describe what each item in your toolbox can be used for. Show how to use three of the tools safely.

   _____

2. Be Ready. With the help of an adult in your family, do the following:

   A. Locate the electrical panel in your home. Determine if the electrical panel has fuses or breakers.

   _____

   B. Determine what sort of fuel is used to heat your home.

   _____

   C. Learn what you would do to shut off the water for a sink, a toilet, a washing machine, or a water heater. If there is a main shut-off valve for your home, show where it is located.

   _____

3. Describe to your Webelos den leader how to fix or make safe the following circumstances with help from an adult:

A. A toilet is overflowing. _____

B. The kitchen sink is clogged. _____

C. A circuit breaker tripped, causing some of the lights to go out. _____

4. Let's Fix It. Select and do eight of the following. You will need an adult's supervision for each of these Fix It projects:

A. Show how to change a light bulb in a lamp or fixture. Determine the type of light bulb and how to properly dispose of it. _____

B. Fix a squeaky door or cabinet hinge. _____

C. Tighten a loose handle or knob on a cabinet or a piece of furniture. _____

D. Demonstrate how to stop a toilet from running. _____

E. Replace a furnace filter. _____

F. Wash a car. _____

G. Check the oil level and tire pressure in a car. _____

H. Show how to replace a bulb in a taillight, turn signal, or parking light, or replace a headlight in a car. _____

I. Help an adult change a tire on a car. _____

J. Make a repair to a bicycle, such as adjusting or lubricating the chain, inflating the tires, fixing a flat, or adjusting the seat or handlebars. _____

K. Replace the wheels on a skateboard, a scooter, or a pair of inline skates. _____

L. Help an adult prepare and paint a room. _____

M. Help an adult replace or repair a wall or floor tile. _____

N. Help an adult install or repair a window or door lock. _____

O. Help an adult fix a slow or clogged sink drain. _____

P. Help an adult install or repair a mailbox. _____

Q. Change the battery in a smoke detector or a carbon monoxide detector, and test its operation. _____

R. Help an adult fix a leaky faucet. _____

S. Find wall studs, and help an adult hang a curtain rod or a picture. _____

T. Take an old item, such as a small piece of furniture, a broken toy, or a picture frame, and rebuild and/or refinish it. Show your work to an adult or your Webelos leader. _____

U. Do a Fix It project agreed upon with your parent or guardian. _____

REQUIREMENT 1 | Put a Fix It Toolbox together.
Describe what each item in your toolbox can be used
for. Show how to use three of the tools safely.

Fixing things can be fun. What's not so much fun is having to search for the tools you need. If you keep your basic tools together, you can take care of many handyman jobs quickly and easily.

A basic handyman toolbox might include the following:

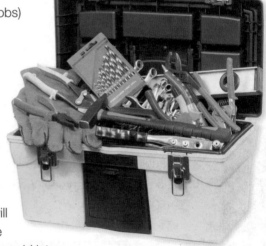

♦ Small and medium slotted screwdrivers

♦ Small and medium Philips screwdrivers

♦ A hammer (a 12- or 16-ounce hammer will handle most jobs)

♦ Scissors

♦ Needle-nose pliers

♦ A roll of duct tape

♦ A measuring tape

♦ An assortment of small nails and screws

♦ A flashlight

♦ Paper and pencil

Choose a box or bag that will hold all your tools. Leave a little space for tools you may want to add later.

A Scout is helpful. Learning how to safely help your family with repairs is a great way to pitch in at home.

REQUIREMENT 2A | Locate the electrical panel in your home. Determine if the electrical panel has fuses or breakers.

All the electricity your home uses comes in on a single line. (If you look outside, you may be able to see where this line enters your home near the electric meter.) Once inside, the electricity goes to a nearby electrical panel, where it is divided into separate circuits. There might be circuits for the washing machine, the refrigerator, the air conditioner, the electricity for each room, and so forth.

To prevent a power overload, which could cause a fire, each circuit is equipped with either a fuse or a circuit breaker. If too much power goes through the circuit, the fuse burns out or the breaker trips (switches off).

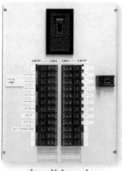

circuit breaker   fuse

> Before working on a circuit's wiring or any electrical task, an adult should always shut off the power by removing the fuse or shutting off the breaker. Scouts should not work with electricity without direct adult supervision.

Your home uses one or more energy sources to generate heat. Common sources include electricity, natural gas, propane, and fuel oil. Others include wood and geothermal energy. Ask your parent what power source or sources your home uses, and find out where heating appliances like the furnace are located.

Wood stove

Radiator

Heat pump

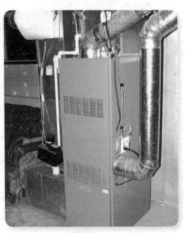
Furnace

When a sink, toilet, or washing machine overflows or a pipe breaks, it's important to shut off the water as quickly as possible. There should be a shut-off valve near where the water supply enters your home.

There should also be a shut-off valve near each sink, toilet, and other appliance that uses water, including the water heater. Your washing machine may have two valves, one for cold water and one for hot. Some shut-off valves have handles like a faucet. Others have levers.

Walk around your house with an adult and find all the shut-off valves. Turn one off and on to see how it works.

REQUIREMENT 3A | A toilet is overflowing.

Have you ever seen a toilet overflow? That can be a messy situation, but you can usually unclog it with a plunger.

First, tell an adult what has happened. Then, help as they do the repair. Turn the water supply off so no more water can enter the toilet. Then, place the rubber bottom of the plunger over the hole in the bottom of the bowl. Push down and pull up several times until the toilet empties. The suction the plunger creates should break up the clog so it can go down the drain. (It helps if the bowl is half full of water.)

Simple clogs will get cleared this way. If the plunger doesn't work, your family may have to get a plumber to unclog the toilet.

To prevent future clogs, only put human waste and toilet paper in the toilet.

REQUIREMENT 3B | The kitchen sink is clogged.

If the kitchen sink is clogged, tell an adult. You can unclog a kitchen sink with a plunger the same way you unclog a toilet. If you have a double sink, put a stopper in the second sink. Otherwise, you won't be able to create suction.

Many clogs happen because people put the wrong things in their garbage disposals. Don't try to grind up potato peels, meat, uncooked pasta or rice, or stringy vegetables like celery. After using the garbage disposal, let the water run another 15 seconds to flush the food waste. Never put your hand inside the garbage disposal.

If some, but not all, of your lights go out, you have lost power on a single circuit, as described in requirement 2a. With an adult, go to the electrical panel and look for the breaker for that circuit. If the circuits aren't labeled, you'll have to do a little detective work and look for a breaker that has tripped. A tripped breaker is usually easy to spot because it will be switched in the opposite direction from the other breakers.

To reset a tripped breaker, simply switch it back on as you would a light switch. You can now check the lights to see if they work. If the breaker trips again, your parent or guardian should call an electrician.

REQUIREMENT 4A | Show how to change a light bulb in a lamp or fixture. Determine the type of light bulb and how to properly dispose of it.

When your parents, grandparents, and great-grandparents were your age, most people used the incandescent light bulb in their homes. Today, people can choose from many types of light bulbs.

Here are the three most common types:

♦ **Incandescent bulbs.** These bulbs produce light by heating a tiny filament until it glows. Incandescent bulbs are cheap, but most of their energy is turned into heat, not light. That's why the most inefficient versions are no longer sold in the United States.

♦ **Compact fluorescent (CFL) bulbs.** These bulbs produce light by using a mixture of argon and mercury to excite a fluorescent coating inside the glass. The same basic technology is used in the long fluorescent tubes found in classrooms, stores, and offices. CFL bulbs use 75 percent less energy than incandescent bulbs.

◆ **Light-emitting diode (LED) bulbs.** These bulbs contain a computer chip that generates photons that illuminate the bulb. They use even less energy than CFL bulbs and can last for 20 years or more. They are also more expensive than CFL bulbs.

You can usually identify the type of bulb by how it looks, as the pictures here show. Sometimes, however, CFL and LED bulbs are made to look more like incandescent bulbs, so you might need to check for a label printed on the bulb.

Changing a light bulb is a very simple task. However, you should still follow the same basic safety practices whenever you handle any electrical device or appliance.

First, turn off the switch or pull the plug. Make sure the old bulb has cooled off before you touch it. Carefully unscrew the old bulb and lay it somewhere that it won't break. Replace the bulb with a new bulb that doesn't exceed the light fixture's maximum wattage. Turn on the switch or plug the fixture back in to test the light.

If the bulb is in a hard-to-reach location, ask for help before you climb a stepladder or crawl behind furniture to reach it.

Discarding Light Bulbs

If the old bulb is incandescent, you can discard it in the trash. If it is a CFL bulb, it should be properly recycled because it contains a small amount of mercury. Check with your local recycling center for more information. The recycling center may also have a plan in place for accepting LED bulbs.

REQUIREMENT 4B | Fix a squeaky door or cabinet hinge.

When a door or cabinet hinge squeaks, you can silence it with machine oil or spray lubricant oil. Spray or squirt a little oil into the hinge at several spots, being careful not to get it on the woodwork. Move the hinge back and forth a few times to distribute the oil. Wipe off any excess oil with a rag.

REQUIREMENT 4C | Tighten a loose handle or knob on a cabinet or a piece of furniture.

The knobs and handles on cabinets and other pieces of furniture are usually held on with screws. Over time, those screws can work loose. The fix is easy. Hold the knob or handle with one hand while you use a screwdriver in the other hand to tighten the screw.

Have your ever thought about what happens when you push down the handle to flush a toilet? It's actually quite simple. When you depress the handle, a chain lifts a stopper called the flush valve in the bottom of the toilet tank. All the water in the tank drains into the bowl, causing the bowl to empty into the sewer pipe. The filler valve then refills the tank to get ready for the next flush.

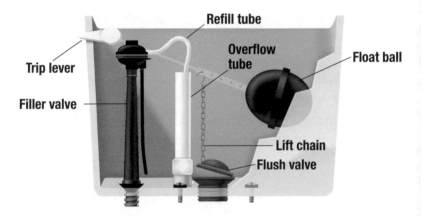

If a toilet is running constantly, the flush valve is letting water through. That usually happens because it didn't fall back into place.

To stop the water from running, do the following:

- Remove the top of the toilet tank, and place the cover out of your way on the floor. Be careful because it is breakable.

- Find the flush valve and position it so it covers the hole. The tank should begin filling right away.

- Carefully replace the cover on the top of the tank.

A toilet can also run if the flush valve is worn out, if the lift chain is too short, or if part of the lift chain gets caught or tangled. An adult can help you fix these problems.

REQUIREMENT 4E | Replace a furnace filter.

Besides keeping your home at a comfortable temperature, your furnace and air conditioner remove dust and other impurities from the air by trapping them in a special filter. This filter should be changed every three months or so. (Note: Some furnaces have permanent filters that are designed to be washed instead of replaced.)

To replace the filter, do the following:

* Turn off the heater or air conditioner if it is running.

* Go to your furnace and look for an access door. It may be near the floor or between the air-intake duct and the furnace itself.

* Open the door. Note exactly how the filter is installed, including which way the arrows point. (These arrows indicate which way the air flows through the filter.)

* Remove the filter, and replace it with one of the same size and type. Be sure the arrows point in the right direction.

* Shut the access door, and turn the heater or air conditioner back on.

* Dispose of the old filter. If it's very dirty, put it in a trash bag before carrying it through the house.

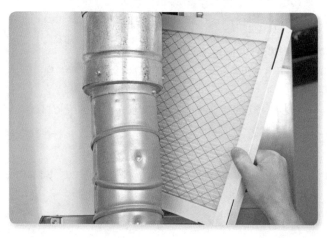

REQUIREMENT 4F | Wash a car.

Washing a car protects the car's finish and helps the car look nicer. It's also a great way for you to cool off on a hot day.

Before you get started, gather your materials: detergent designed for washing cars, a bucket, a soft sponge for scrubbing, rags for drying, and a hose with an automatic shut-off valve (so you won't waste water). Make sure you're not wearing anything that could scratch the car's paint, like a belt buckle or wristwatch. And close the car windows!

Mix up some soapy water in the bucket. Rinse the car with plain water to remove loose dirt. Start washing the top of the car and work down so the suds and dirty water won't streak areas you have already washed. Do a small area—about 3 feet square—at a time. Then rinse by spraying.

You can let the car drip dry, but wiping it dry with a clean rag prevents water spots. Once you're finished, clean the windows inside and out with window cleaner.

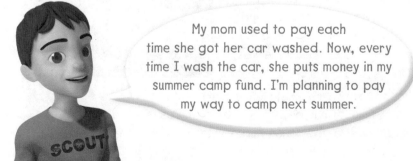

My mom used to pay each time she got her car washed. Now, every time I wash the car, she puts money in my summer camp fund. I'm planning to pay my way to camp next summer.

Oil allows the parts of a car's engine to move easily. It also carries away little bits of metal and other impurities that can damage the engine. That's why it's important to have enough oil in the engine at all times.

Checking the oil level is easy. When the engine is cool, have an adult open the hood and insert the prop rod (if there is one) to hold the hood up. The adult can also help you find the oil dipstick, the metal rod you use to check the oil.

Remove the oil dipstick and wipe it clean. Then, put it back in and pull it out again. Look at the markings near the tip. If the oil level is below the "add" or "min" line, the car needs oil. Put the dipstick back in, and have an adult add some oil to the crankcase.

It's also important to have the right amount of air in a car's tires (including the spare tire in the trunk). That amount, measured in pounds per square inch (PSI), is shown on each tire's sidewall and in the owner's manual. Having the right amount of air makes the tires last longer and saves on fuel costs.

You will need a tire gauge to check tire pressure. When the tires are cool, take the cap off a tire's valve stem. Push the tire gauge hard against the valve. The gauge will show the tire's pressure. If the tire needs more air, tell the car's owner.

Lights on the front and back of a car make driving safer. They are also required by law.

On many cars, the rear lights can be replaced from inside the trunk. See the owner's manual for instructions, because taillight bulbs and installation methods aren't the same for all cars.

Headlights take a little more work and may require special tools. Handle the new bulb only while wearing gloves, or the bulb may burn out faster. Bulbs are sensitive to the oils on your fingers. Because headlights and headlight bulbs aren't the same for all cars, follow the directions in the owner's manual, and have an adult advise you on changing a headlight.

Sooner or later, every driver has a flat tire. That's why knowing how to change a tire is important.

Before you try to change a tire, you must do two things. First, make sure an adult is with you. Second, carefully read the instructions in the owner's manual and make sure you understand them.

> **People talk about changing a tire, but you're actually changing the whole wheel!**

Follow these steps to change a tire:

- Make sure the car is on level ground and a solid surface. Remove the spare tire, jack, and lug wrench from the trunk.

- Set the parking brake as tightly as you can.

- Have an adult put the car in park (if it has an automatic transmission) or first gear (if it has a manual transmission).

- Put wedges or chocks in front of and behind the wheel that is diagonally opposite from the tire you are going to change. For example, if you are changing the back right tire, chock the front left tire.

- Remove the hubcap or wheel cover if one is present. To do this, pry it off with the pointed end of the lug wrench.

- Using the lug wrench, loosen the nuts that hold the wheel on the axle. You may need an adult's help with this. Loosen the nuts about one turn.

- Place the jack under the side of the car near the flat tire, as explained in the owner's manual. If the jack is not placed properly under the car, you could damage the car when you jack it up. It could even fall off the jack and injure you.

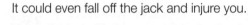

- Using the jack, lift the car so that the flat tire clears the ground.

- Remove the lug nuts. Set them inside the hub cap or somewhere else safe so they don't roll away.

- With an adult's help, remove the flat tire, and replace it with the spare.

- Put the lug nuts back on, and tighten them as much as you can with your fingers.

- Lower the car with the jack until the jack is free of the car.

- Using the lug wrench, tighten one nut as tight as you can. Next, tighten the nut opposite the first one. Continue working back and forth until all the nuts are tight.

- If there's a hubcap or wheel cover, fit it back into its brackets and push it into place.

- Put the jack, lug wrench, and flat tire in the trunk of the car.

The job is done, but the flat tire still needs to be fixed or replaced! Don't delay; many cars have temporary or "doughnut" spares that are only intended for driving to the repair shop.

REQUIREMENT 4J | Make a repair to a bicycle, such as adjusting or lubricating the chain, inflating the tires, fixing a flat, or adjusting the seat or handlebars.

A bicycle is a lot simpler to maintain than a car. But it is a machine, too, so it needs to be taken care of just as a car does.

Adjusting a Bike Chain

If the chain needs tightening, turn the bicycle upside down. Loosen the two axle nuts on the rear wheel with a wrench. (A combination or socket wrench is best so that you don't wear down the nuts over time.) If the bicycle has a coaster brake, loosen the brake arm mounting nuts, too. Now, pull the wheel back until the chain has about a half-inch of play in its center. Tighten the axle nut on the chain side. Make sure that the wheel is centered between the chain stays. Then, tighten the other axle nut and the coaster brake arm mounting nuts.

Lubricating a Bicycle Chain

Oil prevents rust and helps to keep a bicycle running smoothly. To lubricate the chain, turn the bicycle upside down. While using the pedals to make the crank turn, drip lightweight oil on the chain. The oil will spread over the chain as you turn the crank. When all the links of the chain have a light coating of oil, wipe any extra oil from the chain and sprocket with a clean rag.

Inflating the Tires

A bicycle's tires should be kept at the correct pressure. The pressure may be stamped on the side of the tire. If it isn't, check the owner's manual. Use a bicycle tire gauge to check the pressure. Use a hand pump to add as much air as

you need. Some bicycle pumps have a tire gauge built in.

Be sure the pump you use is designed for the valves you have. Some bicycle tires use the same Schrader valves as car tires; others use Presta valves. (Presta valves have a small nut at the end that locks the valve; be sure to loosen this nut before inflating.) Tires with Presta valves require higher pressure than a car tire gauge can read, so you will need a tire gauge designed for bikes.

Presta valve   **Schrader valve**

Fixing a Flat

To fix a flat tire, you will need a tire repair kit. Some kits have a scraper or sandpaper, patches, and cement. Other kits have patches that don't need cement.

Take the wheel off the bicycle, and then remove the tire and tube from the wheel. Taking off the tire can be tricky. You might have to use tools called tire levers to pry the tire off. Ask an adult to help you the first time if you have trouble.

Once the tube is free, examine it to find the leak. If you can't see where the hole in the tube is, pump air into the tube and dunk it into a tub of water. Bubbles will show where the air is escaping. Dry off the area around the hole. Use the scraper or sandpaper to rough up

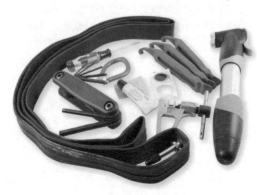

the tube around the hole. If your repair kit includes cement, put a light coating of cement around the hole, and quickly wipe it off. Then, put on another coat of cement, and let it get tacky. (Glue-less patches don't need cement.)

Remove the coating from a patch, and smooth the patch over the hole. Press the patch hard to spread the cement evenly and make a tight seal.

Put the tube back in the tire, and position the tire carefully on the wheel. Be sure the valve stem goes straight through the hole in the wheel and doesn't tilt. Partially inflate the tire, mount the wheel on the bike, and then finish inflating it.

Adjusting the Seat and Handlebars

To adjust the seat or handlebars of your bike, all you need is the right wrench. For some bikes, you'll need a combination wrench; for others, you'll need an Allen wrench. To change the height of the seat, loosen the bolt that keeps the seat post tight in the frame, and then raise or lower the seat post to the height you need. Make sure that the seat post goes at least 2 inches into the frame.

You can also raise and lower the handlebars on your bike and rotate them to make the handles easier to reach. Look at your bike and find the bolts that control these adjustments. Loosen the bolts to make the adjustments. As with the seat post, make sure the handlebar stem goes at least 2 inches into the frame.

How do you know the seat and handlebars are in the right position? When you stand on a pedal, that leg should be slightly bent. When you hold the handlebars, your elbows should be slightly bent, and your shoulders should be relaxed.

Sometimes the wheels or trucks on skateboards, scooters, or skates need to be replaced. It can also be fun to customize your skates or board with new wheels.

You should be able to replace them with compatible wheels and basic tools. Be sure to get help from an expert at your local skate shop or a knowledgeable adult. Your skateboard and skates will be safer and more fun when everything is in working order.

REQUIREMENT 4L | Help an adult prepare and paint a room.

Nothing improves the look of a room more than a fresh coat of paint. You can get information about painting where you purchase paint and supplies, but here are the basic steps:

- ◆ **Clean the walls.** Wipe down the walls with a sponge dipped in water and a little dishwashing liquid. Then, wipe the walls down again with clean water.

- ◆ **Apply painter's tape.** Place painter's tape along the edges of the ceiling, the tops of the baseboards, and the sides of door and window frames. This will keep the wall paint off those surfaces.

- ◆ **Cut in around the edges.** Use a short trim brush to paint a 3-inch strip at the top and the bottom of each wall, around windows and doors, and in the corners—anywhere a paint roller can't reach.

- ◆ **Roll the walls.** Using a paint roller, apply paint starting in one corner. Roll a W that measures about 3 feet by 3 feet, and fill it in. Continue in sections along that wall, and then do the same thing on the other walls.

- ◆ **Apply painter's tape again.** Once the walls are completely dry, remove all the painter's tape. Then, place new tape on the walls where they meet the baseboards and door and window frames. This will keep the trim paint off those surfaces.

- ◆ **Paint the trim.** Paint the baseboards, door frames, and molding with an angled trim brush.

To make sure paint goes just where you want it to, cover the floor (and any furniture you can't move out of the room) with plastic sheeting. Each time you finish a coat of paint, wash your brush or roller thoroughly, and securely close the paint can.

You can replace a ceramic tile by following these steps:

* Remove the grout, which seals the joints between the tiles.

* Break up the old tile with a hammer and chisel. (Be sure to wear gloves and safety glasses.)

* Remove the old tile and all the mortar underneath.

* Apply a new layer of mortar in the empty space.

* Set the replacement tile in place and re-grout the joints.

If a tile is loose and has broken, you may be able to glue it back together and reuse it.

REQUIREMENT 4N | Help an adult install or repair a window or door lock.

Window and door locks keep your home safe from intruders and prevent the wind from blowing windows and doors open. When you buy a new lock, it should come with instructions. Follow those instructions to install it.

REQUIREMENT 4O | Help an adult fix a slow or clogged sink drain.

A drain trap is a J-shaped piece of pipe in a sink drain that creates a low spot to hold water. The trap keeps gas from the sewer from coming into the house. Sometimes it clogs and must be taken off and cleaned out.

To clean a trap, first put down plastic sheeting or newspaper below the trap. The trap is full of water, so protect the area beneath the sink from spills. Use a pan to catch any drips.

Use a large pipe wrench to loosen the two screw collars that hold the trap. They have right-hand threads, which means that you turn them clockwise (the direction a clock's hands move) to tighten them. You will need to turn them the other way (counterclockwise) to unscrew them. They might be tight to start with, so you will need help from an adult with this job.

After each collar has been unscrewed two or three turns with the pipe wrench, you can probably continue by hand. Be careful; the trap is full of water, and other refuse that you won't want to spill. Unscrew the collars with one hand while holding the trap in the other hand so it won't fall off when the collars are completely loosened. Now you can lift out the trap.

HOW TO CLEAN A DRAIN TRAP

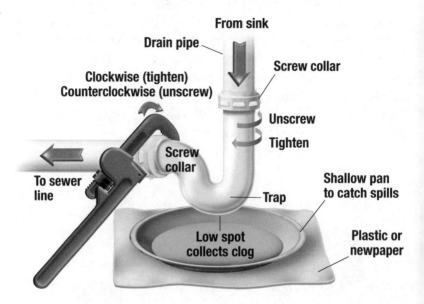

From sink

Drain pipe

Screw collar

Clockwise (tighten)
Counterclockwise (unscrew)

Unscrew

Tighten

Screw collar

To sewer line

Trap

Shallow pan to catch spills

Low spot collects clog

Plastic or newpaper

Next, remove the rubber seals. If they show signs of corrosion, you will need to replace them with new ones. Carefully place the trap in the pan so it won't spill, and carry it to the trash. The water can be poured into another drain, but the sludge and solid material should go in the trash. Flush out the trap outdoors with a hose.

Reverse the steps to replace the trap. Turn both collars at least two turns by hand to make sure the threads are matched up, and then make them as tight as you can with the pipe wrench. An adult should do the final tightening job to make the joints as leakproof as possible. Run some water in the sink to check for leaks. If you see any drips, tighten the screw collars more, or remove the trap and replace the rubber seals before putting it back.

REQUIREMENT 4P | Help an adult install or repair a mailbox.

Whether your mailbox is attached to your house or sits on a post near the road, it needs to be in good condition to keep your mail safe and dry. If you purchase a new mailbox, it will come with instructions. Follow those instructions to install it. If you need to repair your mailbox, ask an adult to help you figure out what to do.

REQUIREMENT 4Q | Change the battery in a smoke detector or a carbon monoxide detector, and test its operation.

Every home should have smoke detectors in the kitchen and bedroom areas and carbon monoxide detectors in the bedroom areas. If your home has more than one floor, it should have detectors on each floor. (Carbon monoxide is an odorless gas that can kill you if you breathe it in.)

> My dad changes our smoke-detector batteries when daylight saving time begins and ends. That's an easy way to remember to change the batteries.

Many smoke detectors and carbon monoxide detectors run on batteries, and all of them have test buttons. It's a good idea to check your detectors regularly—at least twice a year—by pressing the test buttons. If a detector doesn't work, replace the battery with a new one.

If a detector is mounted on the ceiling, you will need a stepladder to access it.

Follow these safety rules when using a ladder:

- ◆ Be sure the ladder's legs are locked into place.
- ◆ Always keep three points of contact with the ladder (two hands and a foot or two feet and a hand) when climbing.
- ◆ Always face the ladder when climbing.
- ◆ Never climb onto the top step of the ladder.
- ◆ Never lean to one side. Keep at least one shoulder between the sides of the ladder.
- ◆ Have an adult hold the ladder while you are using it.

Most faucets include washers and O-rings to prevent water from leaking when the faucet is shut off. Over time, those washers and O-rings can wear out. Every faucet is different, but you can follow these general steps to repair a leaky faucet:

+ Shut off the water to the faucet.
+ Remove the faucet handle and pull out the stem.
+ Remove and replace all the washers and O-rings you find.
+ Replace the stem and faucet handle.
+ Turn on the water.

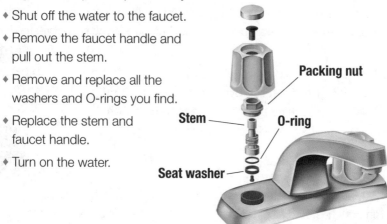

Packing nut

Stem

O-ring

Seat washer

In most homes, the walls are made of wallboard that is nailed onto vertical wooden studs. Wallboard isn't sturdy enough to support things like heavy pictures, curtain rods, shelves, and wall-mounted televisions. They need to be attached directly to a stud.

The best way to locate studs is with an electronic stud finder like the one shown on this page. The stud finder will beep as it passes over the edge of the stud. Mark each edge with a pencil, and you'll know where you can safely drive a nail or a screw.

REQUIREMENT 4T | Take an old item, such as a small piece of furniture, a broken toy, or a picture frame, and rebuild and/or refinish it. Show your work to an adult or your Webelos leader.

Somewhere around your house, there is probably a broken toy, a picture frame, or a piece of furniture that you could make as good as new (or even better!) with a little work. Talk with your parent or guardian about what you can do to rebuild or refinish the item you choose. Be sure to take before and after pictures to show the progress you make.

REQUIREMENT 4U | Do a Fix it project agreed upon with your parent or guardian.

There are many other Fix It projects you could do around your home, from fixing a leaky garden hose to replacing the roof on a doghouse. Use the skills you've learned in this adventure to do a Fix It project agreed upon with your parent or guardian. And be on the lookout for other ways to help out around the house after you complete this adventure. Remember: you can fix it!

GAME DESIGN

SNAPSHOT OF ADVENTURE

Games are fun! In this adventure, you'll learn the elements of games and what makes them entertaining. You'll also get to create your own game and teach an adult or another Scout

how to play it. When it comes time to teach, be patient. Some people didn't grow up playing cool games, so it may take them a while to learn how to play!

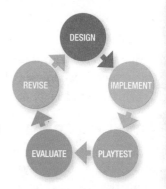

Games can be simple or complex. So can the elements required for designing your own game. This diagram shows the big chunks to start you on a simple path to creating a game. Remember that creating a great game

isn't likely to happen on the first try. It's only by testing, evaluating, and making revisions that a designer can discover what works best for a game. (The Game Design merit badge in Boy Scouts will go further in depth if you want to learn more.)

REQUIREMENT

Do all of these: Approved by

1. Decide on the elements for your game.   _____

2. List at least five of the online safety rules that you put into practice while using the Internet on your computer or smartphone. Skip this if your Cyber Chip is current.   _____

3. Create your game.   _____

4. Teach an adult or another Scout how to play your game.   _____

You know that games are fun, but have you ever thought about what makes them fun? Or what makes one game more exciting than another?

To make fun games (which is fun to do!), you need to know about the elements of games. Below are four elements that make up a game. These will get you started on what to include in your game design.

Narrative or Story

The narrative or story is what your game is about. Is your game about being a ship captain and searching for buried treasure? Is it about being a detective and solving a crime? Is it about exploring space or the sea floor? Is it about a sport like snowboard racing or mountain biking?

Decide early on what your game will be about. That way, you can decide what kind of characters to have, what the scenery will look like, and how the game will be played.

Goals and Mechanics

Next, think about your game's goals and mechanics. A game's goals include how players win and what they must do to advance from one level to the next.

As part of setting the goals, you must also decide how players compete. Is a single player competing against himself or herself? Are groups of players competing on teams? Or are many individual players competing against each other to win?

A game's mechanics include how players move around and interact with the game. What are players doing to advance in the game? There might be a method for scoring points, a race to the finish, a structure to build, or another way for a player to move ahead.

Aesthetics

Aesthetics is a fancy word that describes how your game will look. Do you want your characters to walk in a forest of palm trees or along a busy street? Will your game be very colorful or just have a few colors in it? What will your characters see, feel, smell, and taste?

Medium

The medium is the format of the game and the materials needed to play it. Decide what materials you need to make your game possible. The medium can be any kind of material from paper and pencils to smartphones and computers. Options for your game's medium include physical games and sports, board games, tile games, dice games, party games, cards, and electronic or digital games.

On this page, write down ideas for the basic elements of your game. Use additional paper or a separate notebook, if needed, and jot down any ideas that come to mind. Then review your ideas and decide on the ones you like best. Once you've settled on your basic idea and structure, you can add more details. What will the characters be called? How many levels will there be? How will players earn points?

MY GAME

Narrative/Story _____

_____

Goals/Mechanics _____

_____

Aesthetics _____

Medium _____

As you get into game design, you might want to use the Internet to find ideas for your game. The Internet is an extremely useful tool for you to learn new things and find information.

However, some sites do not offer good information. Instead, they try to steal personal information, like your name or phone number, from you. These sites can look like fun places to play games, chat, and watch videos, but they are not what they seem. Since it's not always easy to spot unsafe sites, it's important to only use the Internet with your parent's or guardian's permission. Also, be sure to let a trusted adult know if anything happens online that makes you feel uncomfortable or nervous.

A Scout is trustworthy. Signing—and following—the Internet Safety Pledge is part of being trustworthy online.

INTERNET SAFETY PLEDGE

1. I will tell my trusted adult if anything makes me feel sad, scared, confused, or uncomfortable.

2. I will ask my trusted adult before posting photos or sharing information like my name, address, current location, or phone number.

3. I won't meet face-to-face with anyone I meet in the digital world.

4. I will respect the online property of others.

5. I will always use good "netiquette" and not be rude or mean online.

The Internet Safety Pledge includes simple rules that you can follow to stay safe when using the Internet. Talk with your parent or guardian about additional rules your family may have.

cyber**CHIP**

THIS IS TO CERTIFY THAT THE BEARER

Has read the Internet safety rules at
www.scouting.org/cyberchip.
He knows how to be responsible online
and what to do if he discovers unsafe
Internet practices. He accepts this
responsibility and is hereby
granted Cyber Rights.

CUBMASTER

BOY SCOUTS OF AMERICA

NOTE: In addition to your parents, other adults, like grandparents, teachers, and Scout leaders, can help you stay safe on the Internet.

Once you've designed your game, it's time to actually create it. You can use a variety of resources you have around the house to turn your idea into a real game.

Many games actually start on paper, even if they will use a different medium for the final product. The designers create rough prototypes on paper and have game testers play them. Game testing is an important part of ensuring your game works and achieves its goal. If

designers see that a change needs to be made, they can make the change easily at this stage. After this testing period, the designers have a better idea of how the game should work when they start creating it.

One option for creating a digital game is to use a game designer website or design software. If using an online game designer website, explore the program first so you understand how it works. Then, use it to create your game. Be sure to ask questions if you need help.

Once you're finished creating your game, share your creation with others to enjoy. If possible, share your game with the other members of your den and try their games. Tell them what you liked about their games and ask them for ideas to make your game better.

There are many free or inexpensive online resources for new game designers. With a parent's or guardian's permission, you might try one of the following sites:

www.scratch.mit.edu   **www.yoyogames.com/studio**
www.kodugamelab.com   **www.stencyl.com**
www.gamestarmechanic.com

You can also check out the Game Design merit badge pamphlet available at your local Scout shop or online at **Scoutstuff.org.**

First, explain the game's characters and story, what the point of the game is, and how to play it. Demonstrate for a few minutes and then watch the person play the game.

Because you are the expert on the game, offer advice if the person gets stuck or has questions. But remember that a Scout is courteous and helpful. Instead of criticizing, be polite and patient, because the person you're teaching won't be as familiar with the game as you are.

Note how the players interact with the game. Are there certain places where they get stuck or seem frustrated? Is everyone having a good time? By observing how other players move through the game, you can make changes or improve your game to make it even more fun.

Don't be surprised if you get better at a game when you teach someone else to play it. A cool thing about teaching is that you always learn something yourself at the same time!

INTO THE WILD

SNAPSHOT OF ADVENTURE

Do you wonder what makes the howling, hooting, whistling, and humming sounds you hear at night? Do you wonder where flocks of birds are going when they fly overhead? Do you wonder why rabbits look like statues in the grass or how deer can end up in a city backyard? When you go "into the wild," you will begin to understand some of the mammals,

birds, reptiles, amphibians, and insects that live with us day and night and how they contribute to the world in which we live.

REQUIREMENT

Do six from requirements 1 through 9:   **Approved by**

1. Collect and care for an "insect, amphibian, or reptile zoo." You might have crickets, ants, grasshoppers, a lizard, or a toad. Study them for a while and then let them go. Share your experience with your Webelos den.   _____

2. Set up an aquarium or terrarium. Keep it for at least a month. Share your experience with your Webelos den by showing them photos or drawings of your project or by having them visit to see your project.   _____

3. Watch for birds in your yard, neighborhood, or town for one week. Identify the birds you see, and write down where and when you saw them.   _____

4. Learn about the bird flyways closest to your home. Find out which birds use these flyways.   _____

5. Watch at least four wild creatures (reptiles, amphibians, arachnids, fish, birds, insects, or mammals) in the wild. Describe the kind of place (forest, field, marsh, yard, or park) where you saw them. Tell what they were doing. _____

6. Identify an insect, reptile, bird, or other wild animal that is found only in your area of the country. Tell why it survives in your area. _____

7. Give examples of at least two of the following:

   A. A producer, a consumer, and a decomposer in the food chain of an ecosystem _____

   B. One way humans have changed the balance of nature _____

   C. How you can help protect the balance of nature _____

8. Learn about aquatic ecosystems and wetlands in your area. Talk with your Webelos den leader or family about the important role aquatic ecosystems and wetlands play in supporting life cycles of wildlife and humans, and list three ways you can help. _____

9. Do ONE of the following:

   A. Visit a museum of natural history, a nature center, or a zoo with your family, Webelos den, or pack. Tell what you saw. _____

   B. Create a video of a wild creature doing something interesting, and share it with your family and den. _____

A great way to learn about living creatures is to watch them. Collect some insects or reptiles and keep them in a box, jar, or other container for a few hours. Be sure they are in the shade and that they have plenty of air. Watch them to see how they behave. Then release them and see what they do next.

Make notes on this page and share your experience with your Webelos den.

My Zoo

Creature 1 _____

Where I Found It _____

Where I Kept It _____

What It Did in the Zoo _____

What It Did When Released _____

Creature 2 _____

Where I Found It _____

Where I Kept It _____

What It Did in the Zoo _____

What It Did When Released _____

_____

Creature 3 _____

Where I Found It _____

Where I Kept It _____

What It Did in the Zoo _____

What It Did When Released _____

State and local laws control what wild creatures can be
captured. Check with a local nature center before you do
this requirement.

Here are tips on finding different insects and reptiles. Whatever you
catch, keep it in a container covered with wire mesh or a lid with air
holes punched in it. Don't let your creatures escape into your house
before you have a chance to release them!

Crickets

Put an inch of moist soil in a small plastic jar or can. Sink the jar or can in the ground so its rim is level with the surface. Put a sweet, gooey mixture in the jar. This might be a mixture of two parts molasses and one part water or some mashed-up overripe fruit. The sweet smell will attract crickets and beetles, and they will tumble in.

You can also look for crickets under rocks and logs. You have to be quick to catch one because they're good jumpers.

Ants

Ants are easy to find because they live in anthills or nests under rocks. Once you find an anthill, stir it gently with a stick or trowel. When the ants come out to investigate, guide them into a jar with a piece of cardboard. Then, put some dirt from the anthill in with them.

Ants like to work in the dark, so keep your jar covered when you aren't watching them.

 Caution: Be sure to avoid fire ants and other biting ants!

Grasshoppers and Walkingsticks

Grasshoppers are usually found on grass and in grain fields. Look for walkingsticks on trees. If you're really quick, you can pick up these insects with your fingers, but a collecting net like the one shown below would work better.

You can also catch many types of insects by using a stick to shake a bush so they will fall off. Hold an umbrella upside down under the bush or spread a large cloth on the ground to catch them. To catch moths and other insects at night, hang up an old sheet and shine a flashlight on it. The insects will be attracted to the light, and you can scoop them off the sheet.

Frogs, Toads, and Lizards

Amphibians, such as frogs and toads, can often be found in wet areas like the banks of streams or ponds. Lizards like to hide under rocks and piles of firewood in moist, undisturbed areas. (So do snakes, so be careful!) At night, lizards can be found around porch lights, which attract the insects they like to eat. In cool weather, they like

to sun themselves on rocks and dead logs. Sneak up on them slowly and capture them with a net. Be sure not to hurt frogs, toads, and lizards by squeezing them. Instead, gently transfer them from your net to a container.

Turtles

You can find turtles around small ponds where the ground is damp and there are plenty of places to hide. Dig a trap that's about 10 inches across and 10 inches deep with steep sides. Put some bait like lettuce in the bottom of the trap and a little more bait around the rim. Eventually, a turtle should venture into the trap and be unable to get out. Grasp the turtle gently by the sides of its shell.

Be sure to check the trap frequently and fill it back in with dirt when you're done.

A Scout is kind. Be sure to release animals soon after you capture and study them so they may return to their natural habitat.

Aquariums

An aquarium is a tank that holds fish and other marine creatures. Aquariums can be really fancy, but you can start with just a simple 10-gallon fish tank, which will hold up to six goldfish and a few snails.

Visit a pet store to get started and find out what you need. Besides a tank, water, and fish, you'll need fish food, gravel or soil for the bottom of the tank, a water heater, a filter to keep the water clean, and a light.

Terrariums

A terrarium is a small garden of plants in an enclosed container. You can use a big bottle or jar with a lid on it, or you can turn an aquarium into a terrarium.

Here's one way to make a terrarium that will support plant life for two or three months.

Use a wide-mouthed gallon jar and build a base to fit it so it doesn't roll around. Put in a half-inch of sand or fine gravel. Sprinkle a half-inch of charcoal chips over that. On top of the charcoal, put two cups of rich soil, such as potting soil from a garden center.

Plant small tropical plants that thrive in low light and high humidity, like aluminum plant, flame violet, and artillery plant. Ask about small tropical plants at a garden center.

Mist the plants lightly with water before screwing on the lid. You shouldn't need to water them again because the moisture will circulate in the jar.

Keep the terrarium where it will get indirect sunlight each day. Don't put it in direct sunlight because the container will heat up too much.

If you want a cactus terrarium, it should have a wide open top so moisture can get out instead of staying in. Cactus plants can't take high humidity. Cacti do need water, but not too often. Give them bright, indirect light, and turn the container occasionally so all the plants get light.

Don't fertilize any terrarium plants. If you do, they may outgrow their containers.

REQUIREMENT 3 | Watch for birds in your yard, neighborhood, or town for one week. Identify the birds you see, and write down where and when you saw them.

Birds are among the easiest wild creatures to see because they generally aren't afraid of human beings. You can attract birds to your yard by setting out birdfeeders. You may also want to build a bird nesting box and put it near a window for a close-up view of birds.

Some birds like to eat things like sunflower seed, dried corn, and thistle. Others like suet (hard cakes of animal fat) and peanut butter. Still others like nectar (a mixture of water and sugar), fruit, and even bread crumbs.

Here's what some common birds like to eat:

- ◆ **Seeds:** Cardinals, goldfinches, mourning doves
- ◆ **Suet:** Woodpeckers, chickadees, nuthatches
- ◆ **Nectar:** Hummingbirds
- ◆ **Fruit:** Orioles, mockingbirds

Nectar

Seeds

Fruit

Suet

Borrow a field guide to birds from a library so you can identify the birds you see. With your parent's permission, you can also use websites and smartphone apps to identify birds.

Birds I Identified

_____

_____

_____

_____

_____

_____

One of the moms in my den was a birder—someone who watches birds for a hobby. She said she had more than 250 species of birds on her life list. I didn't even know there were that many kinds of birds!

Some birds, including starlings, blue jays, sparrows, and nighthawks, stay in one area all their lives. Others, including geese, ducks, herons, and hummingbirds, migrate. That means they fly south each fall to warmer places where they spend the winter. They return to nest and live in their northern homes each spring.

Many birds that migrate use regular routes called flyways. There are four main flyways in North America, as shown on the map. You don't have to live on a flyway to see birds moving in the spring and fall. Some will pass over your town in other parts of the country. But most flocks of birds use the flyways.

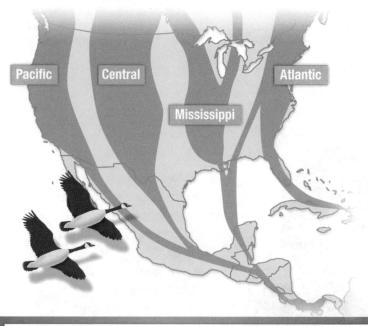

Pacific   Central   Atlantic

Mississippi

The _____ flyway is the flyway that's closest to my home. Birds that use this flyway include _____.

Wherever you live, even in a big city, wild creatures live nearby. Watch four of them and make a record of what you saw.

Wildlife I Saw

Creature 1 _____

Where I Saw It _____

When I Saw It _____

What It Did _____

Creature 2 _____

Where I Saw It _____

When I Saw It _____

What It Did _____

_____

Creature 3 _____

Where I Saw It _____

When I Saw It _____

What It Did _____

_____

Creature 4 _____

Where I Saw It _____

When I Saw It _____

What It Did _____

Here are some tips for observing wild creatures:

- Be as quiet as you can.

- Approach creatures from downwind (with the wind blowing toward you not toward the creature).

- Move slowly and don't make sudden movements.

- Look in places where animals can find food or water.

- Make your observations in the early morning or early evening. Many wild creatures rest during the heat of the day.

- If possible, observe wildlife from a natural or man-made blind, a structure you can hide behind so the creatures can't see you.

Some wild creatures can be found in almost all areas of the country. For example, meadowlarks can be found just about everywhere in the continental United States. Other creatures live in smaller areas.

Here are some birds that live in limited areas within the United States:

- **Anhinga:** swamps and coastal areas in the South
- **Greater roadrunner:** grasslands and woodlands in the Southwest
- **Arctic loon:** Alaska
- **Nene:** Hawaii
- **Black-chinned hummingbird:** the Southwest and inland Pacific Northwest
- **Snowy owl:** states along the Canadian border

Find out from a local nature center or science teacher what wild creatures only live in your part of the country. Learn why that wild creature lives there and not somewhere else.

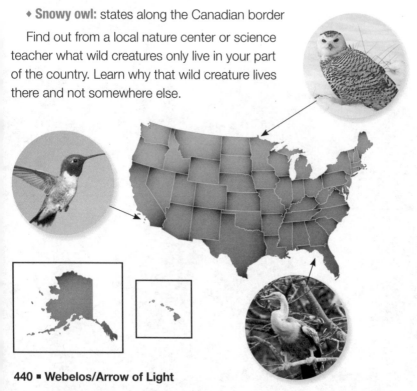

A. A producer, a consumer, and a decomposer in the food chain of an ecosystem

B. One way humans have changed the balance of nature

C. How you can help protect the balance of nature

An ecosystem is a community of plants and animals living in an environment that supplies what they need for life. In an ecosystem, plants and animals depend on their environment and on each other for survival. Energy and food flow through the community in a food chain.

There are many types of ecosystems. For example, forests, deserts, and wetlands all contain different combinations of plants, animals, and environmental characteristics.

Elements of an Ecosystem

Here are the elements of an ecosystem:

+ **The sun:** Without the sun, there would be no life on Earth. The energy of the sun flows through a cycle in the ecosystem. Plants are the first to use this energy.

+ **Producers:** All green plants—trees, shrubs, grasses, flowers, etc.—use the energy of the sun to grow. Plants also take up nutrients and minerals from the soil. The plants produce leaves, bark, fruits, nuts, and seeds that many animals eat.

+ **Consumers:** Animals are consumers. They use the stored energy, nutrients, and minerals in their food to grow and to maintain their health.

+ **Decomposers:** These are the fungi, lichens, bacteria, and insects that break down dead plants and animals. This process returns organic matter and minerals to the soil, making them available to trees and other plants—the producers. Nature is a good recycler.

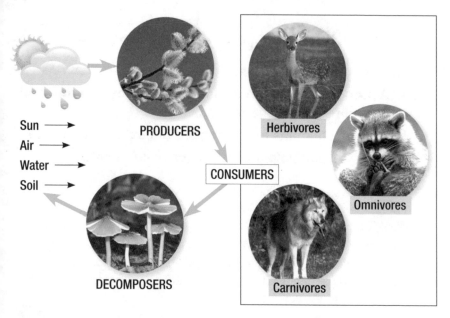

Sun ⟶
Air ⟶
Water ⟶
Soil ⟶

PRODUCERS

CONSUMERS

Herbivores

Omnivores

Carnivores

DECOMPOSERS

You can divide consumers into two categories:

♦ **Primary consumers:** Plant-eating animals, also called herbivores, are called primary consumers because they are the first to benefit by eating the producers. Examples include rabbits, squirrels, deer, seed-eating birds, grasshoppers, and cattle on farms.

♦ **Secondary consumers:** Meat-eating animals, also called carnivores, are called secondary consumers because they benefit from the energy and nutrients stored in their prey, the herbivores. For example, hawks and owls eat mice and rabbits, while mountain lions hunt deer and smaller animals.

	Simplified Examples	
Producer	SEED	GRASS
Consumer	BIRD	HORSE
Secondary Consumers	FOX	WOLF
Decomposer	BACTERIA	FUNGI

Some consumers are called omnivores because they eat both plants and animals. For example, the gray fox hunts rabbits, mice, voles, birds, and insects, but it also eats blackberries, grapes, persimmons, and grass. Human beings (unless they are vegetarians) are omnivores, too.

The Balance of Nature

When you figure out the food chain in an ecosystem, you can see how animals, plants, and their habitat are connected. The ecosystem is in balance when all the necessary parts of its community are present. The ecosystem is out of balance when there is not enough habitat and food for animals to survive.

After some natural events, like a forest fire started by lightning, the original ecosystem may slowly recover. Nature eventually adjusts the balance. The needs and plans of humans often alter the balance of nature quickly and permanently. When people clear forest and brush and turn it into agricultural land, much of the animal life may disappear from the area, except for animals that can adapt to the farming environment. When a huge shopping center is built and surrounded by a paved parking lot, animals cannot adapt to that environment. Pollution of air or water can damage or wipe out an ecosystem.

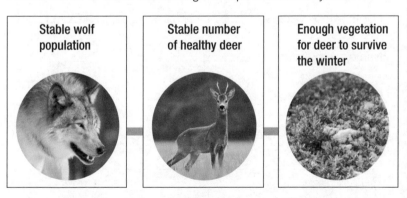

Losing one link in the food chain can upset the balance, too. Here's an example: Wolves hunt deer, and that helps keep the deer population under control. But since wolves also hunt livestock, many ranchers have tried to reduce their numbers. When the wolf population goes down, the deer population goes up because they have fewer natural predators. When that happens, deer begin eating more vegetation than an area can produce. Eventually, overgrazing can cause soil erosion, making it harder for vegetation to grow.

As humans, we can all help maintain the balance of nature. Land developers often plant trees to replace those they cut down for their buildings. When hunters and fishermen buy licenses for their activities, part of the money goes to conservation efforts. Many people volunteer in parks and forests to pick up trash, plant trees, and remove invasive species that crowd out native species. As a Webelos Scout, you can help with those activities. You can also feed native species and conserve natural resources. When feeding native species, be sure to give them appropriate food (such as birdseed instead of table scraps); check with a local nature center for guidelines.

Understanding Ecosystems

Name two producers: _____

Name two consumers: _____

Name two decomposers: _____

Humans have changed the environment for other life forms by

_____

I can protect the balance of nature by

_____

_____

REQUIREMENT 8 | Learn about aquatic ecosystems
and wetlands in your area. Talk with your Webelos
den leader or family about the important role aquatic
ecosystems and wetlands play in supporting life cycles
of wildlife and humans, and list three ways you can help.

Ecosystems don't just occur on dry land. Aquatic ecosystems and
wetlands are very important, too. All living things need water, of course,
and wetlands serve as natural water filters. Rivers and lakes provide
habitat for wildlife and drinking water for human beings. Find out about
the aquatic ecosystems and wetlands in your area, and talk with your
den leader or family about ways you can help protect them.

**Ways I Can Help
Aquatic Ecosystems and Wetlands**

_____

_____

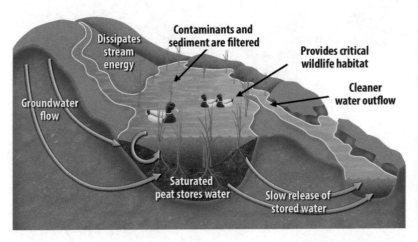

Dissipates
stream
energy

Contaminants and
sediment are filtered

Provides critical
wildlife habitat

Cleaner
water outflow

Groundwater
flow

Saturated
peat stores water

Slow release of
stored water

REQUIREMENT 9A | Visit a museum of natural history, a nature center, or a zoo with your family, Webelos den, or pack. Tell what you saw.

As you've learned, different parts of the country have different plants and animals and face different environmental challenges. The people who know your area of the country best often work at local museums, nature centers, and zoos. Visit one of those places with your family, Webelos den, or pack.

If you've already done other requirements for the Into the Wild adventure, you've probably thought of some questions you would like to ask. Make a list of those questions to ask a staff member or volunteer at the facility you visit.

You may have seen amazing nature videos in school or on television. Now, it's your turn to get behind the camera. For example, you could record the movements of birds, rabbits, or squirrels in your neighborhood or the antics of penguins at a zoo. After you create your video, share it with your family and den.

INTO THE WOODS

SNAPSHOT OF ADVENTURE

Trees and plants play important roles in nature. In this adventure, you will get to learn about the plants and trees in your community by exploring your area on a walk or visit to a local nature center, tree farm, or park.

If you've ever stood beneath a towering redwood or enjoyed the colors of fall leaves or watched pine trees swaying in the wind, you know that trees and plants are beautiful. But they are also important to life on Earth. As you go into the woods in this adventure, you'll learn what trees and plants do for us and for animals and why taking care of them is important to our planet's well-being.

A Scout is reverent. Spending time in nature can provide an opportunity for quiet reflection or prayer.

REQUIREMENT

Do all of these: Approved by

1. Identify two different groups of trees and the parts of a tree.   _____

2. Identify six trees common to the area where you live. Tell whether they are native to your area. Tell how both wildlife and humans use them.   _____

3. Identify six plants common to the area where you live. Tell which animals use them and for what purpose.   _____

4. Visit a nature center, nursery, tree farm, or park, and speak with someone knowledgeable about trees and plants that are native to your area. Explain how plants and trees are important to our ecosystem and how they improve our environment.   _____

5. Develop a plan to care for and then plant at least one plant or tree, either indoors in a pot or outdoors. Tell how this plant or tree helps the environment in which it is planted and what the plant or tree will be used for.   _____

6. Make a list of items in your home that are made from wood and share it with your den. Or with your den, take a walk and identify useful things made from wood.   _____

7. Explain how the growth rings of a tree trunk tell its life story. Describe different types of tree bark and explain what the bark does for the tree.   _____

Unless you live in the desert, on the tundra, or at the top of a very tall mountain, there are probably trees around you—even in the middle of a city. But what kind of trees are they? If you look closely, you will discover that different trees have different characteristics. Some grow very tall, while others grow out as much as they grow up. Some keep their foliage all year round, while others lose their leaves in the fall (often after those leaves have turned brilliant shades of yellow, red, and orange).

Scientists divide most trees into two main groups: coniferous trees and deciduous trees.

Coniferous Trees

Coniferous trees include pines, cedars, firs, and spruces. The seeds in these trees grow in cones, which is where the word "coniferous" comes from. When a cone's scales open up, the seeds fall out, and new trees can take root. Coniferous trees tend to grow tall rather than wide; they have a triangular shape like a Christmas tree.

Evergreens do lose their needles. They just don't lose them all at the same time.

Most coniferous trees are evergreen, meaning they don't lose their leaves (which are called needles) in the fall. However, some coniferous trees, like the bald cypress, do lose their leaves as winter approaches.

Deciduous Trees

Deciduous trees include oaks, maples, poplars, beeches, sycamores, ashes, and many other species. They are called deciduous because they lose their leaves each year.

Instead of having needles, deciduous trees have wide, flat leaves that are good at capturing sunlight. These trees spread out as they grow, and they're often bigger at the top than they are at the bottom. Deciduous trees don't produce cones. Their seeds are contained in nutshells or fruit. Maple trees have special seeds that "fly" to the ground like little helicopters.

A few deciduous trees are actually evergreens. The live oak is an example.

What About Palm Trees?

Palm trees, which are often seen in far southern parts of the United States, don't really fall into either the coniferous or the deciduous category. They don't have cones, and they also don't drop their leaves in the fall.

How a Tree Grows

A tree grows in its roots, trunk, and crown (its top, where all the branches and leaves are). The tree needs food to grow, and its roots and leaves play a part in the process of making food.

> **How far do a tree's roots stretch? A tree's root ball is usually as wide as its branches.**

Crown: The crown is the upper part of the tree, including the branches and leaves. The leaves take in sunlight and use it to make food for the tree in a process called photosynthesis.

Trunk: The trunk is a pathway for water and minerals (food) to move from the soil up through the trunk to the leaves. It grows outward and upward each year. As the trunk grows taller, the crown of the tree grows higher in search of more sunlight. In trees used for lumber, the trunk produces most of the useful wood.

Roots: Roots anchor the tree in the earth. They soak up the water, minerals, and nitrogen from the soil that the leaves need to make food for the tree. A layer of growth cells at the root tips makes new roots each year. Tree roots help slow erosion by holding soil in place. Even when a tree is cut down, the roots may sprout new growth to revive and, perhaps, bring the tree back to life.

Some trees are native to your part of the country and have been growing there for thousands of years. Others, especially those planted in parks and around buildings, may have been imported from other areas. (Some of these are called invasive species; they are pests that tend to crowd out native trees.)

A field guide to trees can help you identify trees in your area. It will show you characteristics that make it easy to tell one kind of tree from another.

When you are looking at trees, take time to look closely at everything. Use a magnifying glass to study tiny details.

Check for:

♦ Type of leaf. Feel it. Is it smooth or rough? Notice the shape.

♦ Leaf edges. Are they smooth or toothed?

♦ Type of bark. Is it smooth, rough, peeling, light, or dark?

♦ Unusual features like thorns, flowers, or berries. Some trees have more than one leaf shape. The sassafras tree has three leaf shapes.

♦ With coniferous trees, notice the length, shape, and grouping of the needles. Spruce needles are sharp and short, with four sides, and they grow separately on the twigs. Pine needles grow in bundles; count the number in a bundle for a clue to the kind of pine it is. Needles of a longleaf pine could be 18 inches long, but jack pine needles are only about 1 inch long.

♦ The size and type of cone or fruit will also provide clues to the identity of the tree. The acorns on most oak trees have small, fairly smooth caps, but bur oak acorns have fringed caps that nearly cover the whole acorn.

How do the trees smell? Some trees, like pines and eucalyptus, give off wonderful scents, especially when the air is moist.

If you look closely, you'll see how trees support other forms of life. Look for woodpecker holes, insects hiding under the bark, mistletoe rooted in the branches, fungi growing on the bark, and the nests of birds and squirrels.

Larger animals use trees, too. Bears mark their territory by clawing and biting tree trunks. Beavers eat tree bark and cut down trees to build dams and homes for themselves. Mountain lions sharpen their claws on trees. Moose, elk, and deer use tree trunks or flexible saplings to rub the velvet off their antlers. They also eat tree bark, leaves, and stems.

Trees Around Me

Name of Tree	Native?	Characteristics	Use

REQUIREMENT 3 | Identify six plants common to the area where you live. Tell which animals use them and for what purpose.

Much like trees, smaller plants and shrubs are important to animals. Bluebirds, catbirds, and mockingbirds eat the red berries of the holly bush. Deer, rabbits, birds, and insects feast on flowers, leaves, fruits, and nuts of both trees and plants. Hummingbirds drink nectar out of flowers. Birds build nests in trees and shrubs.

See what you can learn about the plants in your area. If possible, observe a plant from a distance and watch an animal using it.

Plants Around Me

Name of Plant	Characteristics	Use
_____	_____	_____
_____	_____	_____
_____	_____	_____
_____	_____	_____
_____	_____	_____
_____	_____	_____

An ecosystem is a community of plants and animals living in an environment that supplies what they need for life. Within an ecosystem, tree and plants produce leaves, bark, fruits, nuts, and seeds that many animals eat. They also produce oxygen, which animals need to breathe. In fact, plants and trees produce most of the oxygen on Earth.

Through a process called photosynthesis, plants turn sunlight, water, and carbon dioxide into energy. A byproduct of photosynthesis is oxygen. You know where sunlight and water come from, but where does carbon dioxide come from? It comes from animals and humans every time we breathe out! That's why scientists talk about the oxygen cycle that connects plants and animals.

Atmosphere

Oxygen

Plants create oxygen with photosynthesis

Carbon dioxide

Animals and plants breathe in oxygen

By trapping carbon dioxide, plants and trees keep it out of the atmosphere. That's important because too much carbon dioxide in the atmosphere contributes to climate change.

Plants and trees do some other important things. They stabilize the soil, which prevents erosion, and they provide shade and shelter for animals and humans. They can be harvested to create furniture, building materials, clothing, paper, food, and many other things we use every day.

No plant or tree lives forever. Some die of old age, some get damaged by fire or lightning, and some are cut down to be used for lumber or other purposes. You can help replace lost plants or trees by planting new ones. If you're lucky, you may someday walk beneath the branches of a tree you planted!

A local nursery or garden center can help you select a plant or tree that will grow well in your area. (You wouldn't have much luck growing a palm tree in Minnesota or a Douglas fir in Florida.) It helps to know how much sun the plant or tree will get and what type of soil it will be planted in. Be sure to plant trees in places where they have plenty of room to grow both up and out.

Here are some planting tips:

- Carry seedlings in a bucket or box. Keep the roots damp.

- Place trees at least 6 feet apart. Place plants at least 6 inches apart (but follow the instructions that come with each plant).

- Dig a hole just deep enough to hold the roots. Loosen the sides and bottom of the hole so that tiny roots can push into the soil. The roots should not be stuffed into the hole.

- A seedling should be planted so that its old ground line is about one-quarter inch below the new ground level. (The ground line is the dark mark on the trunk.) Plants should be planted at the same ground level.

- A seedling or other plant should be planted with its trunk straight up. Fill the hole with soil so it is even with the ground. The soil should not be sunken in or mounded up above the ground.

- Press the soil down firmly around the roots to prevent air pockets. If you don't, the tree or plant may die because the air pockets dry out the roots, preventing water and nutrients from reaching them.

- A newly planted seedling needs lots of water, so soak the soil around the seedling with water, and then soak it again if it is planted in the ground.

- If you're planting in a pot, make sure the pot is large enough to allow the plant or tree to grow (at least double the size of the container the plant arrived in). Be sure there are holes in the bottom of the pot to allow excess water to drain and a saucer underneath to catch the water. Place a layer of pebbles in the bottom of the pot to prevent the soil from draining.

- Closely follow the instructions for watering given on any tag or label that comes with the plant or tree. Each type of plant has different watering needs. Be sure to provide water and food as required on a regular basis.

- Cover the ground around the base of a seedling with several inches of mulch—composted leaves, wood chips, grass cuttings, straw, or sawdust. This holds in moisture and helps make the soil richer for the new tree. The mulch should be flat or slope down from the trunk to the ground. Don't make it look like a volcano.

Your plant or tree can help the environment in several ways. Flowering plants provide food for bees and hummingbirds. Fruit and nut trees provide food for wildlife (and people!). Shade trees help keep buildings cooler. Evergreen trees offer shelter from winter winds. All trees provide habitat for wildlife and purify the air by taking in carbon dioxide and releasing oxygen.

Many things in your home are made from wood. In fact, your home itself may be made from wood. If you go into an unfinished attic or basement, you can see some of this wood in the form of studs, joists, and floor boards.

Make a list of everything in your home that is made of wood, or take a walk around your neighborhood or school and look for other wooden things.

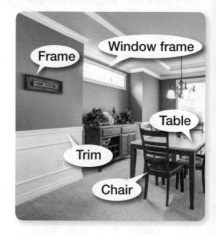

Wood and Plant Uses

♦ Hickory and white ash are used to make baseball bats and tool handles.

♦ Cedar is used to make porches, decks, and shingles for roofs.

♦ Mesquite and hickory chips on cooking fires flavor food.

♦ Paper is made of wood pulp.

♦ Toothpaste contains cellulose gum, which is made from wood fiber.

♦ Cinnamon, nutmeg, and vanilla come from trees.

♦ Some candles are made from the waxy covering of the southern bayberry fruit.

♦ Maple syrup is made from the sap of sugar maples harvested in the early spring.

The Inside Story of a Tree

Inner Bark: Carries food made in the leaves down to the branches, trunk, and roots. It consists of hollow tubes.

Outer Bark: Protects the tree from injuries.

Fire Scar: A tree can be damaged by fire even if it is not burned down. Disease and insects can enter through fire scars.

Sapwood: Carries sap from roots to leaves.

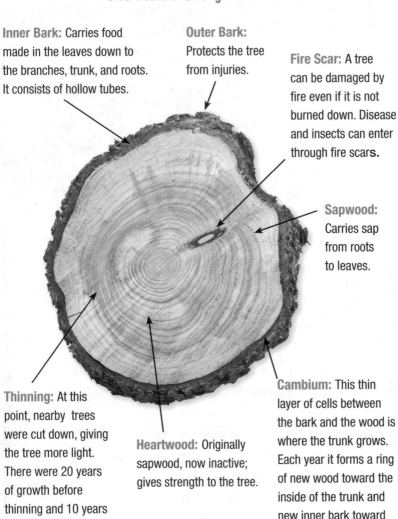

Thinning: At this point, nearby trees were cut down, giving the tree more light. There were 20 years of growth before thinning and 10 years of growth afterward.

Heartwood: Originally sapwood, now inactive; gives strength to the tree.

Cambium: This thin layer of cells between the bark and the wood is where the trunk grows. Each year it forms a ring of new wood toward the inside of the trunk and new inner bark toward the outside of the trunk.

> **Sanding the slice can help bring the rings out.**

Look at a large slice of a tree trunk or thick branch that shows rings. For most types of trees, there will be one ring per year. The width of each ring represents the kind of year the tree experienced. A thin ring may indicate a lack of rain or nutrients. A thick ring may mean plenty of water and food for that year. A scar may mean a fire damaged the tree.

Make a bark rubbing by taping paper to the bark of a tree and rubbing the side of a crayon on the paper to transfer the texture of the bark to the paper. Different types of trees have very different bark. Some bark is thick and deeply furrowed, some bark is smooth with pock marks, and some has flaky outer layers that fall off naturally.

Our den visited a nature center that had a slice from a 200-year-old oak tree. There were little labels that showed historical events going back to before the Civil War. Imagine all of the changes that happened while that tree grew!

LOOKING BACK, LOOKING FORWARD

In 1909, a Scout in London helped a lost American, William D. Boyce. This moment inspired Boyce to bring Scouting to America.

SNAPSHOT OF ADVENTURE

Have you ever wondered what life was like before you were born? Have you ever imagined what things will be like 50 or 100 years from now? In this adventure, you'll get to explore questions like those. You'll take virtual journeys into the past to learn about topics that interest you, and you'll imagine how those topics will change in the future. You'll also get to create a Scouting scrapbook and a time capsule that your children or grandchildren may one day discover!

REQUIREMENT

Do all of these: **Approved by**

1. Create a record of the history of Scouting
   and your place in that history.   _____

2. With the help of your den leader, parent, or
   guardian and with your choice of media, go on a
   virtual journey to the past and create a timeline.   _____

3. Create your own time capsule.   _____

REQUIREMENT 1 | Create a record of the history of Scouting and your place in that history.

As a Webelos Scout, you know that you are part of a den and a pack. But did you know that you are part of an organization, the Boy Scouts of America, that has millions of members and is more than a hundred years old? In this requirement, you will learn more about the story of Scouting and the role you play in that story.

You will also create a scrapbook to record what you have learned. Your scrapbook will have three parts:

♦ Part 1 will contain the history of Scouting.

♦ Part 2 will record your own Scouting story.

♦ Part 3 will explore the future of Scouting.

You can create your scrapbook on paper or on the computer. (Presentation software makes it easy to combine words and pictures and later show your creation to an audience.) Think up creative ways to tell your story.

The Past: Scouting's History

In 1902, British General Robert Baden-Powell came home from war to a big surprise. Boys across England were playing soldier using an army manual he had written called *Aids to Scouting*. Over the next few years, Baden-Powell turned his book into a program for boys that would teach camping, fitness, and citizenship, things boys of the time really needed to learn. He tested his program at a camp on Brownsea Island in 1907 and launched the Boy Scouts the following year.

In 1909, one of Baden-Powell's Scouts helped an American businessman find his way on a London street. The man was so impressed with the Scout's service and attitude that he decided to start a similar program back home. And so the Boy Scouts of America was born.

Back then, you had to be 12 years old to be a Scout, but younger boys wanted to get in on the fun. Eventually, Cub Scouting was created to allow every boy the chance to be a Scout.

With the help of the Internet, your school or local library, or your adult leader, parent, or an adult Scouter, go on a virtual Scouting trip to the past and investigate the questions below. (Before doing any research online, be sure to get permission from a parent or guardian.)

Find out:

- ♦ Who was the American businessman who visited London?
- ♦ What year did the Boy Scouts of America begin?
- ♦ What year did the Cub Scout program begin?
- ♦ What are some ranks and awards that are no longer part of the Cub Scout program?
- ♦ What are two other countries with Scouting programs?

- Do other countries allow girls to be a part of Scouting?
- What are some other differences between Scouting in America and other countries?

In part 1 of your scrapbook, record the answers to these questions and any other interesting facts you discover. Illustrate this part of your scrapbook with photos or drawings of what Scouting was like in the past.

The Present: Your Scouting Story

You are an important part of Scouting's present. In part 2 of your scrapbook, record important dates about your time in Scouting, such as when you joined and when you earned your rank badges. Make a list of the trips you've been on and any special awards you've received. Add pictures or drawings to illustrate your Scouting journey and information on people who have helped you along the way.

The Future: What's Next for You and Scouting

Part 3 of your scrapbook will take some thinking. Go back and review your scrapbook from the beginning to the present. Think about how Scouting has changed since the beginning and how it has remained the same.

Now, think about the future. What do you think Scouting will look like in 20 years? How will it be the same? How will it be different? What would you like Scouts to do in the future?

Illustrate the future of Scouting in part 3 of your scrapbook. List two changes you would like to see happen in Scouting. List one thing you can do to help Scouting be successful in the future.

Our library is decorated with old pictures of our town. It's fun to look at how people dressed and what kind of cars they drove when our great-grandparents were kids!

REQUIREMENT 2 | With the help of your den leader, parent, or guardian and with your choice of media, go on a virtual journey to the past and create a timeline.

For this requirement, you will take another virtual trip into the past and the future.

First, pick two items from this list that you would like to learn more about:

- Ways we communicate
- Ways we travel
- Games we play
- Foods we eat
- Schools we attend
- Buildings we live in
- Music and musical instruments
- Books, movies, and television
- Knowledge of the earth or space
- Changes in our environment
- Changes in medical care
- Another topic of your choice

In your scrapbook, create a timeline like the one shown on the next page for each of the topics you chose. Each timeline should have boxes representing 100, 50, 20, and five years in the past, as well as now and the future. Using the Internet (with a parent or guardian's permission), a library, or people you know, learn more about your topics. Write something about each topic in each box to show how the topic has changed over the years.

The last box—the one for the future—will take some thought. What do you think the future will hold for your community? What would you like to see change about each topic? Are there things you can do to help with the changes? Record your ideas in your scrapbook.

COMPUTER TIMELINE

100 years ago: There were no computers!

20 years ago: People used personal computers to connect to the Internet.

Today: People use computers for everything from shopping to playing games.

50 years ago: Computers were so big they filled entire rooms.

5 years ago: Smartphones and tablets were more powerful than the first computers.

Future: Computers will be able to walk, talk, and think.

To share the information you learned, you could play a matching game with your family or den. Create a set of index cards labeled "100 Years Ago," "50 Years Ago," "20 Years Ago," "Five Years Ago," and "Now." Create another set with the information you learned about one of your topics. Mix up the 10 cards and see how quickly your friends or family members can match up the pairs of cards.

You've probably heard of archaeologists who have dug up artifacts from ancient civilizations. The things they find—pottery, scrolls, clothing, medicine, and other items—help us understand what life was like hundreds or even thousands of years ago.

For this requirement, you will create a time capsule to help future generations understand what life is like right now. To get started, imagine that you could meet with a time traveler from a future century. What would you want to tell him about life today? What objects would you want to show him? Think about your daily activities and the objects you touch every day. Which of those things best tell the story of life today?

Put together a collection of photos, newspaper clippings, and objects that illustrate what life is like today. Some fun things to include would be small toys, a take-out menu from your favorite restaurant, a copy of *Boys' Life*, ticket stubs from a game you attended, an old Cub Scout T-shirt, current photos of family members, and coins that were minted this year.

You might write a letter about things like how you spend a normal day and how you celebrate special family events, etc. Put the date on your letter, then seal it in an envelope for the time capsule.

Once you have assembled your contents, seal everything in a box, label it with your name, today's

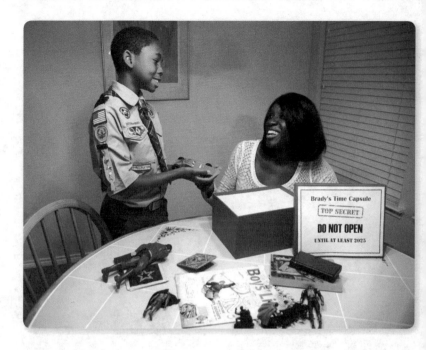

date, and the date when the time capsule should be opened. Then, hide it somewhere that it will be safe until the date you specified.

Your parent or den can help you construct and hide your time capsule. If it will be hidden under the ground, it will need to be completely weatherproof. If it will be hidden in a public area, be sure you have proper permission.

Be sure to create a written record of exactly where the time capsule is hidden so that someone in the future will be able to find it. If your Cub Scout pack or chartered organization has a historian, ask that person for ideas. Also, if you're going to bury your time capsule, make sure it's in a metal box or has metal on its lid so that someone using a metal detector can find it.

You may want to share the contents of your time capsule at your pack meeting before it is sealed and hidden. After all, it will be a long time before anyone looks inside again!

MAESTRO!

SNAPSHOT OF ADVENTURE

A maestro is a musical genius, someone who writes, conducts, or performs music so well that you want to stand up and cheer. Some maestros, such as Ludwig van Beethoven and Wolfgang Amadeus Mozart, lived hundreds of years ago, yet their music is still played today. Others are creating and performing amazing music right now. In this adventure, you'll get to explore the world of maestros. You can learn how music is made, create and play your own instrument, and try your hand at writing songs. So tune up your instrument, and let's start making music!

Ludwig van Beethoven

REQUIREMENT

Do all of these: Approved by

1. Do A or B

   A. Attend a live musical performance.   _____

   B. Visit a facility that uses a sound mixer, and learn how it is used.   _____

2. Do two of the following:

   A. Make a musical instrument. Play it for your family, den, or pack.   _____

   B. Form a "band" with your den. Each member creates his own homemade musical instrument. Perform for your pack at a pack meeting.   _____

   C. Play two tunes on any band or orchestra instrument.   _____

3. Do two of the following:

A. Teach your den the words and melody of a song. Perform the song with your den at your den or pack meeting. _____

B. Create original words for a song. Perform it at your den or pack meeting. _____

C. Collaborate with your den to compose a den theme song. Perform it at your pack meeting. _____

D. Write a song with words and music that expresses your feelings about an issue, a person, something you are learning, a point of the Scout Law, etc. Perform it at your den or pack meeting, alone or with a group. _____

E. Perform a musical number by yourself or with your Webelos den in front of an audience. _____

REQUIREMENT 1A | Attend a live musical performance.

Music is all around you. Depending on where you live, you can find frequent performances by touring pop stars, professional orchestras, community bands, high school choirs, and even music students who are your age or a little older.

With the help of your parent, guardian, or den leader, select a performance or concert to attend. Afterward, make notes on the next page about the performance or concert.

My Musical Outing

Name of performer or musical group: _____

Style of music performed (classical, pop, jazz, gospel,
country, rhythm and blues, etc.): _____

Some of the songs or compositions performed : _____

_____

What I liked about the performance: _____

_____

What I didn't like about the performance: _____

_____

A Scout is courteous. Show respect for performers and other
audience members by listening and applauding. You'll appreciate
the same when you're the musician!

Last year, my family
went to a concert by a jazz
band from New Orleans. It was
really cool to see how the musicians
took turns playing solos. Everybody
got time in the spotlight, and
nobody got left out.

Most musical performances are team efforts. In addition to the musicians you see on stage, there is usually an audio engineer working at a sound mixer in the back of the performance space. Audio engineers also play an important role in creating recordings and live broadcasts.

What is a sound mixer? It is a machine that lets audio engineers mix together the sound that comes from different microphones. Mixers make it possible for you to hear the voice of a soloist over

an entire orchestra or band. They also balance the sound that comes from very loud instruments (such as trumpets and drums) and very quiet instruments (such as clarinets and oboes).

For this requirement, visit a facility that uses a sound mixer, such as a sports arena, radio station, church, or recording studio, and ask someone to show you how it is used. On this page, write down two things you learned about sound mixers.

Two Things I Learned About Sound Mixers

_____

_____

Sound and Musical Instruments

Have you ever thought about what makes the sound in a musical instrument? Every musical instrument—including the human voice—makes sound by sending out sound waves.

Imagine dropping a pebble into a pond. The ripples you see are like sound waves moving away from a musical instrument. Regular sound waves create music; irregular sound waves create noise. Different instruments create unique kinds of sound waves, which is why they all sound different.

When you sing, your vocal cords vibrate to generate sound waves. Place your hand on your throat while you hum or sing, and you'll feel your vocal cords vibrate.

Now, clap your hands. Doing that causes sound waves much like striking a drum. Next, buzz your lips to make a horse sound. That buzzing sound is what starts the sound waves going in a trumpet or trombone. If you stretch out a rubber band and pluck it, you'll make sound like a violin or guitar does.

Here are the main types of instruments:

◆ **Strings** include instruments like violins, cellos, guitars, and banjos. Long, thick strings make low sounds, while short, thin strings make high sounds. A player changes the length of the strings with his or her fingers and then either plucks the strings or runs a bow across the strings to make them vibrate.

◆ **Woodwinds** include instruments like flutes, clarinets, oboes, and saxophones. Vibrating air inside them makes the sounds. With a flute or piccolo, the player blows across a hole to start the sound; with most other woodwinds, a vibrating reed (a thin piece of wood

in the mouthpiece) gets the waves started. Keys on the side of the instrument open and close holes that change the length of the air column inside and make the sounds that come out higher or lower.

♦ **Brass instruments** include trumpets, trombones, tubas, and French horns. Vibrating air inside them makes sounds, but what starts the vibration is a buzzing sound the player makes in the mouthpiece. Brass instruments usually have keys, valves, or slides that change the length of the air column and thus the sound.

♦ **Percussion instruments** include drums, cymbals, gongs, and xylophones. You play a percussion instrument by hitting it or shaking it.

♦ **Electronic instruments** use computer technology to mimic the sound of traditional instruments or to make cool new sounds.

One of the most common instruments is the piano. It combines features of string instruments and percussion instruments. Inside the cabinet are long strings like on a guitar or harp. When the pianist presses keys on the keyboard, hammers strike the strings to create sound.

Now that you know something about how musical instruments work, you will have the opportunity to play an instrument you make yourself!

REQUIREMENT 2A | Make a musical instrument. Play it for your family, den, or pack.

Professional musical instruments take many hours to make and can cost thousands of dollars. However, you can make some musical instruments on your own using items from around your home.

For this requirement, try making your own simple instrument out of some common household items. Here are some ideas.

Storage Container Guitar

Start with a plastic storage container with the lid off. Wrap rubber bands of different sizes and thicknesses around it. Pluck the strings to make music.

Glass Harmonica

Set up a row of glasses on a table. Pour a different amount of water into each one. Lightly thump or rub the rims of the glasses to make music.

Easter Egg Maracas

Put rice, lentils, or dried beans inside a plastic egg or other small plastic container. With duct tape or decorative tape, attach two plastic spoons to the egg for a handle. Shake to make a rhythmic sound.

Paper Towel Horn

Cover one end of a paper towel or wrapping paper tube with waxed paper, and secure it with a rubber band. Punch holes along one side of the roll with a pen. Sing into the open end of the horn to make music.

Bottle Flute

Blow across the mouth of an empty soda bottle to make a sound like a flute. Add a little water to the bottle to change the pitch of the sound.

My Musical Instrument

The instrument I made: _____

_____

The song I played: _____

_____

What I learned: _____

_____

_____

_____

_____

If you can make a musical instrument, so can the other boys in your den! Get each member to make his own instrument, and then form a band. After you've practiced for a while, perform for the other members of your pack.

Our Den Band

The instrument I made: _____

_____

Other instruments in the band: _____

_____

The song we played: _____

What I learned: _____

_____

_____

REQUIREMENT 2C | Play two tunes on any band or orchestra instrument.

Are you learning to play a musical instrument at school? Are you taking private music lessons? Bring your instrument to a den meeting, and play two tunes for your fellow Scouts.

My Instrument

Band or orchestra instrument I play: _____

_____

Tunes I played for my fellow Scouts: _____

_____

REQUIREMENT 3A | Teach your den the words and melody of a song. Perform the song with your den at your den or pack meeting.

Your voice is considered an instrument! Do you have a favorite song to sing? Teach it to your Webelos friends.

To help them learn the words, you may want to write the words on a poster. It can also help to practice one verse at a time. Once everyone knows the song, perform it at a den or pack meeting.

The song I taught my den is _____

_____

You can also create a new song easily. Think of a popular song or a folk song you already know. Using that song's melody, create new words to go with it, and sing it at your den or pack meeting.

For example, some people might wonder if the holidays are coming when they hear "Scout Vespers." That's because the melody is]the same as the traditional German song "O Tannenbaum"]("O Christmas Tree").

My New Song

Name of my song: _____

_____

Melody of my song: _____

_____

Words to my song: _____

_____

_____

_____

_____

_____

_____

A theme song identifies something or someone. Your favorite TV show may start with a song that describes the characters in the show or their situation.

For this requirement, write a theme song for your den. First, think about the members of your den and what makes your den special. Then, compose the words to your song, and fit them to a familiar tune. Practice your theme song, and perform it at a pack meeting.

Words to our den theme song: _____

_____

_____

_____

_____

Songs can be fun, but they can also communicate very important ideas. Every country has a national anthem, and most religions use songs to describe what they believe. Throughout history, people have written songs to express joy, love, sorrow, anger, and other feelings.

The Star-Spangled Banner

Now it's your turn. Here's how you can write your own song to express your feelings:

1. Begin with an idea or theme. Will you write about one of your hobbies, a family member or friend, your Scout experiences, or a favorite sport? Choose an idea and start to write down your thoughts about the idea you have chosen.

2. What might your chorus be? Start with a catchy or really interesting phrase. Think of it as something that will capture everyone's attention.

3. Pick a beat. Find one using your computer or sound equipment or do a search on the Internet (with your parent's permission). Pick a beat that you think sounds like the song you want to sing or chant.

4. Now that you have a good idea of your song's sound and beat, arrange the ideas that you wrote down into lines or verses. Do you want each line to rhyme or every other line to rhyme? Will you put your chorus in between the verses?

5. Now, start to sing your words along with the beat you chose. By practicing your words, you will learn how to make your words fit with the music. Adjust your words so that your theme or message can be easily understood.

Words to my song: _____

_____

_____

_____

_____

_____

_____

_____

For this requirement, perform a musical number in front of an audience, such as your family or your pack. Are you nervous? That's OK. Even some professional musicians get butterflies in their stomachs before they go on stage! You'll feel better if you practice ahead of time so you don't have to worry about forgetting the words or music.

If you don't feel comfortable performing in front of others, record your performance, and share it with an audience later. Get a friend or family member to make a video of your performance using a video camera or smartphone, or use an audio recorder to capture just the sound of your performance.

If you want to perform live for friends or family who can't come to your performance, ask your parent or den leader to help you set up a video link using a computer or smartphone. With a video chat service, friends and family around the world can tune in to your performance and enjoy your music!

My Performance

I performed the following musical number:

_____

_____

_____

I shared my musical performance in the following way:

_____

_____

_____

MOVIEMAKING

SNAPSHOT OF ADVENTURE

Let's make a movie! This adventure will give you the chance to direct your own movie through a visual storytelling experience. Do you ever watch movies and think, "I could do that?" In this adventure, you will get the chance! You will learn about the moviemaking process by exploring storytelling and animation. You'll also get to share your creations with your friends. Are you ready? Lights! Camera! Action!

REQUIREMENT

Do all of these: **Approved by**

1. Write a story outline describing a real or imaginary Scouting adventure. Create a pictured storyboard that shows your story.   _____

2. Create either an animated or live action movie about yourself. Your movie should depict how you live by the Scout Oath and Scout Law.   _____

3. Share your movie with your family, den, or pack.   _____

For thousands and thousands of years, people have been telling stories with pictures. Cavemen drew pictures on cave walls, and artists decorated walls and ceilings in places of worship. Today, we often tell stories with moving pictures and watch them at movie theaters or on television.

Stories are a way to express yourself and connect with other people. Your idea for a story can come from real-life experiences or you can use your imagination. Telling a story about yourself with a movie can allow others to get to know you better. If you tell a story about getting lost on a hike or burning your dinner on a campout, most Scouts will identify with your story because they've experienced something similar!

Today, many people tell stories for a living, including cartoonists, animators, and movie directors. A lot of time can go into planning a great story.

The first step in creating your movie is to write an outline of the story. Next, you'll create a storyboard to show through pictures how the story will progress. A storyboard is much like a comic book, with each picture representing one scene or camera shot. Creating a storyboard lets everyone involved with the movie visualize what it will look like before they get started.

For this requirement, write an outline for your story about a Scouting adventure. Then create a storyboard showing each part of the story.

It should include these story elements:

- **Setting:** When and where the story happens (on a farm, in a castle, during the American Revolution, 500 years in the future, etc.)

- **Characters:** Who appears in your story (a hero, a villain, a monkey, a king, etc.)

- **Plot:** What happens in your story

A good plot has a beginning, a middle, and an end. The beginning introduces the main character and the problem he must solve or the challenge he must overcome. The middle shows the main character working to solve the problem or overcome the challenge. The end shows how things turned out.

Think of a Scouting activity and write a story outline. Your story can take place anywhere you imagine and can include all sorts of fun characters. It can be set in modern times or in the past or future.

Create a storyboard using your outline as a guide. You may use sketches, photos, or a collage. Try to visualize what your story would look like if acted out.

Do you ever watch cartoons? Did you realize that a cartoon is nothing but a series of still pictures strung together, each one slightly different than the one before?

Drawings made by hand or generated on computers can be used to make animation. Photographs of clay figures or moveable objects to simulate motion can also be used.

For this requirement, create a short animated or live-action movie. You should start with the storyboard you created for requirement 1 or write a new story. Writing a more detailed script that contains what each character is doing and/or saying might help. Then, you're ready to get started!

For an animated movie, your setting can be as simple as a photo backdrop or as fancy as a 3-D "stage" complete with props and furniture. Your "actors" can be people, puppets, action figures, clay sculptures, or basically anything you want. Just choose objects that can be adjusted in small ways and will stand on their own. Be sure your camera is on a tripod or a stand so it doesn't move between shots.

Follow these steps to create your animation:

- Place your actors on the set in their starting positions.

- Take a picture.

- Make slight changes to your actors so they progress in whatever action they're doing, like waving, jumping, or walking.

- Take another picture.

- Continue moving your actors and taking pictures until all movements in the scene are complete.

Be sure to include a character in the movie that represents something about you. If you want to show that you are friendly, your avatar could wave at the camera. If you like science, your avatar could wear a lab coat.

Once the scene is complete, you can use free photo-viewer software on a computer to rapidly move through all the pictures and see your animation in action. Ask an adult for permission before going online.

For a live-action movie, be sure to shoot your video with equipment and at a location approved by your parent or guardian.

My dad told me there are 12 different images in every second of a simple animation. That means a 30-minute cartoon would have 21,600 separate images!

REQUIREMENT 3 | Share your movie with your family, den, or pack.

Part of the fun in creating and telling stories is sharing them with others! For this requirement, share your stories with fellow Scouts, your den, or members of your family.

Afterward, ask them what they thought about your stories:
- ◆ What was their favorite part?
- ◆ Were they able to recognize your character?
- ◆ Did they understand the story?

PROJECT FAMILY

SNAPSHOT OF ADVENTURE

Families are groups of people who care for one another and share their lives together. Every family is different, and every family is special in its own way. In this adventure, you'll learn more about your family and the role you play in it. You'll also have the chance make your home safer, to serve your community as a family, and to participate in a fun family activity.

REQUIREMENT

Do 1 through 5, then choose two of 6 through 8:

Approved by

1. Interview a grandparent, another family elder, or a family friend about what life was like when he or she was growing up. Share his or her story with another family member.

2. Talk with members of your family about your family name, history, traditions, and culture. Create a family tree of three generations, or make a poster or Web page that shows the origins of your ancestors. Or choose a special celebration or holiday that your family participates in, and create either a poster, picture, or photo slideshow of it. Share this project with your den.

3. Show your understanding of your duty to family by creating a chart listing the jobs that you and other family members have at home. Choose three of the jobs you are responsible for, and chart them for two weeks.

4. Select ONE of the jobs below that belongs to another family member, and help that person complete it:

   A. Create a grocery shopping list for the week. _____

   B. Complete the laundry for your family one time. _____

   C. Help prepare meals for your family for one day. _____

5. Create a list of community service or conservation projects that you and your family can do together, and present it to your family. Select one project, plan it, and complete it with your family. _____

6. With the help of an adult, inspect your home and its surroundings. Make a list of hazards or security problems you find. Correct one problem you found, and tell what you did. _____

7. Hold a family meeting to plan an exciting family activity. The activity could include:

   A. A family reunion _____

   B. A family night _____

   C. A family outing _____

8. Have your family event. Afterward, tell your parent or guardian what you liked best about the event. _____

A family is a group of two or more people who are related by birth, marriage, or adoption and who live together for the most part. Families come in all shapes and sizes. What is common to all families is that the members take time to care for each other.

You and your family are on an adventure together, an adventure that began a long time before you were born. Stories passed down from generation to generation help tell about your family's adventure. From these stories, you can learn where your family came from, why you celebrate different traditions, and what pieces of your history you will want to pass on.

Think about someone who cares about you, either a family member or someone close to your family. Arrange to meet with this person, and interview him or her about what life was like before you were born. If possible, make a video or audio recording of the interview so you can play it back later.

Afterward, share what you learned with another family member. If the person has really interesting stories to tell, you could even invite him or her to tell those stories at a den meeting.

My Interview

Person I interviewed:

_____

His or her relationship to me:

_____

Sample Questions

Before your interview, make a list of questions to ask. Here are some to get you started. Your parent may be able to suggest other questions based on whom you are interviewing.

- When were you born?
- Where did you grow up?
- What activities did you do when you were my age?
- Tell me about a happy memory from your childhood.
- Was there a time when something was difficult for you? Can you tell me about it?
- What family traditions were important to you?
- What was your family's favorite food? Is there a recipe for it?
- How was childhood different then compared with now?

Have you ever wondered where your name came from or why your family celebrates certain occasions? For this requirement, you will do some exploring to find out about your roots and heritage.

Have an adult in your family help you find family pictures, record family stories from relatives, and visit libraries, cemeteries, websites, or other places where family history might be found. Be your family's historian by interviewing other family members; ask them what their jobs are or were and a few important facts about them. Ask for or take pictures of the people you interview. Then, put together what you learned to tell your family story. Create a family tree of three generations (you and any brothers or sisters, your parents, and your grandparents) or make a poster or Web page that tells about your family members.

Another way to find out about your family's culture is through the way you celebrate special occasions. Choose a special holiday or event that your family participates in, and demonstrate what makes it special for your family. Find out if your family's celebration is something that many other people celebrate or if it is a tradition that belongs to just your family.

I created a _____

Date I shared with my den: _____

REQUIREMENT 3 | Show your understanding of your duty to family by creating a chart listing the jobs that you and other family members have at home. Choose three of the jobs you are responsible for, and chart them for two weeks.

REQUIREMENT 4 | Select ONE of the jobs below that belongs to another family member, and help that person complete it:

REQUIREMENT 4A | Create a grocery shopping list for the week.

REQUIREMENT 4B | Complete the laundry for your family one time.

REQUIREMENT 4C | Help prepare meals for your family for one day.

Living in a family means that you give and receive love and support. When you care about others' feelings, listen to their problems, and try to help, you are being a good family member. Another way to show you care is by doing your share and helping others. When you pick up your belongings, clear the table after a meal, or help a younger family member with homework, you make life more pleasant for the whole family.

As a family member, your first job is to take care of yourself and your belongings. If you don't do that, you add to the work of other family members.

Keep yourself clean by bathing, brushing and flossing your teeth, cleaning your nails, and combing your hair. (Of course, it's OK to get dirty when you're playing or working hard; just be sure to clean up afterward.) These simple things show other family members that you care about yourself and want them to be proud of you.

Next, take care of your bedroom or personal space. It isn't hard to keep your belongings and your surroundings neat. Pick up after yourself. Put your books, games, and sports equipment where they belong. Learn to make your bed and do it every morning. Doing these things shows you care about others in your family.

Once you've taken care of yourself and your personal space, you can take on chores that help the whole family, such as setting the table, helping with the laundry, or caring for your family pet. When you do household chores like these, you show your family that you are responsible and are contributing to making your family work.

My Family's Chores

Who does the chores in your family? Write down who does each chore on this chart. If your family has other chores, write them on a separate page.

Chore	Person Who Does It
Laundry	_____
Grocery shopping	_____
Cooking	_____
Setting the table	_____
Washing dishes	_____
Housecleaning	_____
Caring for pets	_____
Paying bills	_____
Mowing or other outside work	_____

My Chores

List your chores and put a checkmark under each day that you do them for two weeks.

Chore 1 _____

Chore 2 _____

Chore 3 _____

Week 1

Sunday	Monday	Tuesday	Wednesday	Thursday	Friday	Saturday
_____	_____	_____	_____	_____	_____	_____

Week 2

Sunday	Monday	Tuesday	Wednesday	Thursday	Friday	Saturday
_____	_____	_____	_____	_____	_____	_____

REQUIREMENT 5 | Create a list of community service or conservation projects that you and your family can do together, and present it to your family. Select one project, plan it, and complete it with your family.

You can make your family stronger by sharing in chores. Your family can make your community stronger by doing things to help it.

Many people and places in your community need help. Talk with your family about the needs in your community, and find a way you can help.

Here are some ideas:

- Serve a meal at a homeless shelter.
- Pick up trash or plant trees in a park.
- "Adopt" a family by providing holiday gifts.
- Visit residents at a retirement community.
- Participate in a walkathon to raise money for charity.
- Donate gently used clothing and toys to a charity thrift store.
- Send holiday cards to soldiers overseas.
- Collect pet food for an animal shelter.
- Rake leaves or shovel snow for neighbors who need help.

The project my family participated in: _____

I finished the project on (date): _____

It is important to make your home safe. Many accidents occur because of hazards nobody noticed. By inspecting your home and its surroundings, you can find such problems and prevent accidents.

Use the checklist shown here to inspect your home. Make notes of any problems you found and what you did to fix them.

You can do some other things to help make your home as safe as possible:

♦ Have stepladders or stepstools available for reaching items that are stored up high.

♦ If there are young children in the home, install safety plugs in electrical sockets and safety latches on cabinets.

♦ Install no-skid mats in tubs and showers and on bathroom floors.

♦ Make sure everyone in the family knows how to shut off the water in the home.

♦ Make sure everyone in the family knows what to do if they smell gas.

♦ Make sure the family has a fire escape plan and practices it regularly.

♦ Make sure all purses and briefcases, including those belonging to visitors, are placed out of children's reach.

♦ Use the back burners on the stove, and turn pot handles toward the wall.

♦ Dry your hands before touching electrical switches or using electrical outlets.

♦ Never use electrical devices in or near the bathtub or shower.

Home Safety Checklist

Date of inspection: _____

Place	Hazard	Status/Action Taken
Living Room	Toys on floor (tripping hazard)	_____
	Furniture blocking easy passage	_____
	Electric cords under rugs (worn cords can cause shock or fire)	_____
	Curtain cords dangling (can strangle small children)	_____
Bedroom	Toys on floor (tripping hazard)	_____
	Bunk beds missing rails (fall hazard)	_____
	Smoke detector missing or not functioning	_____
	Carbon monoxide detector missing or not functioning	_____
Kitchen	Matches accessible to small children	_____
	Knives accessible to small children	_____
	Cleaning fluids and other poisons exposed	_____
	Fire extinguisher missing or discharged	_____
	Smoke detector missing or not functioning	_____

Bathroom	Medicines accessible to small children	_____
	Hair dryers, radios, and other electrical devices near water source	_____
	Toilet lid open (drowning hazard)	_____
	Water too hot (ask an adult to adjust the water heater)	_____
Stairways	Boxes, toys, and other items left on stairs (tripping hazard)	_____
	Handrail loose	_____
	Stair covering or tread loose	_____
	Light bulb out	_____
	Safety gates at top and bottom are missing when small children are in house	_____
Work/ storage area	Tools left out	_____
	Firearms left unsecured	_____
Furnace area	Waste paper or rubbish near furnace	_____
Outside	Garbage cans not secured	_____
	Swimming or wading pool left uncovered	_____
	Dead trees or large overhead limbs not removed	_____
	Doors or window locks broken	_____
	Entryway not well lit	_____

REQUIREMENT 7 | Hold a family meeting to plan an exciting family activity. The activity could include:

A. A family reunion

B. A family night

C. A family outing

REQUIREMENT 8 | Have your family event. Afterward, tell your parent or guardian about what you liked best about the event.

A family meeting happens when the whole family takes time to talk about what is happening in their lives and to make plans and decisions together. Maybe your family talks about these things around the dinner table, and it doesn't seem like a meeting at all. Or maybe you set a special time to talk about family business or make plans for the upcoming weekend.

Hold a family meeting to plan a family activity that everyone can enjoy together. There are many ways a family can have fun. Some don't cost any money and are easy to plan; others cost money and take a long time to get ready for. Your job is to think of some fun activities that your family can do together, and then come up with a plan for your adventure.

Here are some ideas:

- ♦ A family reunion
- ♦ A family game night or a family talent show
- ♦ A night filled with music where you all enjoy your favorite songs to sing or listen to
- ♦ A sport you can play together
- ♦ A dinner you all participate in making and eating together
- ♦ A picnic, hike, or camping trip
- ♦ A trip to go fishing, swimming, bowling, or ice skating
- ♦ A visit to a museum, zoo, or park

A Scout is loyal to his family. Spending time with your family can help you appreciate the ways that your family is special.

Our Family Meeting and Event

We held our family meeting on (date): _____

We talked about: _____

_____

_____

Our family adventure was: _____

We did it on (date): _____

What I liked about our family event: _____

What I would do differently next time: _____

For our project, my family served lunch at a shelter for homeless families. Afterward, I got to play games with some of the kids who were staying there. It made me feel really lucky to have a nice place to live.

SPORTSMAN

SNAPSHOT OF ADVENTURE

America is a sports-loving country. We go to games and watch all kinds of sports on television. Big events like the Olympic Games and national championships capture the attention of millions of people. It's fun to watch sports, but the real adventure happens when you get on the field or court yourself. In this adventure, you will get to play both individual and team sports. You may even try a sport that you will like enough to enjoy all of your life.

REQUIREMENT

Do all of these: **Approved by**

1. Show the signals used by officials in one of these sports: football, basketball, baseball, soccer, or hockey.   _____

2. While you are a Webelos Scout, participate in two individual sports.   _____

3. While you are a Webelos Scout, play two team sports.   _____

4. Complete the following requirements:

   A. Explain what good sportsmanship means.   _____

   B. Role-play a situation that demonstrates good sportsmanship.   _____

   C. Give an example of a time when you experienced or saw someone showing good sportsmanship.   _____

If you've ever been to a sporting event or watched one on TV, you know how loud an arena or stadium can get. That's why officials use hand signals to communicate with the players, coaches, fans, and even each other. Like the Cub Scout and Boy Scout signs, these signals can share important information quickly.

When you're a sports fan, understanding signals helps you enjoy the game more. When you're a player, understanding them helps you know what to do next.

For this requirement, learn the signals for one team sport. Then, the next time you watch a game, see if you can follow the action without needing a play-by-play announcer to tell you what's going on.

If you'd like, learn the signals for more than one sport. Look for examples of signals that are shared between sports.

OFFICIALS' SIGNALS

Soccer

| Corner Kick | Substitution | Offside | Throw In | Goal Kick |

| Penalty Kick | Indirect Free Kick | Play On (Advantage) | Caution or Expulsion | Direct Free Kick |

Football

Touchdown or Field Goal

Illegal Action

False Start

Safety

Illegal Shift

Illegal Participation

Intentional Grounding

Delay of Game

Clipping

Pass Interference

Roughing Passer

Roughing the Kicker

Offside

Time Out

• Incomplete Pass
• Penalty Declined
• No Play • No Score

Illegal Use of Hands (Holding)

Illegal Pass or Handing Ball Forward

First Down

Start the Clock

Grabbing Face Mask

Baseball

Safe

Time Out or Foul Ball

Out or Strike

Fair Ball

Foul Tip

Do Not Pitch

Play Ball

Hockey

Fighting (Roughing)   Slow Whistle   "Wash Out"   Penalty Shot   Slashing   Delay Calling of Penalty

Elbowing   Butt-Ending   Holding   Boarding   Charging   Interference

Hooking   Holding Face Mask   Misconduct   Cross-Checking   Goal Scored   Icing

High-Sticking   Checking from Behind   Unsportsmanlike Conduct Time Out   Spearing   Tripping   Kneeing

Basketball

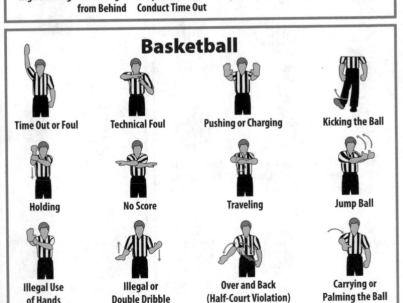

Time Out or Foul   Technical Foul   Pushing or Charging   Kicking the Ball

Holding   No Score   Traveling   Jump Ball

Illegal Use of Hands   Illegal or Double Dribble   Over and Back (Half-Court Violation)   Carrying or Palming the Ball

REQUIREMENT 2 | While you are a Webelos Scout, participate in two individual sports.

An individual sport is one you play by yourself. That doesn't mean there's no competition, however. You'll want to learn and practice so you can do your best when you compete against another person—or when you compete against your own previous performance.

Every sport is different. Tennis requires agility, which means being able to move quickly in different directions. Cycling requires endurance, which is the ability to keep going for a long time. Archery requires good eye-hand coordination. Gymnastics requires flexibility and balance. Fishing requires patience.

Just because you don't have those skills right now doesn't mean you can't learn them. Part of participating in sports is trying things you haven't done before and getting better at them.

Think about all the individual sports you know about. Which ones interest you? _____

Ask your friends about sports they enjoy that you have not played. What are they? _____

_____

My uncle runs marathons, which are races of 26.2 miles—a long way! He knows he may never come in first, so he tries each time to set a new personal record. That way he's a winner even if 100 runners finish ahead of him.

A Scout is clean. Sports help you keep your body and your mind fit. Just find the sport that's right for you.

My Individual Sports

Sport No. 1 _____

When I Played _____

How I Did _____

What I Liked _____

What I Didn't Like _____

What I Learned _____

_____

Sport No. 2 _____

When I Played _____

How I Did _____

What I Liked _____

What I Didn't Like _____

What I Learned _____

Team sports offer all the variety that individual sports do. Some require strength, some require agility, some require quick thinking, and some require endurance. And they all require teamwork. In fact, teamwork can be more important than the specific skills the sport requires. Players with average skills who work together as a team will often beat players who are good at the sport but bad at teamwork.

Team members depend on one another to play well and to win. They practice together and figure out ways to use each other's abilities to benefit the whole team. And they encourage each other during practices and games, especially when things aren't going well.

For this requirement, play one team sport with your den, other dens, or your pack, and play another team sport with your den or a group of friends. Choose sports that everyone wants to play or learn how to play.

My Team Sports

Sport No. 1 _____

When We Played _____

How the Team Did _____

How I Did _____

What I Liked _____

What I Didn't Like _____

What I Learned _____

_____

Sport No. 2 _____

When We Played _____

How the Team Did _____

How I Did _____

What I Liked _____

What I Didn't Like _____

What I Learned _____

REQUIREMENT 4A | Explain what good sportsmanship means.

REQUIREMENT 4B | Role-play a situation that demonstrates good sportsmanship.

REQUIREMENT 4C | Give an example of a time when you experienced or saw someone showing good sportsmanship.

Sportsmanship is how you act when you are playing a sport. A good sport plays by the rules and never cheats. Playing fairly is a matter of honor and self-respect, as well as respect for opponents. Play hard and play to win—but play fairly.

When you win, you might want to jump for joy or dance or cheer out of excitement. These feelings are natural, but remember that while you are celebrating, the other team is feeling unhappy about its loss. Be a gracious winner; do not put the other team down. Take time to tell your opponents they played a good game, and always shake hands.

If you lose, try to take the loss bravely. Congratulate the winners, and shake their hands. Don't complain about bad luck or blame the officials or your teammates. Instead, practice, do your best, and see what happens the next time you compete.

In my own words, good sportsmanship means

_____.

A situation that demonstrates good sportsmanship is

_____.

A time when I observed good sportsmanship was

_____.

SPECIAL AWARDS YOU CAN EARN

The following awards can be earned while you are a Cub Scout. Check with your pack leaders or go to **Scouting.org** (with a parent's or guardian's permission) to learn more.

Conservation Good Turn Award

The Conservation Good Turn is an award packs may earn by partnering with a conservation or environmental organization to choose and carry out a Good Turn in their home communities.

Outdoor Activity Award

Tiger, Wolf, Bear, and Webelos Scouts have the opportunity to earn the Cub Scout Outdoor Activity Award. Scouts may earn the award in each of the program years as long as the requirements are completed again each year. Cub Scouts complete specific requirements for each rank, including a number of different outdoor activities.

National Summertime Pack Award

The National Summertime Pack Award encourages packs to be active when school is out for the summer. Youth and adult pack members can earn the award by taking part in one activity per month in June, July, and August.

Outdoor Ethics Awareness Award
Outdoor Ethics Action Award

Cub Scouts who are interested in learning more about outdoor ethics and Leave No Trace may earn the Outdoor Ethics Awareness Award. The Outdoor Ethics Action Award asks Scouts to use their new knowledge to take steps to improve their outdoor skills.

STEM/Nova Awards

The Nova awards for Cub Scouts are for Wolf, Bear, and Webelos Scouts who are interested in learning more about science, technology, engineering, and mathematics. These awards may not be earned by Tiger Scouts.

For their first Nova awards, Scouts have the opportunity to earn the Nova award patch, followed by three more π pin-on devices. The patch and the three devices represent each of the four STEM topics. The Supernova awards have more challenging requirements and recognize more in-depth, advanced achievement in STEM-related activities.

World Conservation Award

The World Conservation Award for Cub Scouts provides an opportunity for individual Wolf, Bear, and Webelos Scouts to "think globally" and "act locally" to preserve and improve our environment. This program is designed to make youth members aware that all nations are closely related through natural resources, and that we are interdependent with our world environment.

Requirements for this award must be completed *in addition to* any similar requirements completed for rank. This award may not be earned by Tigers.

Bobcat Trail

Your name _____

Fill in seven tracks to earn the Bobcat badge.

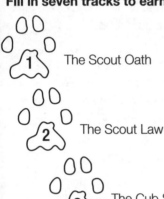 The Scout Oath

The Scout Law

The Cub Scout sign

 The Cub Scout handshake

 The Cub Scout motto

 The Cub Scout salute

 Exercises in *How to Protect Your Children From Child Abuse: A Parent's Guide*

Webelos and Arrow of Light Adventure Tracking

Webelos Required Adventures

Cast Iron Chef

1 ___ 2 ___ 3 ___ 4 ___ 5 ___

Duty to God and You

Do either requirement 1 OR requirement 2. For
requirement 2, complete at least three of requirements 2a–2d.

1 ___ 2a ___ 2b ___ 2c ___ 2d ___

First Responder

1 ___ 2a ___ 2b ___ 2c ___ 2d ___ 2e ___ 3 ___
4 ___ 5a ___ 5b ___ 5c ___ 5d ___ 5e ___ 5f ___
5g ___ 5h ___ 5i ___ 6 ___ 7 ___ 8 ___

Stronger, Faster, Higher

1 ___ 2a ___ 2b ___ 2c ___ 2d ___ 2e ___
2f ___ 3 ___ 4 ___ 5 ___ 6 ___

Webelos Walkabout

1 ___ 2 ___ 3 ___ 4 ___ 5 ___ 6 ___ 7 ___ 8 ___

Arrow of Light Required Adventures

Building a Better World

1 ___ 2 ___ 3 ___ 4 ___ 5 ___

6 ___ 7 ___ 8 ___ 9 ___ 10 ___

Camper

1 ___ 2 ___ 3a ___ 3b ___ 3c ___

4 ___ 5 ___ 6 ___ 7 ___

Duty to God in Action

Do either requirement 1 OR requirement 2. For
requirement 2, do requirement 2a and any two from 2b–2e.

1 ___ 2a ___ 2b ___ 2c ___ 2d ___ 2e ___

Scouting Adventure

1a ___ 1b ___ 1c ___ 1d ___ 1e ___ 2a ___

2b ___ 2c ___ 2d ___ 3a ___ 3b ___ 3c ___ 3d ___

4 ___ 5a ___ 5b ___ 6 ___

Webelos and Arrow of Light Elective Adventures

Adventures in Science

1 ____ 2 ____

Complete any four of the following:

3a ____ 3b ____ 3c ____ 3d ____ 3e ____

3f ____ 3g ____ 3h ____ 3i ____

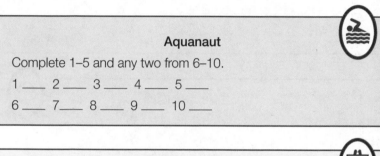

Aquanaut

Complete 1–5 and any two from 6–10.

1 ___ 2 ___ 3 ___ 4 ___ 5 ___

6 ___ 7 ___ 8 ___ 9 ___ 10 ___

Art Explosion

1 ___ 2 ___ Do two of 3a-3i: 3a ___ 3b ___ 3c ___

3d ___ 3e ___ 3f ___ 3g ___ 3h ___ 3i ___ 4 ___

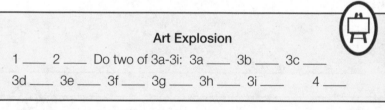

Aware and Care

1 ___ 2 ___ 3 ___ 4 ___ 5 ___ 6 ___

Do two of the following: 7a ___ 7b ___ 7c ___

7d ___ 7e ___ 7f ___ 7g ___ 7h ___

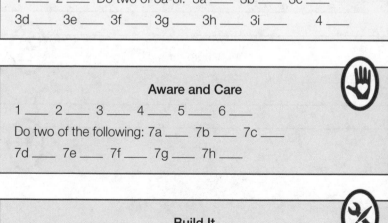

Build It

1 ___ 2 ___ 3 ___ 4 ___ 5 ___

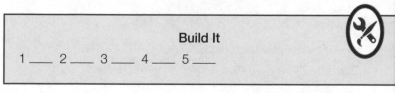

Build My Own Hero

1 ___ 2 ___ 3 ___ 4 ___ 5 ___ 6 ___

Castaway

Do two of these:

1a ___ 1b ___ 1c ___

Do all of these:

2a ___ 2b ___ 2c ___ 2d ___

2e ___ 2f ___ 2g ___ 2h ___

Earth Rocks!

1a ___ 1b ___ 1c ___ 2 ___ 3a ___ 3b ___

3c ___ 4a ___ 4b ___ 5 ___ 6a ___ 6b ___ 6c ___

Do either 7a or 7b: 7a ___ 7b ___

8 ___

Engineer

1 ___ 2a ___ 2b ___ 2c ___ 3 ___ 4 ___

Fix It

1 ___ 2a ___ 2b ___ 2c ___ 3a ___

3b ___ 3c ___

Choose eight of these:

4a ___ 4b ___ 4c ___ 4d ___ 4e ___ 4f ___ 4g ___

4h ___ 4i ___ 4j ___ 4k ___ 4l ___ 4m ___ 4n ___

4o ___ 4p ___ 4q ___ 4r ___ 4s ___ 4t ___ 4u ___

Game Design

1 ___ 2 ___ 3 ___ 4 ___

Into the Wild

Do six from requirements 1 through 9:

1 ___ 2 ___ 3 ___ 4 ___ 5 ___ 6 ___

7 ___ 8 ___ 9 ___

Into the Woods

1 ___ 2 ___ 3 ___ 4 ___ 5 ___ 6 ___ 7 ___

Looking Back, Looking Forward

1 ___ 2 ___ 3 ___

Maestro!

Do a or b: 1a ___ 1b ___

Do two of the following: 2a ___ 2b ___ 2c ___

Do two of the following: 3a ___ 3b ___ 3c ___

3d ___ 3e ___

Moviemaking

1 ___ 2 ___ 3 ___

Project Family

Do 1 through 5, then choose two of 6 through 8:

1 ___ 2 ___ 3 ___ 4 ___ 5 ___ 6 ___

7 ___ 8 ___

Sportsman

1 ___ 2 ___ 3 ___ 4a ___ 4b ___ 4c ___

GET SET FOR BOY SCOUTING!

You did it! I'm sure it's hard to believe you've finished the Cub Scouting adventure! You've met new people, tried new activities, learned a ton about Scouting, and probably laughed a lot too.

Now I hope you're excited about joining a Boy Scout troop like mine. You have so much to look forward to! Who knows? Maybe I'll see you at the next jamboree. I'll be the guy in the Boy Scout uniform.

The Adventures of Boy Scouting Await You!

As an Arrow of Light Scout you've learned a lot about the next program level, Boy Scouting, by completing the Scouting Adventure. You've learned they work in patrols instead of dens, that the leadership of the troop is boy-led with adult guidance in the Scoutmaster and assistant Scoutmaster. You've learned that they have a different motto, "Be Prepared," as well as a different sign and handshake.

Adventure! That's what you've been experiencing in Cub Scouting, and adventure is what you will continue to experience in Boy Scouting. You're standing at the doorway to the most exciting adventures you can imagine. As you step into the world of Boy Scouting, you can hike along trails, canoe across misty lakes, and camp under the open sky. You can smell fresh rain in the woods and fill your mouth with the taste of wild strawberries. At the end of a patrol bike hike, plunge into a cool mountain lake. Cook your meals over a camp stove. Travel the backcountry without leaving a trace, and live well with only what you carry in your pockets and pack. Observe wildlife close up, and study nature all around you.

Scouting is also a doorway to friendship. Other boys who have not been in your Webelos den might be joining your troop, and you'll meet a lot of other Scouts along the way. Scouting is a worldwide brotherhood many millions strong. Almost anywhere you go, you'll find Scouts excited about the same activities you enjoy. Scouts know how to find their way, how to stay warm and dry in stormy weather, and how to give proper first aid. When you master important Scouting skills, you can teach others what you know.

Everyone helping everyone else—that's part of Scouting, too. People have always relied on Scouts to Be Prepared in times of need. Your troop leaders will show you meaningful ways to help your family, community, nation, and world. The acts of kindness you perform every day will improve the lives of others. In an emergency, you'll be ready to do whatever the situation requires.

Outdoor adventures, service projects, leadership in your patrol and troop—Scouting will give you experiences and responsibilities that will help you mature. The Scout Oath and the Scout Law provide the guidelines you need to become a strong, confident adult. The knowledge and attitudes you develop as a Scout will be with you the rest of your life. And Scouting is fun! You can look around during Scouting activities and see everyone sharing and learning. Are you ready to get in on all the fun of Boy Scouting?

First, review the joining requirements to becoming a Boy Scout. Many of the requirements will look familiar to you! Next, schedule a meeting with the Scoutmaster of the troop you've selected to join, and fulfill these requirements to earn your first rank in Boy Scouting, the "Scout" rank.

Scout Rank Requirements

All requirements for Scout rank must be completed as a member of a troop. If you already learned these as a Webelos Scout, simply demonstrate your knowledge or skills to your Scoutmaster or other designated leader after joining the troop.

1. **Complete all of the items below:**

   a. Repeat from memory the Scout Oath, Scout Law, Scout motto, and Scout slogan. In your own words, explain their meaning.

   b. Explain what Scout spirit is. Describe some ways you have shown Scout spirit by practicing the Scout Oath, Scout Law, Scout motto, and Scout slogan.

   c. Give the Boy Scout sign, salute, and handshake. Explain when they should be used.

   d. Describe the First Class Scout badge and tell what each part stands for. Explain the significance of the First Class Scout badge.

   e. Repeat from memory the Outdoor Code. In your own words, explain what the Outdoor Code means to you.

2. **After attending at least one Boy Scout troop meeting, do the following:**

   a. Describe how the Scouts in the troop provide its leadership.

   b. Describe the four steps of Boy Scout advancement.

   c. Describe what the ranks in Boy Scouting are and how they are earned.

   d. Describe what merit badges are and how they are earned.

3. Do the following:

    a. Explain the patrol method. Describe the types of patrols that are used in your troop.

    b. Become familiar with your patrol name, emblem, flag, and yell. Explain how these items create patrol spirit.

4. Do the following:

    a. Show how to tie a square knot, two half hitches, and a taut-line hitch. Explain how each knot is used.

    b. Show the proper care of a rope by learning how to whip and fuse the ends of different kinds of rope.

5. **Demonstrate your knowlege of pocketknife safety.**

6. **With your parent or guardian, complete the exercises in the pamphlet *How to Protect Your Children from Child Abuse: A Parent's Guide* and earn the Cyber Chip Award for your grade.***

7. **Since joining the troop and while working on Scout rank, participate in a Scoutmaster conference.**

* If your family does not have Internet access at home AND you do not have ready Internet access at school or another public place or via a mobile device, the Cyber Chip portion of this requirement may be waived by your parent or guardian.

INDEX

T

Team sports participation, 523–24
Team Tiger, 536–39
Telegraph machine, 379–80
Telling your story with pictures, 494–96
Tents, 12, 154, 155, 156, 202
Tiger rank, 5, 6, 8, 17, 526, 527
Time capsule, 472–73
Tool safety, 296–97
Tools, 292–95, 298–99, 388
Tracking
    Arrow of Light adventures, 530, 531–34
    Bobcat Trail, 528
    Webelos adventures, 529, 531–34
Trail summary, Bobcat, 528
Trees identifying, 451–55
Turtles, 431

U

Uniforms and insignia, 15–18, 31, 53, 126, 143, 154, 186, 193, 200. *See also* Badges
United States flag, 122–27
    displaying and flying, 123–25, 127
    folding, 125
    history of, 122–23
    saluting, 31, 125–26, 186
Universal emergency signal, 335

V

Venomous reptiles and snakes, 104–7
Visiting an art museum, 253–54

W

Walkabout. *See* Webelos Walkabout
Watching and studying birds, 434–35, 436
Watching creatures in the wild, 437–39, 447
Water, how to purify, 332–33

Water activity
    adventures, 228–49
    gear, 233, 234, 238, 239, 248, 249
    rescues, 238–39
    safety, 231–33, 248
Weather emergencies, 157–59
Weather vane, 382–83
Webelos
    badge, 13, 17, 34
    elective adventures, 205–525. *See also* specific adventure
    history of, 5–6
    rank, about, 6, 8, 13, 17, 33
    required adventures, 36–117. *See also* specific adventure
    what it stands for, 13
Webelos den
    about, 6–7, 13–14, 15, 17, 34, 35, 145, 195, 466
    chief, 14
    inviting guests, 64, 247, 283, 308, 503
    leadership, 4, 6, 7, 8, 11, 13, 14, 39, 54, 101, 102, 191
    overnight campouts, 11–12, 219
Webelos Walkabout adventure, 98–117
Wetlands, 441, 445
Whipping rope ends, 201, 203
Whittling Chip card, 112, 154, 204, 326
Wolf rank, 5, 6, 8, 17, 526, 527
Wood, identifying types and uses, 461
World Conservation Award, 527
World Crest badge, 201
World Crest patch, 143
World Friendship Fund, 54, 144
Worship service, planning, 54–55

Z

Zoo, making your own, 427–31
Zoo, visiting, 211, 446, 514

Acknowledgments

The Boy Scouts of America gratefully acknowledges the contributions of the many Cub Scouts, Scouters, subject experts, and staff throughout the nation for their help in preparing the *Webelos Handbook*.

Photo/Illustration Credits

Illustration

Anomie/CC-BY-SA-3.0 Public Domain—page 123 (*today's flag*)

brdad/CC-BY-SA-3.0 Public Domain—page 163 (*Leatherman variant of international geocaching logo*)

BSA—page 187

Choosemyplate.gov— page 42

DevinCook/CC-BY-SA-3.0 Public Domain—page 122 (*bottom*)

Jeff Ebbeler—pages 66, 69, 71, 73, 155, 215, 265, 266, 270, 272, 278, 281, 321, 324, 331, 366, 372 (*top*), 402, 412, 469, 486, 494, and 495

Chris Folea—pages i, 22, 33, 37, 43, 49, 51, 53, 57, 59, 64, 85, 87, 92, 97, 99, 107, 108, 117, 119, 125 (*bottom*), 130, 139, 147, 149, 152, 160, 167, 169, 177, 179, 185, 196, 198, 210, 243, 273, 280, 305, 315, 332, 347, 365 (*bottom*), 383, 399, 413, 423, 435, 463, 469, 478, 498, 515, 521, and 535

Hoshie/CC-BY-SA-3.0 Public Domain—page 122 (*middle*)

Aleksey Ivanov—pages 89–90, 238, 241, 242, 244, 245, and 246

jacobolus/CC-BY-SA-3.0 Public Domain—page 123 (*Flag of 1818*)

Carl Lindberg/CC-BY-SA-3.0 Public Domain— page 123 (*top*)

John McDearmon—pages 16 and inside back cover

Grant Miehm—page 313

Rob Schuster—pages 48, 68, 84, 103, 123–125 (*flags*), 162, 201–203 (*knots*), 217, 218, 236–237, 258, 267–268, 292–297 (*all*), 302–303, 352, 365 (*top*), 372 (*bottom*), 373, 376–379 (*all*), 382, 391, 397, 400, 411, 414, 417, 431, 433, 436, 445, 457, and 518–520

Mr.Taz/CC-BY-SA-3.0 Public Domain— page 122 (*top*)

Photography

Courtesy of Lee Berger—page 227 (*Lee Berger*)

Ed Bronson—page 178

Dan Bryant—pages 8, 23, and 134

BSA—pages 5, 30 (*bottom*), 53, 97, 112 (*top*), 145 (*top*), 146, 171, 180–181, 188, 191, 192 (*bottom*), 194–195, 196, 200, 204 (*top*), 259, 313, 326, 337 (*top*), 464, 465, 466, 467, 468 (*meeting*), 477 (*fiddle*), and 479

160, 161, 166, 175, 182, 183, 185, 186, 189, 193, 197, 199, 204 (*bottom*), 206, 230, 231, 232, 232–233, 234, 248, 249, 260–262, 263, 271, 282, 285–287, 289, 307, 309, 319, 320 (top), 343 (*bottom*), 351, 359, 360, 370, 375, 384, 393, 396, 408, 409, 413, 415, 423, 454, 468 (*frog*), 472, 473, 482–484, 487 (*top*), 501, and 525

Courtesy of Shutterstock.com—pages 19 (*ladybug*, ©Slavko Sereda/Shutterstock), 39 (*matches*, ©Volegzhanina Elena), 40 (*bucket*, ©Sergei Rozvodovskii), 43 (*family eating*, ©Monkey Business Images), 44 (*fruits and vegetables*, ©Serg64), 45 (*journal background*, ©Ghenadie; *vegetable art*, ©mahmuttibet), 52 (*background*, ©Galyna Andrushko), 54 (*Bible*, ©4Max), 60-61 (*ambulance*, ©Glen Jones), 65 (*notebook background*, ©Prapann), 69 (*man holding arm*, ©Giideon), 70 (*AED*, ©Baloncici), 78 (*tick*, ©Henrik Larsson; *bee*, ©irin-k; *chigger*, Kletr), 79 (*brown recluse spider*, ©Steve Collender; *black widow*, ©Peter Waters), 80 (*copperhead*, ©Eric Isselee), 82 (*first aid kit*, ©Alena Brozova), 88 (*running track*, ©sippakorn), 91 (*boy on track*, ©racorn), 100 (*forest background*, ©Candia Baxter), 103 (*notebook background*, ©Ohishiapply), 104-106 (*notebook background*, ©Ohishiapply), 104 (*gila monster*, ©fivespots; *Eastern Diamondback*, ©Eric Isselee; *Western Diamondback*, ©Ryan M. Bolton; *Timber rattlesnake*, ©Erick Isselee), 105 (*prairie rattlesnake*, ©Nashepard; *horned snake*, ©Matt Jeppson; *coral snake*, ©Patrick K. Campbell; *water moccasin*, ©Leighton Photography & Imaging), 106 (*copperhead*, ©fivespots; *wasp*, ©irin-k; *tick*, ©Sarah2; *chigger*, ©kletr), 107 (*black widow spider*, ©Peter Waters; *brown recluse spider*, ©Steve Collender), 109 (*recipe background*, ©margouillat), 110, (*trail mix*, ©Elena Elisseeva; *orange*, ©EM Arts), 111 (*stream*, ©pyansetia2008), 113 (*hiking boots*, ©ppart), 120-121 (*Washington Monument*, ©Zack Frank), 126 (*flags*, ©Sergey Tarasenko), 127 (*flags*, ©Denise Kappa), 128 (*voting sign*, ©Kenneth Summers; *bilingual voting sign*, ©Frontpage), 129 (*children at school*, ©bikeriderlondon), 131 (*stop sign*, ©Sean Pavone), 133 (*receipt*, ©NAN728), 137 (*light bulbs*, ©maxstockphoto), 140 (*recycling symbols*, ©Baloncici), 156 (*tent near lake*, ©InkaOne), 158 (*lightning*, ©cephotoclub), 159 (*forest fire*, ©Anupan Praneetpholkrang), 170-171 (*candles background*, ©Vladyslav Starozhylov), 172 (*family praying*, ©Monkey Business Images), 174 (*boy with Bible*, ©Terrie L. Zeller), 209 (*sunflower*, ©Mariola Kraczowska), 209 (*sunflower plant*, ©Miramiska), 212 (*journal background*, ©mexrix), 213 (*planting tools*, ©tobkatrina; *sand pile*, ©tobkatrina) 219 (*constellations in sky*, ©tanais), 220 (*spiral background*, ©kanate), 222 (*bottle of vinegar*, ©Jo De Vulder; *baking soda*, ©simoly), 229 (©B Calkins), 247 (©Charles F McCarthy), 251 (*art supplies*, ©Gvictoria), 253 (*expressionist painting*, ©Clarence Bowman), 254 (*impressionist painting*, ©Mikhail Zahranichny; *pop art*, ©Denis Simonov; *surrealistic art*, ©Paul Fleet), 256 (*art supplies*, ©Africa Studio), 257 (*water color paints*, ©Olga Kovalenko; *art brushes*, ©Alexandru Nika), 258 (©basel101658), 264 (©Sergey Karpov), 269 (*scout and computer*, ©Catalin Petolea; *art for computer*, ©R lion O), 277 (©Alsu), 279 (©Oksana Shufrych), 284 (*wheelchair tennis*, ©Nicholas Rjabow; *young woman and elderly woman*, ©Alexander Raths), 288 (*service dog*, ©Brois Djuranovic; *disabled parking sign*, ©Nickylarson974), 301 (©kosam), 304 (©4Max), 305 (©Pressmaster), 308 (©Monkey Business Images), 309 (*bus driver and volunteer*, ©bikeriderlondon; *teacher and student*, ©Monkey Business Images), 310 (©Sferdon), 311 (©artenot), 314 (©Danomyte), 318 (©sp. VVK), 319 (*top*, ©Suzanne Tucker), 325 (*emergency blanket*, ©Bogdan ionescu), 327 (*tape*, ©gcpics; *fishing line*, ©Coprid; *hooks*, ©Mr. Suttipon Yakham), 328 (©Diego Cervo), 329 (©BrAt82), 330 (©Sean MacD), 335 (©mangojuicy), 337 (©silky), 339 (©Madlen), 340 (©holbox), 341 (©beboy), 343 (*hammer/chisel*, ©Balefire; *mineral* pad, ©Triff; *magnifier*, ©gualtiero boffi), 345 (*basalt*, ©Tyler Boyes; *gabbro*, ©Tyler Boyes; *granite*, ©Coprid; *obsidian*, ©mikeledray; *pumice*, ©servickuz; *breccia*, ©Siim Sepp; *conglomerate*, ©sonsam; *limestone*, ©Siim Sepp; *sandstone*, ©michal812; *shale*, ©Siim Sepp), 346 (*slate*, ©Tyler Boyes; *metaquartzite*, ©Tyler Boyes; *green schist*, ©kavring; *marble*, ©Siim Sepp; *gneiss*, ©Siim Sepp; *gold*, ©scyther5; *copper*, ©Epitavi; *biotite*, ©akiyoko), 347 (©Hanze), 348 (©ventdusud), 349 (*water erosion*, ©Lee Prince; *leaf fossil*, ©alice-photo), 353 (©Ranier Lesniewski), 354 (©Orhan Cam), 355 (©Orhan Cam), 356 (©Paul B. Moore), 362 (*bio-chemical engineer/plants*, ©Monika Wisniewska), 363 (©Marcin Balcerzak), 369 (*Golden Gate Bridge*, ©S. Borisov), 371 (©Forewer), 380 (©Zorandim), 386 (©Daleen Loest), 388 (©yevgeniy), 389 (*circuit breakers*, ©entafern; *fuse box*, ©Stocksnapper), 390 (*wood stove*, ©ARENA Creative; *radiator*, ©Click Images; *furnace*, ©ARENA Creative; *propane gas heater*, ©GSPhotography), 391 (©ermess), 392 (©Kues), 394 (*incandescent bulb*, ©Chones, *fluorescent bulb*, ©Chones), 395 (©Chones), 398 (©Serenethos), 399 (©bikeriderlondon), 403 (©Winai Tepsuttinum), 405 (*bike Dunlap and Shrader valves for tire*, ©Nils Z; *reuseable bike Dunlap and Schrader valves for tire*, ©Nils Z ; *bike tool kit and tire replacement*, ©David Watkins), 406 (©Pressmaster), 407 (*replacing wheel*, ©plastique; *building skateboard*, ©BarracudaDesigns), 410 (©linerpics), 417 (©dominique landau), 418 (©Franck Boston), 420 (©Blend Images), 421 (*game controller and disc*, ©Nata-Lia; *game controller*, ©BonD80), 422 (©Monkey Business Images), 425 (©Erni), 426 (©Weihenmayer), 427 (©Hurst Photo), 429 (*cricket*, ©alexsvirid; *ants*, ©Mirek Kijewski), 430 (*grasshopper*, ©anat chant; *Cub with net*, ©Matt Jeppson; *hands with frog*, ©Matt Jeppson), 432 (©S-F), 434 (*hummingbird*, ©Tim Roberts Photography; *cardinal*, ©Mike Truchon; *bird with coconut*, ©Gerald Marella; *woodpecker/feeder*, ©Gerald A. DeBoer), 435 (©Mike Truchon), 437 (©Potapov Igor Petrovich), 438 (©martellostudio), 439 (©Brian Lasenby), 440 (*hummingbird*, ©Tom Reichnerl; *snowy owl*, ©Chris Hill; *Anhinga*, ©Thomas Barrat; *map*, ©silver tiger), 441 (©Aleksandr Kurganov), 442 (*pussy willows*, ©Alexandr79; *deer*, ©Guy J Sagi; *raccoon*, ©worldswildlifewonders; *wolf*, ©Daniel Korzeniewski; *mushrooms*, ©Choosakdi kabyubon; *sun and clouds*, ©kirbyedy), 443 (*grey wolf*, ©karl umbriaco; *deer*, ©Martin Hesko; s*now/bush*, ©Ruud Morijn), 444 (©Budimir Jevtic), 446 (©Anan Kaewkhammul), 447 (©Denise Kappa), 449 (©Wildnerdpix), 450 (©Albert Pego), 451 (©Serg64), 452 (*deciduous trees*, ©filmfoto; *palm trees*, ©Peter Zachar), 453 (©Potapov Alexander), 455 (*squirrel*, ©Kellis; *bear*, ©Dennis Donohue), 456, (*bluebird/berry*, ©Bonnie Taylor Barry; *hummingbird*, ©bonjangles), 457 (©Norikazu), 458 (*lettuce farm*, ©Ivonne Wierink; *logging*, ©juras), 461 (©Iriana Shiyan), 462 (©J. Helgason), 468 (©Lukiyanova Natalia), 470 (*typewriter/phone/ books*, ©BrAt82; *children in line*, ©Elzbieta Sekowska), 471 (*old computer*, ©Fer Gregory; *man/cell phone*, ©EdBockStock; *old computer mainframe*, ©Everett Collection; *kids/tablets*, ©EpicStockMedia; *robot*, ©koya979), 475 (©Georgios Kollidas), 476 (©bikeriderlondon), 477 (*outdoor concert*, ©Andrey Armyagov; *jazz musicians*, ©bikeriderlondon), 480 (*sound waves*, ©Eliks; *violin*, ©grafvision; *clarinet*, ©Vereshchagin Dmitry), 481 (*brass instrument*, ©Vereshchagin Dmitry, *electronic keyboard*, ©Petr Malyshev; *drums and tambourine*, ©Skylines), 485 (©arek malang), 487 (©advent), 490 (©Glenda), 493 (Maxx-Studio), 502 (©FernandoMadeira), 504 (©slava17), 505 (©Monkey Business Images), 507 (©Erika Cross), 508 (©pio3), 511-512 (©TAGSTOCK), 513 (©FernandoMadeira), 514 (©Apples Eyes Studio); 517 (©Galina Barskaya), 522 (©John Wollwerth), 523 (*lacrosse*, ©4736202690; *ice hockey*, ©ifoto), 524 (©Suzanne Tucker), 538-539 (©silky), 550 (©Judy Kennamer)

THE OUTDOOR CODE

As an American, I will do my best to—

♦ Be clean in my outdoor manners,

♦ Be careful with fire,

♦ Be considerate in the outdoors, and

♦ Be conservation minded.

LEAVE NO TRACE PRINCIPLES FOR KIDS

Know Before You Go

Choose the Right Path

Trash Your Trash

Leave What You Find

Be Careful With Fire

Respect Wildlife

Be Kind to Other Visitors

*The member-driven Leave No Trace Center for Outdoor Ethics teaches people how to enjoy the outdoors responsibly. This copyrighted information has been reprinted with permission from the *Leave No Trace Center for Outdoor Ethics: www.LNT.org.*